TRANSACTIONS

of the

American Philosophical Society

Held at Philadelphia for Promoting Useful Knowledge

VOLUME 80, Part 5

Le Lai de l'Oiselet
An Old French Poem of the Thirteenth Century
Edition and Critical Study

LENORA D. WOLFGANG

Department of Modern Foreign Languages and Literature
Lehigh University

AMERICAN PHILOSOPHICAL SOCIETY

Independence Square, Philadelphia

1990

Library of Congress Catalog
Card Number 90-55268
International Standard Book Number 0-87169-805-6
US ISSN 0065-9746

To
WILLIAM ROACH

PREFACE

This edition of the *Lai de l'Oiselet* was undertaken in order to provide a complete and accurate text of a poem that has long been available only in outdated or partial editions. The critical study was intended to bring up to date and to gather in one place as much information as possible about the origins of the story and its many analogues.

Throughout the time it has taken to prepare this volume I have incurred many debts of gratitude that it is now a pleasure for me to discharge.

I wish to thank the National Endowment for the Humanities and the American Philosophical Society whose grants have enabled me to consult the manuscripts of the *Lai de l'Oiselet* in the Bibliothèque Nationale and to prepare the critical study.

I also wish to thank my colleagues at Lehigh University who granted me a sabbatical leave, and my colleagues in the field who have supported my work by writing letters of recommendation for me and who have read portions of the typescript.

I owe special thanks to Selma Pastor, who typed the manuscript of this book in its several incarnations, to my husband, Marvin E. Wolfgang, and to the rest of my family, who have been patient and understanding throughout this long process — *ars longa*. . . .

I am very pleased to acknowledge my gratitude to the American Philosophical Society that accepted my book for publication and to the Editors and Staff who have seen it through to its final incarnation.

But it is to Professor William Roach that I address my final words of acknowledgment and gratitude for generously giving of his time and experience to help bring this project to its conclusion.

CONTENTS

Ne pleure ce c'onques n'eüs
Ne croire qanque tu oz dire
. . . ce que tu tiens en tes mains,
Ne le giete jus a tes piez
Le Lai de l'Oiselet

INTRODUCTION

The *Lai de l'Oiselet* is a charming little poem preserved in five French manuscripts of the thirteenth and fourteenth centuries. It was first published in 1756 by Etienne Barbazan, and subsequently in 1808 by Dominique Méon, in 1884 by Gaston Paris, and in 1927 by Raymond Weeks. All these editions are partial or incomplete. In 1756 and 1808 not all the manuscripts were known, and in 1884, although Gaston Paris had access to all of them, he chose not to give any variants in his edition. The same was true of Raymond Weeks, who printed only the text found in B.N. *f.fr. 837.* The present edition is thus the first to provide the full text from all five of the manuscripts.

Gaston Paris, who explored the rich literary background of the *Lai de l'Oiselet* more than once referred to it as a "joli récit indien" or a "charmant conte indien," and even placed it among the fabliaux in his *Littérature française au moyen âge* (§ 77). These vague but unequivocal characterizations of the poem led me to two areas of investigation: the idea of genre, and the oriental origins of the story of the *Oiselet*. The results of the former are set forth in section IV.E of the Introduction, and of the latter in sections IV.A-C of the Introduction and in the Appendix.

In section I of the Introduction I outline the poem in somewhat longer detail than usual. This was done in order not to trivialize a text that depends more on nuance and inference for its effects than on character portrayal or action. In section II of the Introduction the manuscripts are listed and detailed, and in sections V.A-C they are again discussed in terms of the selection of the base manuscript.

The Bibliography is complete, listing all works that have been used to prepare the edition and critical study. A few additional items used only in the Textual Notes are listed at the beginning of that section. In order not to duplicate bibliographic detail, short titles and authors' last names only appear in the footnotes.

The text of the *Lai de l'Oiselet* is given according to the base manuscript with a list of rejected readings. It is followed by a complete diplomatic and synoptic presentation of the other four manuscripts. This has been done in order to facilitate comparisons among manuscripts that have complex rearrangements of lines.

The Textual Notes and Glossary elucidate and facilitate a reading of the base text, but several notes discuss words and structures in the other manuscripts that present special interest or difficulty.

1

I. SYNOPSIS OF THE STORY

It happened more than a hundred years ago that there was a villein who was rich in everything that a nobleman should have: woods, fields, streams, and a manor with a magnificent hall and tower. The property was surrounded by a river, and in the center was a garden encircled by water and air. This had all been made for a great knight. His son inherited it after him, but sold it to the villein. Thus does property decline through bad inheritance!

(1–26)

The garden was filled with flowers and herbs that had healing powers. It was formed in a perfect circle surrounded by tall trees. A great pine tree gave shade there, and in the middle there was a fountain of clear water.

(27–70)

Twice a day a bird came to sing in the garden. His song had the power to bring joy to the unhappy and to inspire love where it was not even thought of before. And there was another marvel: unless the bird came to sing there, the garden would wither and the fountain would dry up.

(71–123)

The villein used to come to the garden each day to the fountain under the pine tree. One day the bird was singing in the tree a song about God and love, but when he saw the villein under the tree looking at him, he sang in a different way: "River, cease flowing! Tower, perish! Hall, crumble! Flowers, fade; herbs, wither; trees, shed your foliage! This place used to be dear to courteous lovers, but now this envious, covetous villein listens to me. He prefers wealth to love and looks at me with the idea of eating!"

(124–192)

Saying this, the bird flew away, and the villein decided to trap him. He placed a snare where the bird sat most often, and thought about how he would sell him dearly, or he would put him in a cage so that he would sing for him morning and night. The bird returned in the evening, and was caught in the trap. "That is the payment you receive," says he, "for serving a villein!" He then says to the villein that he has done wrong to snare him, because he is so small and insignificant. "But no," says the villein, "I will put you in a cage, and you will sing to me as long as I want." — —"I used to sing in liberty," says the bird, "never will I sing in a cage!" — —"Well then, I will eat you!" says the villein. — —"Let me go. You will commit a sin if you kill me." — —"Never!" says the villein. — —"If you let me go," says the bird, "I will teach you three truths that no one of your lineage ever knew." The villein agrees and releases him.

(193–258)

The bird flies up into the tree and smooths his ruffled feathers, and the villein presses him to tell the three truths. The bird tells him the first one: "Do not cry for what you have never had" (271). The villein is very angry and says that that is something everyone knows. The bird taunts him and then tells him the second truth: "Do not believe everything you hear" (301), and the villein frowns in anger, since, he says, he knew this too and, if he still had hold of him, he wouldn't mock anyone anymore! "But," says he, "if you kept your promise to me, you would teach me the third truth." — —"Pay attention here," says the bird, "and I will tell you. The third one is such that he who knows it will never be a poor man." The villein is eager to know this one since, he says, he really does like wealth! "It's time to eat," says he, "teach me it right away." When the bird hears this, he says: "I warn you, villein: what you have in your hands, do not throw at your feet" (326–27). The villein was now in a rage and said, "Is that all? Isn't there something more? These are childish words, and a poor man knows them as well as you." — —"Well," says the bird, "if you knew these things before, you would not have let me go." — —"True," says the villein. Then the bird goes on, "The third truth is worth a hundred times the other two." — —"How's that?" — —"How? I'll tell you, monstrous wretch. If you had killed me, you would have found a precious stone inside me weighing three ounces which would have given you everything you would ask for." Learning this, the villein wrings his hands, tears his clothes, calls himself a miserable wretch, and scratches his face to pieces with his nails. The bird is beside himself with glee as he watches him from the tree. When he sees what the villein has done, the bird says to him: "Miserable villein, when you held me in your hands I was lighter than a sparrow, a tomtit, or a finch. I did not weigh half an ounce." The villein admits that this is true, and the bird says to him that now he will prove that the villein knew nothing of the three truths he told him, since he sees him crying over what he never had, and he says to him: "It is a good thing to learn wisdom. They say that he who listens does not hear: He talks much about wisdom and has little; he talks about courtesy and would not know how to practice it; and he believes himself wise and is guided by folly."

(259–398)

With these words, the bird flew away, never to return to the garden. The foliage fell from the tree, the garden faded, the fountain ran dry, and the villein lost his pleasure of them. Now know you well, ladies and gentle men, the proverb says it quite clearly: He who covets all loses all.

(399–410)

II. THE MANUSCRIPTS

The *Lai de l'Oiselet* is preserved in five manuscripts:

A B.N. f.fr. 837 (formerly *7218*; XIIIth century)
This famous collection of 247 works has served as base manuscript for many of the works it contains and has been described many times in editions and catalogues. A facsimile was published in 1932 by Henri Omont.[1]

---

[1] For descriptions of this manuscript, see: Paulin Paris, *Les Manuscrits françois*, 6: 404–16; *Cat. des Manuscrits fr. Anciens fonds*, 1: 94–96; Omont, *Fabliaux, dits et contes*, v-vii, 1–28, 89–92; Legry-Rosier, "Manuscrits de contes," 40; Bédier, *Lai de l'Ombre* (1913), xxiii, xlii, and "La Tradition manuscrite du *Lai de l'Ombre*," 93; Delbouille, *Lai d'Aristote*, 6–13; Lecoy, *Chevalier au barisel*, iii; Ménard, *Fabliaux*, 1: 9, 160–61; Nykrog, *Les Fabliaux*, viii, xi, xliii, 25, 30, 46;

The *Lai de l'Oiselet* occupies folios 45a to 46d (modern foliation), and is piece number XIII (old numbering). The 362 vellum folios measure 315 × 210 mm. They contain two columns, fifty lines to the column. The first capital of the *Lai de l'Oiselet* is an "I." It is the only large capital in the poem and is decorated in blue, red, and gold. The handwriting is generally clear and easy to read. The *Lai de l'Oiselet* contains 390 verses in this manuscript.

The explicits of the poem are by the hand of the copyist, but the titles were added later by another hand and in a blacker ink.[2]

B B.N. nouv. acq. fr. 1104 (formerly 6865; XIIIth century)[3]

This manuscript was first described by Gaston Paris in 1878 shortly after the Bibliothèque Nationale acquired it.[4]

The *Lai de l'Oiselet* occupies folios 77a to 77c, and is the last piece in this collection of 23 lais. The 92 folios are of vellum and measure 290 × 195 mm. They contain two columns, forty lines to the column.[5] The handwriting is generally easy to read.

The first letter of the *Lai de l'Oiselet* is a capital, measuring 50 mm and is decorated in blue, red, and gold. There are ten other large capitals at lines 51, 71, 93, 169, 189, 209, 259, 299, 343, and 375 of the manuscript. The *Lai de l'Oiselet* contains 410 verses in this manuscript.

C B.N. f.fr. 25545 (formerly Notre Dame no. 2 or 274 bis; XIVth century)[6]

This manuscript served as the base for the editions of the *Oiselet* by Barbazan, Méon, and Gaston Paris.[7]

NRCF, 1: 164; Stuip, *Chastelaine de Vergi*, 38–39; Weeks, *Medieval Studies*, 341–53; Mihm, *Songe d'Enfer*, 21–23.

[2] Omont, *Fabliaux*, vi; P. Paris, *Manuscrits*, 405 n. 1.

[3] For descriptions of this manuscript, see: Gaston Paris, *Romania*, 7: 1–21 and 8: 29–42; Delisle, *Mélanges de Paléographie*, 438–40; Omont, *Cat. général, nouv. acq. fr.*, 1: 145–46; Legry-Rosier, "Manuscrits de contes," 43–44; Baum, *Recherches*, 49–50; Bédier, *Ombre* (1913), xxxvi-xxxix, and "Tradition manuscrite" (repr. 1929), 7, 21, 66–67, 69–70, 98–99; Delbouille, *Lai d'Aristote*, 6–13; Ewert, *Marie de France. Lais*, xix-xx; Grimes, *Lays*, 40; Hoepffner, rev. Warnke, *Lais, Neophilologus*, 11: 143, and "Tradition manuscrite," *op. cit.*, 12: 1, 2, 4, 6, 7, 85–86, 88–95; Orr, *Lai de l'Ombre*, xx; Rychner and Aebischer, *Lai de Lanval*, 14–15; Rychner, *Lais de Marie de France*, xxi, xxiii; Tobin, *Lais anonymes*, 11–12; Zenker, *Lai d'Espine*, 235–55.

[4] Gaston Paris did not use this manuscript for his privately printed edition of 1884, although he published other lais from it in *Romania*, 7: 1–21, 407–415, and 8: 29–72.

[5] Folios 80 to 89 are smaller than the rest of the manuscript: folios 80 to 83 are 205 × 167 mm and 84 to 89 are 250 × 160 mm. They contain prose works. See Omont, *Cat. Gen. nouv. acq.*, 1: 145–46; Delisle, *Mélanges de Paléographie*, 440. Legry-Rosier gives the dimensions of the ms as 290 × 200 mm: p. 43.

[6] The first description of this manuscript is in Barbazan, *Fabliaux et contes* (1756), 1: lv-lvi: "Li Lais de l'Oiselet. Tiré du Ms. de l'Eglise de Paris, N. 2. Il est aussi dans le Ms. du Roi 7218." In vol. 3, in the *Table*, Barbazan refers to the first manuscript as "Manuscrit de l'Eglise de Paris Cote N. No 2." In the "Préface," p. xxxv, of vol. 1, it is referred to as "manuscrit de l'Eglise de Paris cotté N. no 2." In the 1808 edition of Barbazan by Méon, there is a reference to four manuscripts, vol. 3: 114: 7218, 7615, M. 21/3 and N. 2 de Notre-Dame (= 837, 1593, 24432, 25545). For other descriptions, see: Omont, *Cat. Gen.*, 2: 633; Gaston Raynaud, "Chastelaine de Vergi," *Romania*, 21: 147; Långfors, *Romania*, 44: 87–91; Stuip, *Chastelaine de Vergi*, 42–44; Legry-Rosier, "Manuscrits," 43 (the dimensions are given as 217 × 145 mm). In the sixteenth century, this manuscript belonged to Claude Fauchet. See Espiner-Scott, *Claude Fauchet*, 191, 192 n. 5, 199, and Baum, *Recherches*, 61.

[7] Gaston Paris used 25545 as his base because he said that he felt the order of the sens given in *CE* was the original (*Légendes du Moyen Age*, 272); Méon in 1808 said the following of his edition:

In the manuscript, the *Oiselet* occupies folios 151*a* to 154*a* (modern numbering; another numbering, 39 to 42, is crossed out). The poem ends at line 8 on folio 154*a*.

This manuscript of 37 works is made up of at least three different collections, which is shown by the three different numbering systems for folios 84 to 109.

The 167 vellum folios measure 215 × 145 mm, and they contain two columns, 36 lines to the column. The title is in a modern hand, and the explicit is in a different modern hand.

The initials were never filled in, but spaces were left for them at lines 1, 29, 42, 52, 73, 113, 124, 136, 168, 191, 204, 210, 214, 218, 230, 241, 252, 257, 266, 283, 296, 317, 330, 340, 362, and 397 of the manuscript. The handwriting is generally clear and not difficult to read. The *Lai de l'Oiselet* contains 410 verses in this manuscript.

D B.N. f.fr. 24432 (formerly Notre Dame 21/3, then 198)[8]

The version of the *Oiselet* in this manuscript is the longest (505 verses).[9] Of the 90 pieces in ms *D*, at least 56 are called "dits," according to the *Catalogue général*, which may explain why the *Oiselet* is called a "dit" in both its title and explicit.[10]

The *Oiselet* occupies folios XLII*a* to XLV*b* (old notation), or 43*a* to 46*b* (new notation). The 443 parchment folios measure 310 x 220 mm. They contain two columns, 38 lines to the column. Capital letters are to be found at lines 1, 11, 21, 31, 47, 61, 73, 81, 103, 129, 151, 171, 189, 205, 229, 255, 277,

---

Toutes les Pièces qui composent ce volume sont déjà connues, puisqu'elles font la presque totalité des Fabliaux et Contes donnés par M. Barbazan en 1756. . . . Je les ai toutes revues sur les Manuscrits originaux, et, . . . non-seulement j'ai corrigé quelques fautes échappées au premier Éditeur, mais les différentes copies que j'ai trouvés des mêmes Contes, m'ont fait découvrir des différences et des augmentations dont j'ai cru devoir faire usage. Le lecteur pourra les apprécier en les comparant dans les deux éditions (vol. 3: xxx).

Gaston Raynaud said of this manuscript for the *Chastelaine de Vergi*: "Ce ms. [25545] a servi de base principale au texte de Méon; ses leçons sont généralement bonnes et ont quelques points de communs avec *E* [B.N. *f.fr.* 2136]," *Romania*, 21: 147. Barbazan has a text of 410 verses; Méon adds 14 verses for a text of 424, and Gaston Paris has a text of 410 verses, but different from those of Barbazan and the manuscript.

[8] This manuscript was not mentioned by Barbazan in 1756. Méon, however, does list it in 1808 as M 21/3 (vol. 3: 115). Omont, *Cat. gen. Anciens petits fonds*, 2: 368, says that this manuscript was formerly Notre-Dame 198 and that it contains 443 folios plus 198*a-g*. This latter number does in fact appear in the manuscript, p. 1, at the top. Legry-Rosier, "Manuscrits," 37–38, describes the manuscript, but does not give any former number. The dimensions given by Legry-Rosier are 310 × 215 mm. Omont, *Cat. gen. Anciens petits fonds*, 362, says that the *Oiselet* appears two times in Méon, in vol. 2, p. 140, and vol. 3, p. 114. What is in vol. 2, p. 140, is not the *Lai de l'Oiselet* but the *Chastoiement d'un père à son fils* from ms 19152. Omont also says that the edition by Gaston Paris in 1884 is a "réimpression" of Méon's edition of 1808. This statement is also untrue. Méon's version in 1808 has 424 verses and G. Paris's edition has 410. Morever, Gaston Paris had access to *nouv. acq.* 1104, unknown to either Barbazan or Méon. Baum, *Recherches*, indicates seven places where the manuscript has a date, ranging from 1313 to 1345 (p. 56). See also Bastin, *Recueil général des Isopets*, 2: xiii.

[9] Line 102 (= *B* 92) is missing.

[10] Legry-Rosier lists the contents of this manuscript: "Manuscrits," 37–38. Omont, *Cat. gen. Anciens petits fonds*, 2: 361–68, characterizes the contents. See also Baum, *Recherches*, 55, who says "une soixantaine environ, sont qualifiées de dits." See also Hoepffner, "Tradition manuscrite," 8, 9, 95; Lecoy, "Le dit de l'espervier," *Romania*, 69: 528–31; Rychner, *Contribution à l'étude des Fabliaux*, 1: 67–84, and *Lais*, xx, 220–26.

291, 307, 325, 343, 355, 385, 397, 407, 425, 439, 465, and 495 of the manu-
script. The handwriting is large but sometimes difficult to read.

E B.N. f.fr. 1593 (formerly *7615*; XIIIth century)[11]

The *Lai de l'Oiselet* is number 57 in the list of 75 works in this collectio. ,
and it occupies folios 169*b* to 171*b*. There are three foliations, and it is the
second one that is used in the catalogues. The 220 vellum folios measure 250
× 185 mm.[12] They contain two columns, 41 lines to the column.[13] The *Lai
de l'Oiselet* has no large initials or capitals in this manuscript, but there is
a space left for the rubricator at line 1, indicating a letter to be filled in later.

The handwriting is fairly clear and readable, and the text contains 341 verses
in this manuscript.[14]

III. EDITIONS OF THE *LAI DE L'OISELET*

The *Lai de l'Oiselet* was published for the first time in 1756 by Etienne Bar-
bazan from ms *C*.[15] In 1808, Dominique Méon published what he called a
new edition of Barbazan, but his text is essentially that of Barbazan with four-
teen verses taken from *A* added to it. Méon also indicated that he had access
to manuscripts *D* and *E*.[16]

The poem was reprinted several times, and translations into German and
English quickly followed.[17] The English version of G. L. Way, "The Lay of
the Little Bird," for example, became well known, and was often reprinted.[18]

---

[11] For descriptions of this manuscript, see: *Cat. des manuscrits fr. Anciens fonds fr.*, 1: 266–68;
Bédier, *Ombre*, xxiii, and "Tradition manuscrite," 17 passim (1593 = *B*); Delbouille, *Lai d'Ari-
stote*, 6–13; Ménard, *Fabliaux*, 1: 160–61; *NCRF*, 1: 163–65; Legry-Rosier, "Manuscrits," 40–41;
Warnke, *Die Fabeln der Marie de France*, v; Gaston Paris, *Légendes*, 271, gives the date of this
manuscript as fourteenth century.

[12] Legry-Rosier does not distinguish parchment and vellum. According to this description, the
manuscript measures 245 × 180 mm.

[13] On the first *feuille de garde*, dated 15 September 1892, it says that the manuscript had be-
longed to Président Fauchet, that the marginal notes are in his hand, that the volume contains
217 folios, plus Feuillet A préliminaire, plus Feuillet 101 *bis*, 102 *bis*, 123 *bis*, and that folio 19
is "mutilé." According to the editors of the *NRCF*, folio 217 is actually 220 (vol. 1: 163).

[14] Verse 49 (= *B* 47) is missing.

[15] The name of the editor, Etienne Barbazan, is not on the title page. The text of the poem
is in vol. 1: 179–99. For an estimate of Barbazan, see Wilson, *A Medievalist*, xi–xii, 61–62, 67,
209–12, 221, 270. Another interesting observation is in Grimes, *Lays of Desiré, Graelent*, 43,
where she points out that La Curne de Sainte Palaye did not make his own transcriptions but
copied from the printed book of Barbazan! A prose adaptation was made of the poem and printed
twice by Le Grand d'Aussy, in 1779, vol. 3 of his *Fabliaux et contes*, 113–21, and in 1881, vol.
3: 430–39, of a *Nouvelle édition* of the *Fabliaux et contes*. The Le Grand text was published a
third time, in 1829, and the *Lai de l'Oiselet* is in vol. 4: 27–34.

[16] The text of the poem by Méon, 1808, is in vol. 3: 114–28, of his *Fabliaux et Contes*. Méon
adds 14 verses to the 410 in the text of Barbazan.

[17] For the text of these translations, see Tyroller, *Die Fabel von dem Mann und dem Vogel*
(1912). This book contains 73 texts on the theme, including the texts of Lydgate, *The Chorl and
the Bird*, C. M. Wieland, *Die Vogelsang oder die drei Lehren*, and Way's *The Lay of the Little Bird*.

[18] The *Fabliaux et contes* of Le Grand d'Aussy were translated into English by G. Ellis in
1796–1800. The "Lay of the Little Bird" is in vol. 1: 50–59 (notes 166–72) of the 1815 edition
of the Ellis translation. The text of the "Lay of the Little Bird" is printed (in entirety) in the note
to story 167 of the *Gesta Romanorum*, trans. Charles Swan (1888), 415–18. A. A. Renouard

Gaston Paris began to publish the poems and lays from manuscript B. N. *nouv. acq.* 1104 in 1878 in *Romania*,[19] but he did not publish the *Oiselet* from this manuscript, choosing rather to use *C* for his privately published edition.[20] This same text was reproduced in 1903 (posthumously) in *Légendes du Moyen Age.*[21]

No variants from the other manuscripts were provided with his edition, and the following remarks are all he says about the manuscripts:

> Je dirai brièvement que les cinq manuscrits remontent à deux copies différentes du manuscrit original perdu : *ABD* descendent de l'un, *C* représente l'autre, *E* paraît être le produit d'une fusion des deux. Ce qui distingue *CE* de *ABD*, c'est que l'ordre des *sens* de l'oiseau n'y est pas le même : le *sens* qui est le premier dans *CE* est le second dans *ABD*, ce qui amène naturellement à cet endroit d'assez fortes divergences. J'ai considéré l'ordre de *CE* comme l'original, parce qu'il concorde avec celui de Pierre Alphonse : dès lors l'établissement du texte était tout indiqué. La bonne leçon devait résulter de la comparaison des deux familles entre elles : je n'entre pas dans le détail de cette comparaison ; je dirai seulement qu'elle donne comme résultant un texte qu'on peut regarder comme partout satisfaisant. En ce qui concerne les formes, qui varient dans les manuscrits divers et souvent dans un seul et même manuscrit, j'ai adopté celles qui se rapprochent le plus du français normal.[22]

The rest of his study concerns the origins of the story and the sources of the poem.

The last publication of a text of the *Oiselet* was in 1927 by Raymond Weeks. It is, as has already been mentioned, simply a transcription of the text in *A.*[23]

IV. SOURCES AND ANALOGUES OF THE *LAI DE L'OISELET*

A. The *Barlaam and Josaphat*

The story of the *Oiselet* first appears as a parable in the saints' lives, *Barlaam and Josaphat*. This work is considered to be a Christianized version of the

---

makes mention of this translation in the 1829 edition of the *Fabliaux et contes* of Le Grand d'Aussy, vol. 1: vi-vii. Gaston Paris also mentions it in *Légendes du Moyen Age,* 270.

[19] *Romania,* 7: 1–21, 407–15, and 8: 29–72.

[20] I would like to thank Professor William Roach for permission to consult his copy of this edition.

[21] The "Lai de l'Oiselet" is on pp. 225–91 of this collection of five essays by Gaston Paris. The text itself is in the Appendix. The 1903 printing of the 1884 edition does not include the six-page dedication, the last paragraph on pp. 71–72, and the first note to verse 3 where Gaston Paris explained the case-system of Old French to facilitate the reading of the poem by his nephew and new niece. Both editions have the same error where note to verse 246 is meant for 247. G. Paris mentioned that a former "auditor" of his had made variants from the five manuscripts. On p. 69 of the 1884 edition, he says, "Son travail sera, je l'espère, publié quelque jour avec le développement qu'il comporte." In 1903 this sentence is simply removed from the introduction to the poem (*Légendes,* 271), and nothing further is heard again about variants. All the notes at the bottom of the page for the text are translations of difficult passages for the reader. Pauphilet reproduced Gaston Paris's text in *Poètes et romanciers du Moyen âge,* 445–508.

[22] *Légendes,* 272.

[23] *Medieval Studies in Memory of Gertrude Schoepperle Loomis,* 341–53.

life of Buddha, and the earliest version we have is usually traced to the seventh or eighth century A.D. The *Barlaam* has a long and complex history.[24] Gaston Paris gives a complete summary of the Greek version,[25] which I do not give here since the Greek version and translations and summaries of it are readily available.[26] Some of the parables in the *Barlaam* were detached from it and appeared in independent collections of stories (see Appendix, section I).

In the *Barlaam* parable, there are several elements that characterize the story and those versions that derive from it: (1) the bird is generally called a nightingale; (2) the man is a hunter or a bird-catcher; (3) the bird is liberated *after* he tells the three truths; (4) the precious stone is a pearl and compared in size to an ostrich egg; and (5) the three truths are: never try to attain the unattainable, never regret the thing past and gone, and never believe the word that passes belief.[27]

In subsequent discussions, the stories that stem from the *Barlaam* will be called *pleurer croire* stories. This designation refers to the ordering of the three truths or "sens" within the story. The sens "never regret the thing past and gone" is referred to as *pleurer,* and the sens "never believe the word that passes belief" is referred to as *croire.*

---

[24] For versions of the *Barlaam and Josaphat* in Greek, see Sonet, *Le Roman de Barlaam et Josaphat,* 1: 53–68; Boissonade, *Anecdota graeca,* 4: 79–81; Bolton, "Parable, Allegory and Romance," *Traditio,* 14: 359–66; Migne, *Patrologiae graeca,* 96: cols. 941–44; Peeters, "La première traduction latine," *Analecta Bollandiana,* 49: 276–312; Woodward and Mattingly, *Barlaam and Joasaph,* 134–39. For versions of *Barlaam* in Latin, see: Sonet, *Roman de Barlaam,* 1: 11–49, 73–116; Migne, *Patrologiae latina,* 73: cols. 479–80; Graesse, *Légende dorée,* 811–23. For versions in Romance languages, see: Sonet, 1: 119–95; Keller and Linker, *Barlaam e Josaphat* (Spanish); Appel, *Gui von Cambrai, Balaham und Josaphas* (French); Armstrong, *The French Metrical Versions of Barlaam and Josaphat;* Chauvin, *Bibliographie des Ouvrages arabes,* 3: 83 ff.; Hunt, *Beiträge zum romanischen Mittelalter,* 217–29; Koch, *Chardry's Josaphaz;* Kuhn, "Barlaam und Joasaph," *Abhandlungen,* 1–88; Meyer, "Fragments d'une ancienne traduction française," *Bibliothèque. de l'Ecole des Chartes,* 313–30; Mills, *L'Histoire de Barlaam;* Vermette, "Champenois Version"; Zotenberg and Meyer, *Barlaam und Josaphat.* For oriental versions, see: Budge, *Baralâm and Yěwâsěf* (Ethiopian); Gimaret, *Bilawhar et Bûdâsf* (Arabic); Lang, *Balavariani* (Old Georgian). In English, see F. S. Ellis, *The Golden Legend* (Caxton); Joseph Jacobs, *Barlaam and Josaphat.* In Japanese, see Matsubara, "Un conte japonais." For a collection in various languages, see Tyroller, *Die Fabel von dem Mann und dem Vogel.* For adaptations, see Crane, *The Exempla of Jacques de Vitry;* Hervieux, *Les Fabulistes Latins,* vol. 4; Oesterley, *Gesta Romanorum;* Budge, *Laughable Stories* (Syriac); Basset, *Mille et un Contes,* 2: 269–77; Gaster, *The Exempla of the Rabbis;* Wagner, *El Libro del cauallero Zifar,* 259–62. On dates, see Kazhdan, "Where, when, and by whom was the Greek *Barlaam and Joasaph* not written." For discussions of versions in Hebrew, see Gaster, Campbell and Schwartzbaum; also Salo Wittmayer Baron, *A Social and Religious History of the Jews* (2nd. ed., vol 7, New York: Columbia University Press, 1958); Israel Zinberg, *A History of Jewish Literature. The Arabic-Spanish Period* (Cleveland and London: The Press of Case Western Reserve University, 1972); and Haim Schwartzbaum, *Mishlé Shu 'alim* (Kiron, Israel: Institute for Jewish and Arab Folklore Research, 1979). I wish to thank Harriet L. Parmet for bringing these latter three publications to my attention.

[25] *Légendes,* 227–28.

[26] Migne, *Patrologiae graeca* and *latina* (*loc. cit.*); Boissonade, *loc. cit.*; Sonet, *loc. cit.*; and Woodward and Mattingly, *loc. cit.*

[27] In Migne, *Patrologiae graeca* and *latina* (*loc. cit.*), the word for the bird is *luscinia* and the hunter *auceps;* in the Latin of Jacobus de Voragine, the word is *philomela* for the bird and *sagittarius* for the hunter (Graesse, 815); in French, the bird is *rosignoil* and the hunter, *archier* (Mills, 62–63); in Gui de Cambrai, the bird is *lousignot* and the hunter *archier* (Appel); in Jacques de

B. The *Disciplina clericalis*

It is difficult to determine the exact relationship between the *Barlaam and Josaphat* and the *Disciplina clericalis*. The latter is often called the Latin "translation" of the former, but this is misleading. The actual translation of the Greek *Barlaam* into Latin is to be found in versions like the one in Migne.[28] What Petrus Alfonsi did, in the twelfth century, was to *laicize* a saint's life into a series of edifying stories. Some of these stories were detached from the *Disciplina* and appeared in independent collections (see Appendix, section II). The *Disciplina clericalis* was in turn rewritten in French and called the *Chastoiement d'un père à son fils*.[29]

Gaston Paris maintained that the Latin *Disciplina clericalis* of Petrus Alfonsi was the immediate source of the *Lai de l'Oiselet*.[30] The following is the *exemplum* of the *Disciplina clericalis* from the edition of Hilka and Söderjhelm:

Alius: Ne desideres res alterius, et ne doleas de amissis rebus, quoniam dolore nihil erit recuperabile. Unde dicitur quod

XXII. Exemplum de rustico et avicula.

Quidam habuit virgultum, in quo rivulis fluentibus herba viridis erat et pro habilitate loci conveniebant ibi volucres modulamine vocum cantus diversos exercentes. Quadam die dum in suo fatigatus quiesceret pomario, quaedam avicula super arborem cantando delectabiliter sedit. Quam ut vidit et eius cantum audivit, deceptam laqueo sumpsit. Ad quem avis: Cur tantum laborasti me capere, vel quod proficuum in mei captione sperasti habere? Ad haec homo: Solos cantus tuos audire cupio. Cui avis: Pro nihilo, quia retenta nec prece nec pretio cantabo. At ille: Nisi cantaveris, te comedam. Et avis: Quomodo comedes? Si comederis coctam aqua, quid valebit avis

---

Vitry, *exemplum* 28, the bird is *phylomena* and the man *homo* (Crane, 10–11); in the Latin of Odo of Cheriton, Fable 77, the bird is *philomela* and the man *sagittarius* (Hervieux, 4: 252). In Georgian the bird is a nightingale and the man a fowler (*oiseleur*) (Lang, *Balavariani*, 96–98); in Italian the bird is a nightingale *rusignuolo* and the man a hunter *arcadore, uccellatore, cacciatore* (*Storia de' SS. Barlaam e Giosaffatto*, 37–38); in Spanish, the bird is a nightingale *rruyseñor* and the man a hunter *caçador* or *vallestero* (Keller and Linker, *Barlaam*, 92–94) or *filomena* and *sagitario* (Keller and Linker, *Barlaam*, 380–81); in Arabic the bird is a sparrow (*passereau*), and the man simply a man (*homme*) (Gimaret, *Bilawhar*, 108–109); in Ethiopian, the bird is a "*shâḥrûr*" (bird) and the man a hunter (*chasseur*) (Budge, *Baralâm and Yĕwâsĕf*, 2: 63–65); in the *Mille et un contes* the bird is a sparrow (*moineau*) (2: 269–77). The precious stone is a *margarita* (in Graesse); an *ūnio* (in Migne); as big as an ostrich egg (in Gimaret); and in the *Mille et un contes* it is "worth all the taxes in Egypt and Syria" (in Basset).

[28] Migne, *Patrologiae graeca*, 96. cols. 941–44; *Patrologiae latina*, 73: cols. 179–80.

[29] For discussions of the *Disciplina clericalis* of Petrus Alfonsi see Sonet, *Roman de Barlaam et Josaphat*, 1: 20; Vermette, "Champenois Version," 12–14; Jones and Keller, *The Scholar's Guide*, 18–19. For editions of the *Disciplina*: Labouderie, *Disciplina clericalis*; Hilka and Söderhjelm, *Die Disciplina clericalis des Petrus Alfonsi*. For editions of the *Chastoiement*: Barbazan, *Castoiement* (No. 22, *Du Vilein et de l'Oiselet*, is *not* in the 1760 edition, since Barbazan says he gave the "longer version," the *Lai de l'Oiselet*, in 1756!. Méon prints the *Du Vilein et de l'Oiselet* in 1808, 2: 140–43); Labouderie, *Disciplina*, 241–467 (*Oiselet*, 397–403); Hilka and Söderhjelm, *Petri Alfonsi*, vol. 3; Montgomery, *Chastoiement*. There are three versions of the *Chastoiement* in verse, according to Hilka: the first in B.N.*f.fr.* 10289 (ed. Hilka, vol. 3; Montgomery, *Chastoiement*, and Labouderie, *Disciplina*, 397–403). The second is in B.N.*f.fr.* 19151 (ed. Barbazan, 1760; Méon, 1808). The third is in Harley 527 (ed. Hilka and Söderhjelm, 3: 153–54).

[30] *Légendes*, 233–34.

tam parva? Et etiam caro erit hispida. Et si assata fuero, multo minor ero. Sed si me abire dimiseris, magnam utilitatem ex me consequeris. At ille contra: Quale proficuum? Avis: Ostendam tibi tres sapientiae manerias quas maioris facies quam trium vitulorum carnes. At ille securus promissi avem abire permisit. Cui avis ait: Est unum de promissis: ne credas omnibus dictis! Secundum: quod tuum est, semper habebis! Tertium: ne doleas de amissis! Hoc dicto avicula arborem conscendit et dulci canore dicere coepit: Benedictus Deus qui tuorum oculorum aciem clausit et sapientiam tibi abstulit, quoniam si intestinorum plicas meorum perquisisses, unius ponderis unciae iacinctum invenisses. Hoc ille audiens cepit flere et dolere atque palmis pectus percutere, quoniam fidem dictis praebuerat aviculae. Et avis ait illi: Cito oblitus es sensus quem tibi dixi! Nonne dixi tibi: non crede quicquid tibi dicetur? Et quomodo credis quod in me sit iacinctus qui sit unius unciae ponderis, cum ego tota non sim tanti ponderis? Et nonne dixi tibi: Quod tuum est, semper habebis? Et quomodo potes lapidem habere de me volante? Et nonne dixi tibi: Ne doleas de rebus amissis? Et quare pro iacincto qui in me est doles? Talibus dictis deriso rustico avis in nemoris avia devolavit.

Philosophus castigavit filium suum dicens: Quicquid inveneris, legas, sed non credas quicquid legeris.[31]

The French works that are based on the Latin *Disciplina* are a version in French prose,[32] the *Chastoiement* in verse,[33] the *Donnei des Amants*,[34] the *Trois Savoirs*,[35] the *Récits d'un menestrel de Reims*,[36] and a so-called Aesopic fable.[37]

The versions based on the *Disciplina* are characterized by the following: (1) the bird is simply called a little bird; (2) the man is a farmer, peasant, or simply a man; (3) the bird is released *before* the three truths are given; (4) the precious stone is sometimes a hyacinth or simply a precious stone with a weight in ounces; and (5) the three truths are: do not believe everything you hear; you will have what you are destined to have; and do not grieve for what you have lost.[38]

---

[31] Hilka and Söderhjelm, *Petri Alfonsi* (Helsinki, 1911), 1: 30–31. The text is also in Heidelberg, 1911, 33–34.

[32] Hilka and Söderhjelm, *Petri Alfonsi*, 2: 26; Labouderie, 167–69.

[33] Hilka and Söderhjelm, *Petri Alfonsi*, 3: 57–60 (*A*), 119–21 (*B*), 153–54 (*h*). The *A* version is also in Montgomery, *Chastoiement*, 136–40, and Labouderie, *Disciplina*, 397–403. The *B* version is in Méon (1808), 2: 140–43.

[34] Gaston Paris, "Le Donnei des Amants," *Romania*, 25: 497–541.

[35] Paul Meyer, *Romania*, 37: 217–21. Paul Meyer gives excerpts from the manuscript. I have supplied lines 15–24 and 110–212 from my own transcription of Phillipps 25970. See Wolfgang, ed., *Trois Savoirs*.

[36] Natalis de Wailly, *Récits d'un menestrel de Reims*, 237–39.

[37] The translation into French of the fable in Steinhöwel by Julien Macho is the origin of Caxton's "Aesop's" fable. See Keidel, *PMLA*, 24: 218; Brunet, *Manuel du Libraire*, 1: pt. 1, col. 93. The text is printed in Tyroller, 242–43, and edited by Pierre Ruelle, vol. 3, *Recueil général des Isopets*, 237–39.

[38] In the *Disciplina* in Latin, the bird is *avicula* and the man *rustico*; in French prose, *oiselet* and *païsant* or *vilain*; in *Chastoiement B*, *oiselet* and *prudum*; in the *Donnei des Amants*, *oiselet* and *vilain*; in the *Trois Savoirs*, *oiselet* and *vilain*; in the *Récits*, *masenge* and *païsan/vilains*. The stone in Latin is "unius ponderis unciae iacinctum"; in French, "jagonce" or "hyacinthe," that weighs an ounce. In the *Chastoiement* prose, it is a "jagonse une onche pesant"; in *Chastoiement A*, "jacintus/pierre preciose/une once peise"; *B*, *jagunce*; in Harley 527, *jagunce*; in *Donnei*, *jagunce*; *Trois savoirs*, *jagounce*; *Récits*, "pierre precieuse ausi grosse comme uns oes de geline qui vaut cent livres."

In subsequent discussions, the stories that stem from the *Disciplina* will be called *croire pleurer* versions. This designation reflects the ordering of the three *sens* within the story. The *sens* "do not believe everything you hear" is referred to as *croire*, and "do not grieve for what you have lost" is *pleurer*.

The *Lai de l'Oiselet* is a *Disciplina*-type story according to the five narrative elements listed above, with one exception: in manuscripts *ABD* the order of the *sens* is not *croire pleurer* but *pleurer croire*. The three truths appear (in the text of *B*) as follows:

(1) Ne pleure ce c'onques n'eüs	(271)
(2) Ne croire qanque tu oz dire	(301)
(3) . . . ce que tu tiens en tes mains,	
Ne le giete jus a tes piez	(326–27)

It is the order in which the *sens pleurer* and *croire* appear in the texts which divides the *Oiselet* manuscript into two groups: *CE* (*croire pleurer* manuscripts) and *ABD* (*pleurer croire*), and it is this distinction that caused Gaston Paris to choose the version *CE* for his edition and to dismiss the version in *ABD* as not representing the "original."

C. The *Chastoiement*, *Trois Savoirs*, and *Donnei des Amants*

In the discussions that follow, I analyze the closest analogues to the *Oiselet*: the *Chastoiement*, the *Donnei des Amants*, and the *Trois Savoirs*,[39] in order to discover (1) their specific textual relationships with the *Oiselet*, and (2) any precedents in these texts to account for the *pleurer croire* version of the story in manuscripts *ABD* of the *Oiselet*.

The most striking example of textual similarity among these poems is a couplet in ms *E*, unique to that manuscript, and one in the *Chastoiement A*:

Bien savez quant je ceré cuit	
En vo bouche en porroit tex uit	(E 234ab)

Quer quant en l'eve m'avras cuit	
Tu en metreies bien teus uit.	(*Chastoiement A* Hilka, 3473–74; Montgomery, 3379–80)

Another line in *E*, also unique to that manuscript, recalls two lines in the *Donnei*:

Qu'ainz n'ama joie en sa vie	(E 184a)

Donnei:

Quant en joie ne se delite	(28)
Le vilein n'ad de joie cure	(63)

Another line in the *Donnei*, used twice, is also used twice in *E*:

---

[39] See notes 31–35.

Quant li vilein ad ço oï   (1021)
Quan ço oï li fol vileins   (1087)

Et quant li vilains l'oï   (E 317)
Quan li vilains a ce oï   (E 361a)

The following line in the *Donnei* (460):

A la fonteinne suz le pin

describes the fountain in the same way as the *Oiselet* (127):

A la fonta[inn]e souz le pin.

In addition to these fairly explicit examples of similarity, the following par-
tial lists of words and images in the *Chastoiement*, *Trois Savoirs*, and *Donnei
des Amants* suggest parallels with the *Oiselet* text:

The *Chastoiement A*: the catching of the bird with a snare (*laçon* Hilka,
3439–42; Montgomery, 3345–48); the villein climbs the tree to get the bird
(Hilka 3444; Montgomery 3350).

The *Trois Savoirs*: the description of the enclosed garden and fountain with
healing waters (3–14); the song of the bird is a *miracle* (24); the use of the
words *servise* (48, 49); *folie* (56, 167); *feintise* (73); *sens* (97); the idea that
he who would have the precious stone would not be poor (153–54); the villein
is *irascu* (174; cf. *B* 272); the use of *oblie* (181, 212); *proverbe* (213); the use
of *gabez* (232, 233); the use of *croire* in the conclusion (234–35; cf. *E* 384ab).

The *Donnei des Amants* has parallels in its *Oiselet* passage proper (929–1160)
as well as in other parts of the poem:[40] the description of the *fel vilein* (26–84);
the verb *grucer* (29, 65; cf. *B* 376); the contrast of the *gelus* and those of *franc
quer*, and the contrast of the young and old (44–58, 173–208); the use of *fine
amour* (282; cf. *E* 154, 156); *provance* (290); the oiselet who knows how to
imitate the song of other birds (938–42); the use of *se pourpensa* (945; cf. *E*
194b); *servise* (962, 963); *feintise* (993); *sens* (1023); *irascu* (1108); *oblié* (1115,
1129, 1146); *proverbe* (150, 1147); *gabez* (1156–57); *folie* (1160, 65); *secles*
(1189); *deners* (1206); *aver* (1026); *ensample(s)* (1216, 1236); *dit* (150, 156);
fable (155), *fablette* (159); *lai* (156).

What is suggested by a comparison of these texts is a progression from the
short Latin exemplum in the *Disciplina* to increasingly longer versions in French
verse. The order of the texts in terms of length is: the *Disciplina clericalis*;
the versions *h*, *B* and *A* of the *Chastoiement*; the *Trois Savoirs*; the *Donnei
des Amants*; the *Oiselet* in manuscripts *E*, *A*, *BC*, and finally *D*.[41] The out-

---

[40] The *Trois Savoirs* and the *Donnei des Amants* are closely related texts. See remarks by
Meyer, *Romania*, 37: 217–18.

[41] The lengths of the texts are: *Disciplina*, 24 lines plus two-line introduction and two-line
conclusion (in Hilka-Söderjhelm, Helsinki, 1911; in the Heidelberg 1911 printing, the exemplum
is 36 lines and a three-line introduction and a three-line conclusion); the *Chastoiement h* is 50
verses, plus 12 verses of introduction and conclusion; *B*, 92 verses plus 14 of introduction and
conclusion; *A*, 152 verses, plus ten of introduction and conclusion; ms *E*, 342 verses; *A* 390 verses;
BC 410 verses each; and *D* 506 verses.

line of the story remains constant in each text, but the dialogue and descriptions of the garden and the bird increase in length with each subsequent version.

Gaston Paris said that he chose *C* as representing the authentic version of the *Lai de l'Oiselet* because it had the order of the three *sens* as found in the *Disciplina clericalis*, which is, as we have seen: (1) do not believe everything you hear (*croire*); (2) you will have what you are destined to have; and (3) do not grieve for what you have lost (*pleurer*). In the five *Oiselet* manuscripts, the order of the three *sens* compared to the *Disciplina* is: 1 3 2 in *CE* and 3 1 2 in *ABD*, so that the real issue is the order of *croire* and *pleurer*, since all the manuscripts put 2 last. In fourteen texts based on the *Disciplina* that I analyzed, I found that they all consistently place *croire* first.[42]

The order of the three *sens* in the *Barlaam* is: (1) never try to attain to the unattainable; (2) never regret the thing past and gone (*pleurer*); and (3) never believe the word that passeth belief (*croire*). In the *Oiselet* manuscripts, the order of the three *sens* compared to the *Barlaam* is: 3 2 1 in *CE* and 2 3 1 in *ABD*, so again the essential element is the order of *croire* and *pleurer*, not the overall order of the three *sens*. In seventeen *Barlaam* texts that I analyzed, I found that *pleurer* precedes *croire* in all of them.[43]

The *Lai de l'Oiselet* turns out, then, to be a hybrid in terms of the three *sens*: *pleurer* precedes *croire* in *ABD* and thus might reflect the order of the three *sens* in the *Barlaam*, and *croire* precedes *pleurer* in *CE* and thus reflects the order of the *sens* in the *Disciplina*. The four narrative elements in the five *Oiselet* manuscripts are consistent with the *Disciplina* version of the story.

For Gaston Paris only the ordering of the three *sens* in the *Oiselet* manuscripts was the determining factor in his choice of *C* as the original and there-

---

[42] Texts where *croire* comes before *pleurer*: Latin *Disciplina clericalis* (ed. Hilka and Söderhjelm, vol. 1 [Helsingfors, 1911]: no. 22, pp. 30–31, and [Heidelberg, 1911] no. 22, pp. 33–34; ed. Labouderie, no. 20, pp. 166–70); French Prose *Disciplina* (ed. Hilka and Söderhjelm, 2: 26; ed. Labouderie, no. 20, pp. 167–71); French verse *Chastoiement* (ed. Hilka and Söderhjelm, 3: 59, 120, 154; ed. Labouderie, no. 19, pp. 397–403; ed. Méon [1808], 2: 140–43; ed. Montgomery, no. 19, pp. 136–40); English *Disciplina* (ed. Hulm, no. 17, pp. 47–48); Lydgate's *Churl and Bird* (ed. Hammond, 104–10; ed. MacCracken, 2: 468–85 [lines 197–217]); Steinhöwel's *Aesop* (ed. Oesterley, no. 147, pp. 312–13); Julien Macho's French *Aesop* (Ruelle, 237–39); Caxton's *Aesop* (ed. Jacobs, 269–71, ed. Lenaghan, 201–203); Spanish *Esopo* of 1489 (González Palencia, 223–25); *Menestrel de Reims* (ed. Wailly, 237–39); *Donnei des Amants* (ed. G. Paris, 519); *Trois Savoirs* (ed. Wolfgang, lines 111–210); *El libro de los Enxemplos* (ed. Gayangos, no. 53, p. 460; ed. González Palencia, no. 22, pp. 152–54); *El libro de los exenplos por a.b.c.*, ed. Keller, 110–11; Japanese *Aesop* (trans. Matsubara, 204–205).

[43] Texts where *pleurer* precedes *croire*: Gui von Cambrai, *Barlaam* (ed. Appel, 67–70; ed. Zotenberg and Meyer, 60–62); *Mille et un contes* (ed. Basset, no. 39, vol. 2: 274); Greek *Barlaam* (ed. Migne, *PG*, 96: cols. 941–44, *PL*, 73: cols. 479–80; Boissonade, 4: 79–81; Woodward and Mattingly, 134–39); Ethiopian *Barlaam* (ed. Budge, 1: xxii–xxiii, and 2: 63–65); Syriac, *Barlaam* (*Laughable Stories*, ed. Budge, no. 382, p. 93); *Exempla* of Jacques de Vitry (ed. Crane, no. 28, pp. 10–11); Caxton's *Barlaam* (ed. Ellis, vol. 1. 3: 91–93; ed. Jacobs, Appendix 10, pp. 13–14); *Exempla of the Rabbis* (ed. Gaster, no. 390, pp. 149–50); Arabic *Barlaam* (ed. Gimaret, 108–109); *Legenda aurea* (ed. Graesse, ch. 180: 815–16; trans. Ryan and Ripperger, 725–26); *Fables* of Odo of Cheriton (ed. Hervieux, 4: 252, no. 77; trans. John C. Jacobs, 160–61); Perry, *Aesopica*, no. 627, pp. 643–44, and ed. Loeb, no. 627, pp. 551–52; Georgian *Balavariani* (ed. Lang, no. 11, pp. 96–97); Spanish *Barlaam* (eds. Keller and Linker, 92–94, 380–82); French Prose *Barlaam* (ed. Mills, 62–63); *Gesta Romanorum* (ed. Oesterley, no. 167, pp. 554–56; trans. Swan, no. 167, pp. 318–19); Italian *Barlaam* (trans. Bottari, 37–38); Japanese *Barlaam* (trans. Matsubara, 206–207).

fore best version of the story. This determination ignores the fact that three of the five manuscripts preserve a different order. In trying to discover why *pleurer* was placed first in *ABD*, I analyzed the number of lines devoted to this *sens* in these texts, and I discovered that the greatest number of lines were allotted to the *sens pleurer* in all five of the manuscripts even when *pleurer* was not placed first: *pleurer* is referred to in 12 lines (*B* 271, 279–80, 263–65, 369–70, 385–88); *croire* is referred to in five (*B* 301, 378–81); and the third *sens* in four (*B* 326–27, 340–41).

This emphasis on *pleurer* is also reflected in other *Disciplina*-type texts. For example, in the *Chastoiement A*, only *pleurer* is referred to in the introduction:

Fiz, encor te voil chastïer
Qu'autrui chose ne coveitier,
Ne ja mar trop grant *duel* feras
Quant la toue chose perdras,
Quer bien seiz que par *doloser*
Ne porreies rien recovrer   (Hilka, 3397–3402)

This same emphasis on *pleurer* is in the *Disciplina* itself, which begins the following way: "Ne desideras res alterius et ne *doleas* de amissas rebus, quoniam *dolore* nihil erit recuperabile."

The texts of *E* and *C*, which place *croire* first, reflect a slightly different number of lines allotted to this *sens* and to the third one, but *E* and *C* also retain more lines of text devoted to *pleurer* than to the other two. *E* has an additional two lines that refer to *croire* and is the only text to refer to the *sens croire* in the concluding admonition of the bird to the villein:

On ne doit pas tot le mont croire
Tu deïs orains, c'est la voire   (*E* 382ab)

The text of *C*, although it also has *croire* first in order, does not have *E* 382ab in its text. It, rather, has an additional two lines that refer to the third *sens*, and is the only one with this *sens* in the conclusion of the admonition of the bird to the villein:

Et quant me tenis en tes las
Ce qu'an mains eüs as piez ruas   (*C* 388ab)

It seems clear, then, that there are precedents for both orders of *sens*. The order *croire pleurer* reflects the order in all the *Disciplina* versions of the story except in manuscripts *ABD* of the *Oiselet*, and the order *pleurer croire* in *ABD* reflects the order of importance conferred on the *sens pleurer* by the actual amount of space allotted to it in telling the story and in the number of times this *sens* is referred to in the text.

It would be tempting to conclude that the order *pleurer croire* also reflects the order of the *sens* in the *Barlaam*, but there is no other evidence that the *Barlaam* influenced the *Oiselet* except indirectly as a source of the *Disciplina*. The most difficult question about the five *Oiselet* manuscripts is, however: which came first, the version *ABD* or *EC*? Did one scribe/poet actually reverse the version he found in his copy? If *ABD* reversed *EC*, was this done in recognition of the emphasis conferred on *pleurer* as opposed to *croire*? If *EC* reversed *ABD*, was this done to bring it into line with the *Disciplina* versions of the story? Discussions of these questions are to be found in section V of the Introduction and in the Textual Notes, especially to lines 270–312, where clues to the answers are sought among the patterns of lines of the individual manuscripts and from the copying practices of the scribes.

D. THEMATIC SOURCES: THE *LOCUS AMOENUS*

One of the most dramatic differences between the exemplum of the *Lai de d'Oiselet* in the *Barlaam and Josaphat* or the *Disciplina clericalis* and its realization in the *Lai de l'Oiselet* is length.

As Gaston Paris said, the *Lai de l'Oiselet* is based on a parable in the *Disciplina clericalis*, but "transformé presque complètement,"[44] and this almost complete transformation of the story is due in large measure to the amplification of the description of the garden. The garden, which assembles elements from classical and Biblical sources, is transformed into a symbolic milieu, suggesting, in its most complete manifestation, the Earthly Paradise or, in more general terms, the so-called *locus amoenus*.

There is a vast amount of scholarship dealing with this theme,[45] and there are numerous texts which have passages illustrating it.[46] In thirteenth- to fourteenth-century literature the most complete example of it is, of course, the *Roman de la Rose*.[47]

---

[44] *Légendes*, 253.

[45] For studies of the theme of the *locus amoenus*, see Badel, *Introduction à la vie littéraire*, 119–23, 148–55; Baum, "Eine neue Etymologie," 17–78; Chandler, "The Nightingale," 78–84; Camparetti, *Virgil and the Middle Ages*, passim; Curtius, *European Literature and the Latin Middle Ages*, 183–202; Dragonetti, *Technique poétique*, 163–69, 170–72, 177, 181–83; Dronke, *Medieval Latin and the Rise of European Love-Lyric*, 2: 5–6; Empson, *Some Versions of Pastoral*, passim; Fleming, *The Roman de la Rose*, passim; Faral, *Recherches sur les sources latines*, 251–69, 369–72; Frappier, *Amour courtois et Table Ronde*, 143–52; Giamatti, *The Earthly Paradise*, passim; Graf, *Mitti, leggende e superstizioni*, passim; Gunn, *The Mirror of Love*, 95–118, 478–96, 643–84, 701–708; Hensel, *Die Vögel*, 584–670; Hubaux and Leroy, *Le Mythe du Phénix*, 29, 35; Johnston, "The Description of the Emir's Garden"; Kelly, *Medieval Imagination*, 57–95; Lee, "Il giardino rinsecchito," 66–84; Patch, *The Other World according to Descriptions in Medieval Literature*, passim; Piehler, *The Visionary Landscape*, 98–105; Poirion, *Le Merveilleux*, passim, and *Le Roman de la Rose* (Hatier); Ross, "Rose und Nachtigall," 55–82; Spargo, *Virgil the Necromancer*, passim; Stevens, *Medieval Romance*, 119, 139; Thoss, *Studien zum locus amoenus*, passim; Watson, *The Garden of Love*, passim; Wilhelm, *The Cruelest Month*, passim.

[46] For an exhaustive collection of texts, see Thoss, *Studien von locus amoenus*. The traditional points of departure for discussions of the *locus amoenus* are the *Works and Days* of Hesiod, lines 167–69 (Loeb Classical Library, 14–15), and Biblical passages in *Genesis, Song of Solomon*, and *Revelation*. Other texts are: the *Odyssey*, 5, lines 63–91; the *Aeneid*, 6, lines 843–97; Ovid, *Metamorphoses*, 3 (*Narcissus*), 6 (*Philomela*); Alain de Lille, *Anticlaudianus*, 1, lines 55–151. In medieval French literature, the *Roman d'Alexandre*, 7 (ed. Armstrong); *Romanzen und Pastourellen* (ed. Bartsch); *Philomela* (ed. de Boer); *Roman de Troie* (ed. Constans); *Floire et Blanceflor* (ed. Edélestand du Méril); *Partonopeu de Blois* (ed. Gildea); *Li Fablel dou Dieu d'Amours* (ed. Jubinal); *Le Roman de la Rose* (ed. Langlois; ed. Lecoy); *Erec et Enide* (ed. Roques); *Yvain* (ed. Roques).

[47] Lecoy, *Rose*, note to 1595–97.

The garden in the *Oiselet* is round in shape (52);[48] it is enclosed by air and water (19), planted with medicinal herbs (27–38), and made by *nigromance* (49). These details recall passages in several early romances, such as the *Erec* of Chrétien de Troyes, the *Roman d'Alexandre*, and the *Roman de Troie*. The following excerpts from these romances show striking similarities with details in the *Oiselet*:

Erec:

> El vergier n'avoit an viron
> mur ne paliz, se de l'air non;
> mes de l'air est de totes parz
> par nigromance clos li jarz,
> si que riens antrer n'i pooit,
> se par un seul leu n'i antroit,
> ne que s'il fust toz clos de fer.
> Et tot esté et tot yver
> y avoit flors et fruit maür;
> et li fruiz avoit tel eür
> que leanz se lessoit mangier,
> mes au porter hors fet dongier;
> car qui point an volsist porter
> ne s'an seüst ja mes raler,
> car a l'issue ne venist
> tant qu'an son leu le remeïst.
> Ne soz ciel n'a oisel volant,
> qui pleise a home an chantant
> a lui desduire et resjoïr,
> qu'iluec ne poïst l'an oïr
> plusors de chascune nature.
> Et terre, tant com ele dure,
> ne porte espice ne mecine,
> qui vaille a nule medecine,
> que iluec n'i eüst planté,
> s'an i avoit a grant planté.[49]

Alexandre:

> El bois ot un vergié de grant antiquité,
> Poires i ot et pumes et fruit a grant plenté
> Et dates et amandes et yver et esté,
> Cherubins et nardiers, mil arbres de bonté;
> I vinrent par nature, ainc n'i furent planté,
> De la forest tenoient une lieue de lé;

---

[48] The second garden in the *Rose* is also round in shape. Cf. *Rose* (ed. Lecoy), 20264–67. See also note to line 19 of the *Oiselet*. The garden of the Apocalypse may also be suggested here.

[49] Ed. Roques, lines 5689–5714; ed. Foerster, 5739–64.

Et entre les devises du vergié ot un pré
De toutes chieres herbes garni et asasé.
Hom ne demande herbe ne vient en pensé
Dont iluec ne trovast tout a sa volenté.
Il n'a sous ciel cel home tant enferm n'engroté,
De poison ne de poudre tant fort envenimé,
De dolor ne de mal tant fort enraciné
Ne le cuer entoschié ne le foie entamé,
Se il pooit tant faire qu'il en eüst gousté
Et le col en eüst en petitet passé
Et un poi i eüst dormi et reposé,
Que il ne s'en alast tous liés et en santé
De la flairor des herbes et de la sanité.
N'a sous ciel damoisele, tant ait ris ne joué,
S'ele a a son ami son gent cors presenté,
Entre ses bras tenu, baisié et acolé,
Se une seule nuit i avoit reposé
Et son cors trestot nu sor les herbes posé,
Au main ne fust pucele s'eüst sa chasteé
De l'odour des espices et de la douceté.

Molt fu biaus li vergiers et gente la praele,
Molt souef i flairoit riquelisse et canele,
Garingaus et encens, citouaus et tudele.
Tres en mi lieu du pré sort une fontenele
Dont la dois estoit clere et blanche la perrele,
A rouge or espanois pesast on la gravele.[50]

and the *Roman de Troie*:

Devant la sale aveit un pin
Dont les branches furent d'or fin
Tresgetees par artimaire,
Par nigromance e par gramaire.[51]

The fountain (*Oiselet*, 51–57) and pine (58–70) also have parallels in *Floire et Blancheflor*[52] and *Yvain*:

Yvain:

La fontaine verras qui bout,
s'est ele plus froide que marbres.

---

[50] Ed. Armstrong, *Alexandre*, vol. 7, lines 3299–3330. The healing garden is also mentioned in *Blancheflour et Florence* (ed. Meyer, *Romania*, 37: 221–34).

[51] Ed. Constans, lines 6265–68. The motif of the garden with magical qualities and enclosed by a wall of air recalls the legends of Virgil as a magician. See Graf, *Miti, Leggende e superstizioni del medioevo*, esp. vol. 1: xi–xxiii, 16–43; Comparetti, *Virgilio nel medioevo*, trans. Benecke, esp. 102–103, 106–18, 141–49, 233–35, 250–52, 258–63, 292–93, 337–39; and Spargo, *Virgil the Necromancer*, esp. 1–68, 111, 114–15, 138–39.

[52] Ed. Leclenche, lines 1979–82, 1995–2012, 2021–54.

Onbre li fet li plus biax arbres
c'onques poïst former Nature.
En toz tens sa fuelle li dure,
qu'il ne la pert por nul iver.[53]

The following two poems have a villein whose presence in a garden enrages
a singing bird (cf. *Oiselet*, 170–92):

Romance:

En mai au douz tens nouvel,
que raverdissent prael,
oisoz un arbroisel
chanter le rosignolet.
　saderala don!
　tant fet bon
　dormir lez le buissonet.

Si com g'estoie pensis,
lez le buissonet m'assis:
un petit m'i endormi
au douz chant de l'oiselet.
　saderala don! *etc.*

Au resveillier que je fis
a l'oisel criai merci
q'il me doint joi de li:
s'en serai plus jolivet.
　saderala don! *etc.*

Et quant je fui sus levez,
si conmenz a citoler
et fis l'oiselet chanter
devant moi el praelet.
　saderala don! *etc.*

Li rosignolez disoit:
par un pou qu'il n'enrajoit
du grant duel que il avoit,
que vilains l'avoit oi.
saderala don! *etc.*[54]

Fablel dou Dieu d'Amours:

Je me levoie par .i. matin en may,
Por la douchor des oysiaus et del glai,
Del loussignot, del malvis et dou gai.
Qant fui levés en .i. pré m'en entrai.

---

[53] Ed. Roques, lines 380–85. cf. *Oiselet*, 51–70.
[54] Ed. Bartsch, *Romanzen und Pastourellen*, Bk. 1, no. 27, pp. 22–23. Gennrich, *Altfranzösische Rotrouenge*, 47–48, gives the music to this song.

Je vos dirai com faite estoit la praerée;
L'erbe i fu grande par desous la rousée.
Herbe ne flors n'i fust ja perparlée,
S'ele i fust quise, qu'ele n'i fust trovée.

De paradis i couroit uns rouissiax,
Parmi la prée, qui tant ert clere et biax,
N'a tant viel home en cités n'en castiax,
S'il si baignast, lues ne fust jovenenciax.

Ne dame nule tant éust mesivé,
Mais qant nul jor n'éust enfant porté,
Se .i. petit éust asavouré,
Ne fust pucèle, ains qu'ele issist del pré. . . .

De tel manière estoit tous li vergiés,
Ains n'i ot arbre, ne fust pins u loriés.
Cyprès, aubours, entes et oliviers.
Ce sont li arbres que nous tenons plus ciers.

Fuelles et flors ont tos tans li ramier,
Et sont de roses bien carchié li rosier.
Jà par yvier n'aront nul destorbier;
Nient plus que may ne criement il feurier. . . .

Ains ne fust eure se vilains i venist,
Et ce fust cose que ens entrer volsist,
Oustre son gré, qant sor le pont venist,
Levast li pons, et li porte closist.

Tout ensi fust de soi k'il s'en ralast,
Car ne voloient que vilains i entrast;
Et ausi tost que il s'en retornast,
Ouvrist li porte, et li pons ravalast. . . .

Laiens entrai sans nesun contredit.
Qant jou oï des oisyllons le crit,
D'autre canchon en che liu ne de dit,
N'eusse cure, che saciés tout de fit.

Sous ciel n'a home, s'il les oïst canter,
Tant fust vilains ne l'esteut amer;
Illuec m'asis por mon cors deporter.
Desous une ente ki mult fait à loer.[55]

The most complete assemblage of these motifs is in the *Roman de la Rose*.[56] The villein of the *Rose* is Dangier, who, like the villein of the *Oiselet* (170–71), was under the tree (3651–93; 3713–17). Dangier provokes the wrath of Amor,

---

[55] *Li Fablel dou Dieu d'Amours*, ed. Jubinal, lines 13–28, 37–44, 57–64, 77–84.
[56] Particular passages that recall the *Oiselet* are (ed. Lecoy) lines 469–94, 643–711, 1321–1436, 20244–67, 20549–66.

Nature, and Genius the way the villein of the *Oiselet* provokes the wrath of
the bird.

E. Generic and Stylistic Observations

The *Lai de l'Oiselet* appeared in medieval manuscript collections that also
included fabliaux, contes, and dits, but it has been excluded from modern
collections, which have been divided into the categories of fabliaux, lais of
Marie de France, lais anonymes, and lais de Bretagne. Because the *Oiselet*
appears in B.N. *nouv. acq.* 1104, which is called a collection of *lais de Bretagne*,
the *Oiselet* is mentioned in discussions of such lais, but quickly excluded, since
its setting is not explicitly Breton. In most studies of lais and fabliaux, the
Oiselet is thus grouped with a small number of works, like the *lai d'Aristote*,
that do not fit into the standard categories of definitions of lai, fabliau, or
other genres.[57]

One of the first scholars to point out that the *Oiselet* did not fit into clear-
cut categories of lai or fabliau was Joseph Bédier,[58] and later, Jean Frappier
remarked that the *Oiselet* was "aux confins du lai et du fabliau."[59]

There is a mixture of elements in the *Oiselet* associated with both the lai
and the fabliau. The bird, his message, the garden (*locus amoenus*), all be-
long to the world of the lai, whereas the villein and the action of *dupeur dupé*
belong to the world of the fabliau. In the case of the version in manuscript
D, the fabliau elements are even more exaggerated.[60] The bird is the hero who
seeks vengeance, and the villein is the butt of "anti-bourgeois" satire.[61]

The word lai itself has various interpretations, among them: a short narra-
tive, courtly poem; a song; and birdsong. In the *Oiselet* these elements are
all combined: a bird sings a lai within a narrative poem entitled lai.

The "action" of the poem, however, is not courtly: a *dupeur* (the villein)
is outwitted and punished (*dupé*). This kind of action is more often associated

---

[57] The following works have been consulted concerning the definition of the genres lai and
fabliau: Baader, *Die Lais*; Baum, *Recherches sur les oeuvres attribuées à Marie de France*, and
"Les Troubadours et les lais"; Bédier, *Les Fabliaux*; van den Boogard, "L'Exemplum"; Burgess, *Marie
de France, an Analytical Bibliography*; Day, "A Structural Analysis"; Dees, "Considérations théo-
riques"; de Riquer, "La 'aventure,' el 'lai' y el 'conte'"; Donovan, *The Breton Lay*; Dragonetti, *La
technique poétique*; Dubin, "The Parodic Lays"; Dubuis, *Les Cent Nouvelles Nouvelles*; *Epopée
Animale*; Ewert, *Marie de France. Lais*; Foulet, "Marie de France et les lais bretons"; Frappier,
"Remarques sur la structure du lai"; Guiette, *Fabliaux et Contes, Introduction*; Jodogne, "Le Fab-
liau"; Kahlert, "The Breton Lay and Generic Drift"; Keidel, "The History of French Fable
Manuscripts"; Kroll, *Der narrative Lai*; Ménard, *Les Fabliaux. Contes à rire au Moyen âge*, and
Les Lais de Marie de France; *New Grove Dictionary of Music and Musicians*, "Lai"; Nykrog,
Les Fabliaux; Payen, *Le Lai narratif*; Ringger, *Die Lais*; Rychner, *Contribution à l'étude des Fab-
liaux*, "La critique textuelle de la Branche III (Martin) du *Roman de Renart*," and "Les Fabliaux";
Schenck, *The Fabliaux, Tales of Wit and Deception*; Sempoux, *La Nouvelle*; Sienaert, *Les lais
de Marie de France*; Tobin, *Les Lais anonymes*; Williams, "The Genre and Art of the Old French
Fabliaux"; Zumthor, "La brièveté comme forme," *Essai de poétique médiévale*, and *Langue et
techniques poétiques*.

[58] Bédier, *Fabliaux*, 34 n. 1.

[59] Frappier, "Remarques sur la structure," 34 and n. 2.

[60] See discussion of ms *D*, pp. 5–6, 24–26.

[61] See Alter, *Les Origines de la satire anti-bourgeoise*, 124. Lee, "Il giardino rinsecchito," also
calls attention to the satire of the rich villein.

with the fabliau, but, when when one looks for the act committed by the villein that causes him to be so severely punished, all we find is that the villein caught a bird, threatened it, and let it go again. But the villein was severely punished for this action: the garden withers, the fountain dries up, and the villein loses his property and the enjoyment of it.

The real meaning of the poem is thus not in the action, a *dupeur dupé*, but in the bird's message. The message of the lai is that one should love God, practice courtesy and largess, and that those who do not are to be scorned and punished. The villein represents a creature whose appetites and actions outrage God, love, and beauty, symbolized by the bird. Ultimately, the bird signifies *poésie* and the villein is *ignorance*, a philistine, whose very presence in the garden profanes the sacred place and causes it to perish and die. It is not necessary for the bird to be killed, as in Marie de France's *Laustic*, but just for it to be caught, menaced, and ruffled (profaned), for a crime or sin to be committed.

The text of the *Oiselet*, however, plays with the idea of genre: the bird sings a lai within the lai, and the word itself is mentioned three times in the poem (lines 89, 133, 137). Other genre words used are *chant* (lines 85, 95, 107, 117, 169, 187); *chanter* (lines 97, 116, 131, 173, 199); *son* (lines 89, 116); *chançon* (lines 90, 216); *rotrüenge* (line 90); *essample* (line 134); *fable* (line 12); and *sens* (lines 251, 267, 270, 275, 307, 312, 339, 389).

The idea of genre is directly related to style. The *Oiselet* combines themes and motifs that have been called courtly (garden, fountain, birdsong) with non-courtly satire or fabliau themes and motifs (the villein, the *dupeur dupé*, mockery). This mixture of elements from genres traditionally opposed is frustrating perhaps only to an effort to put the *Oiselet* into one definitive list or another, lai or fabliau, and this effort is, perhaps, unnecessary.

The two protagonists of the poem, the bird and the villein, are clearly actors from two different worlds. The villein is the traditional object of mockery and hatred in the fabliau. The bird, a courtly porte-parole, is the "tragic hero," a victim of brutality and base instincts, of the creature who "prefers making money to making love," and, in ms *D*, who prefers peas and lard to blond young women! However, both the bird and the villein lose at the end of the poem: the villein loses his property and the pleasure of it (*deduit*), and the bird flies away and disappears forever. It is this combination of come-uppance and tragedy, of mockery and seriousness of purpose, that, I believe, led Jean Frappier to situate the *Oiselet* "aux confins du lai et du fabliau."

Gaston Paris, however, seemed less ambiguous in his view of the *Lai de l'Oiselet*,[62] and his edition of the poem betrays his strong bias in favor of a courtly lai by his manipulation of manuscript *C*. Gaston Paris chose to use this manuscript because he believed it was the authentic, original version going back to the *Disciplina clericalis* of Petrus Alfonsi, and he wanted to use his edition of it as a wedding present for his nephew.

---

[62] Despite the "slip" in categorizing that Bédier caught! In his *Fabliaux*, 34, n. 1, Bédier points out that G. Paris had called the *Oiselet* a fabliau in his *Littérature française au moyen âge*, § 77.

The text, as Gaston Paris presents it, is delightfully appropriate for the occasion, but there is a serious omission of text, the presence of which would have made it less so. There is no doubt that the poem, with its description of a garden, birdsong, and wise sayings in a clever little plot, made a lovely epithalamium. But, as the bird said, we cannot believe everything we hear, especially if we do not hear everything, such as the last four lines of manuscript *C* that Gaston Paris omitted entirely from his edition:

> Ci faut li lais de l'oiselet,
> Dou vilains ne donroie un pet;
> Il perdi par son couvoitier
> Et son deduit et son vergier.[63]

So, one may ask, is this a lai or a fabliau after all, masquerading behind garden, birdsong, and talk of God, just waiting to reveal itself at the very end? Is the poem just a nasty little joke about an evil-minded little peasant done in by a sharp-talking bird? If genre is related to tone, as Jean Frappier and Robert Guiette put it so well,[64] then manuscript *C* must move over and join the peas and lard of ms *D*!

It seems that Gaston Paris manipulated his text, conveniently published without variants and *leçons rejetées*, so that it reflected both his idea of the authentic and original version of the poem, and is also a charming, courtly lai, proper in tone for a wedding present.

The idea of genre, then, seems to be behind some of Gaston Paris's alteration of the poem, and it is the idea of genre that has disturbed the literary scholars from the beginning, who left the *Oiselet* out of their lists of lais or fabliaux. I would like to propose that the *Oiselet* is a unique entity, with elements of both the traditional lai and fabliau, and so it accomplishes the goals of both: it celebrates the courtly and punishes the non-courtly; it extols God and love, and exposes the nasty, brutish, gluttonous villein to scorn and derision. The obscenity, which had been removed from the poem without a trace, might indeed have been inappropriate for an epithalamium, but its deeper significance does not destroy the poem as a lai. The obscenity of the poet, rather, destroys the villein, the incarnation of violence and blindness to beauty, of indifference to *poésie* and to the whole meaning of the courtly world. Rather than spoiling the genre lai, the conclusion of *C*, exultant, brutal, and direct, underscores the message. The bird is *poésie*, the villein is *ignorance*, and the act is rape. The villein, the materialist, the brute, the dragon in the garden, must be annihilated, and we, the poet, the bird, cannot hate the villein enough,

---

[63] "Here ends the lai of the oiselet, And of the villein I don't give a fart; Through his covetousness he lost Both his pleasure and his garden." Only Barbazan (1756) and Méon (1808) have texts with this ending. Långfors (*Romania*, 44: 90–91) notes that the copyist of ms *C* suffered from "la maladie de la versification," and that he added endings that do not appear in other manuscripts of the same poems.

[64] Frappier, "Remarques," 26, said, "De l'esthétique des tons à l'esthétique des genres la distance ne me paraît pas infinie." He also quotes Robert Guiette: "Le ton nous paraît au contraire nettement déterminé par le caractère même de l'oeuvre, de telle sorte qu'il ne pouvait guère y avoir de confusion [pour les fabliaux] avec les 'lais', bretons ou autres, ou avec les histoires sentimentales relevant de la pensée et de la symbolique courtoises" (loc. cit).

the enemy of God, love, courtesy, and poetry, and so we destroy him with the obscenity of our scorn and deep hatred and are left with the tragedy of our loss.

In short, the *Lai de l'Oiselet* incorporates the best of both worlds, lai and fabliau, the light and the dark, and is thus neither and both.[65]

V. THE PRESENT EDITION

A. The Choice of the Base Manuscript

In the discussions that follow, the lines in manuscripts *CDE* and *A* are described in terms of the line numbers of *B*, the base manuscript. Each manuscript was considered as a possible base, and the main reasons for eliminating each in favor of *B* are outlined in turn.

1. Ms *C*[66]

Gaston Paris had based his choice of manuscript *C*, as we have seen, on literary reasons. For him, *C* represented his idea of the original version of the *Lai de l'Oiselet*. He said that *CE* reflected the original "parce qu'il concorde avec celui de Pierre Alfonse," but he did not want to enter "dans le détail de cette comparaison."[67] He classified the manuscripts the following way: "les cinq manuscrits remontent à deux copies différentes du manuscrit original perdu: *ABD* descendent de l'un, *C* représente l'autre, *E* paraît être le produit d'une fusion des deux."[68]

However much Gaston Paris said he based his choice of *C* on the so-called authenticity of the order of the sens, he nevertheless altered more than two-thirds of the 410 lines of his base manuscript *C*, sometimes choosing readings that "se rapprochent le plus du français normal,"[69] which was not surprising since the poem was meant to be an epithalamium and not a scholarly edition.

More serious, however, was his adding, dropping, and changing of words and lines from ms *C*. Without any variants or notes, one gets a distorted version of the poem in *C* especially, as we have seen, in his omission of the last four lines of the manuscript. The following passage is another example:

	G. Paris		Ms *C*
109	S'il oïst de l'oisel le chant	109	S'oïst de l'oisillon le chant
	Si li semblast il maintenant		Si cuidast il tout maintenant
	Qu'il fust meschins et damoiseaus		Estre ammerres de dammes beles
	Et si cuidast estre si beaus		
	Qu'il fust amés de damoiseles,		
	De meschines et de puceles.		De meschines et de puceles.

---

[65] A point of departure for some of these ideas is in Frappier, "Remarques," 25–35, and Ménard, *Le Rire et le Sourire*, 172. Some of my remarks in this section were in a paper presented at the convention of the Modern Language Association, 28 December 1984.
[66] See above, pp. 4–5.
[67] G. Paris, *Légendes*, 272.
[68] See p. 7 for full citation.
[69] G. Paris, *Légendes*, 272.

In this instance, line 111 and the two added lines in Gaston Paris's text are from ms B.

Ms C has been studied by various editors of lais and fabliaux who generally rejected it as a base when there were other choices. Only Gaston Raynaud in his edition of the *Chastelaine de Vergi* found "ses leçons généralement bonnes."[70]

Ms 25545 contains 410 verses, the same number as B, but it adds 22 verses to B and omits 22.[71] In its additions, the two lines after 388 in C make the only reference in any of the manuscripts to the words of the third sens in the conclusion of the poem:

> Et quant me tenis en tes las,
> Ce qu'an mains eüs, as piez ruas.

Ms C has not been chosen as base for two reasons: (1) it represents the minority version (*croire pleurer*) of the five texts supported by E but opposed by ABD; and (2) it would require many more emendations than B to produce a satisfactory text.

Despite a few interesting lines, such as 388ab, the faults of C far outweigh its virtues. For specific observations about the text of C, see the Textual Notes to lines 10, 151–68, 187–92, 270–312, 331, 335–60, 382–98, and 399–410.

2. Ms D[72]

Ms D, like C, is a fourteenth-century manuscript and is the longest one of the five, with 505 verses (D 102 [= B 92] is missing). D adds 116 verses to B and omits 20,[73] and has 19 hypometric verses (including hiatus) and 6 hypermetric verses.[74]

Ms D is very eccentric in terms of its many added lines, and other editors have almost universally condemned it for its faults. Rychner, Hoepffner, and Lecoy, in particular, are quite outspoken against D,[75] although Rychner does find some virtues in it. He says it is, despite its faults, a manuscript of "expression imagée, d'allure proverbiale et populaire"; that it uses a language that implies "conscience sinon intention"; and that the orientation of the poet is of a "jongleur qui récitait . . . devant un public différent de celui pour lequel

---

[70] See *Romania*, 21: 147. Other editors who discussed C are Rychner, *Contribution*, 1: 53–58; Stuip, *Chastelaine*, 60; Långfors, *Romania*, 44: 90; and Verhulsdonck, "Le ms B.N. 25.545," *Marche Romane*, 28: 193–97.

[71] Verses added are 2 after 10, 130, 152, 182, 216, 304; 3 after 310; 1 after 312; 2 after 388; 4 after 410; verses omitted are 109–110, 131–32, 143–44, 153–54, 187–88, 217–18, 305–306, 341–46, 400, 406. Hypermetric verses: 34, 230.

[72] See above, pp. 5–6.

[73] Verses added to B: 2 after 2, 8, 10, 16, 26, 58, 119, 130, 144, 160, 190, 216, 228, 232, 258, 270, 310, 328, 346, 364, 368, 370; 1 after 169, 403, 404; 3 after 170; 4 after 220, 336; 8 after 168, 206; 12 after 110; 12 after 214; 20 after 192; verses omitted: 3–4, 131–32, 207–208, 211–12, 217–18, 221–22, 311–12, 347–48, 365–66, 400, 406.

[74] Hypometric verses (including hiatus): 14, 74, 104, 125, 154, 190a, 192p, 198, 200, 201, 206g, 214l, 224, 265, 300, 370a, 377 (-2), 388 (-2), 394; hypermetric verses: 12, 110f, 182, 192n, 276, 328b.

[75] Rychner, *Contribution*, 1: 67–84; Hoepffner, *Trad*, 89–95; Lecoy, "Le dit de l'espervier," *Romania*, 69: 528–34, and 70: 408–409.

il avait été écrit."[76] These remarks can also be applied to the additions that D makes to the *Oiselet*, particularly the long ones: 12 lines after 110, 8 after 168, 20 after 192, 8 after 206, and 12 after 214.

In the 12 lines after 110, D continues the comparison already begun about the effect of the birdsong on the hearer. Not only would he think himself handsome enough to be loved by *danzelles*, *dames*, and *pucelles* (111–12), but also as handsome as Partonopeu and Narcissus. These allusions to popular stories and famously handsome men show an author who specifically wants to relate his poem to contemporary works. According to Anthime Fourrier, *Partonopeu de Blois* was the third great "sommet de notre littérature médiévale" after Tristan and the Grail.[77] Romances of Narcissus were also very popular in the thirteenth and fourteenth centuries, and the story was told at length in the *Roman de la Rose*.[78]

In the 20 verses added after 192, D continues the condemnation of the villein and his gluttony: Devils made him come to the garden; he has no joy or love; and he would prefer to have a plate of "fromage blanc," beans, and peas with lard than to listen to lays about love or to embrace a blond gentle woman!

The 12 verses added after 214 elaborate the dialogue at the moment the villein seizes the bird caught in the snare. He says to the bird that he will sing to him: "Malesgré vostre nes devant" (214c).

In the 8 lines added after 206, the poem introduces the motif of catching a bird using *glu* (birdlime). Not only is this a "courant réaliste" in the poem, but it also picks up a detail often mentioned in the fables,[79] and that had been used in the *Trois Savoirs* and the *Donnei*.

The *Oiselet* in ms D is called a *dit* in its title and explicit, and the word *dit* also appears in line 247. How much the poem owes its designation to being destined for a collection of *dits* and *fabliaux* cannot be determined. Conversely, the poem may be in such a collection because it had been expanded and transformed with fabliau elements. Interestingly enough, the poet of D, although enormously expansive, increasing the number of lines in B by a quarter, shows himself also to be very conservative, omitting only 14 verses in B, and no more than two at a time. In important passages, like the one of the three sens, D is conservative, adding only two lines and deleting none, and following AB very closely in wording. The reaction of D, then, to the *Oiselet* is very much that of an amplifier rather than a *remanieur*.

Although most of the text of D (excluding what D adds) can be shown to be close to AB, D also shows some slight reflection of E: in 304 both D and E have the pronoun *les* (see note to 270–312), which is an error in E but not in D; and in 377 both D and E are -2.

---

[76] Rychner, *Contribution*, 1: 78–79, 83.

[77] Fourrier, *Le courant réaliste dans le roman courtois*, 1: 315. See Gildea, *Partonopeu de Blois*, 1: lines 551–78.

[78] In the edition of *Narcisus* by Pelan and Spence, 20–21, the editors mention that Narcissus is alluded to in the *Alexandre*, *Troie*, *Cligés*, *Flamenca*, *Galeran de Bretagne*, *Florimont*, *Floris et Liropé*, and the *Roman de la Rose*. In the *Rose* (ed. Lecoy), the story is told in lines 1436–1520.

[79] See Perry, *Aesopica*, numbers 39 (Halm 417), 437 (Halm 105), 437a (Halm 106), and 576 (*Romulus* IV, 7).

Some of the additions by *D* to the text are banal and repetitious, such as the following:

Dist li oissiaus, "ce poisse moy,
Vous me tenez, ce poisse moy."   (220*ab*)
Que je vous diré une note
Qui ne doit pas estre frivole   (144*ab*)
(Ombre li faissoit un bel arbre)
Que la gent apeloient pin:
Tous temps ert vert soin et matin   (58*ab*)
Li oisellés dist au vilain
Un mot qui ne dit pas en vain   (228*ab*)
("Par foi, et je te mengerai,")
Dit le vilain, "puis que te tien
Desorenavant seras mien."   (232*ab*)
Or oez que dit li oissiaus
Qui tant fu avenans et biaus   (270*ab*)
Dit li vilains [mistake for *oissiaus*], "Entent a moi,
Que tu ne ses ne ce ne quoi   (346*ab*)
Avoit de ce ne faut pas dire
Liez hons estoit sanz nessun ire   (8*ab*)

In sum, the short additions of lines are mostly "filler," whereas the longer additions often represent interesting contributions to the poem.

The tone of the poem in *D*, however, begins to approach that of the fabliau, as in 214*c*:

Malesgré vostre nes devant,

in line 240:

Dit li vilains: "Or vous tessiez,"

and in the twenty-line passage after 192. Such lines would almost qualify the *Oiselet* of ms *D* as a fabliau.[80]

3. Ms *E*[81]

The text of ms *E* is the shortest of the five, 341 verses (47*E* [= 49*B*] is missing), and is the most defective. *E* adds 40 lines to *B* and omits 108.[82] It has 35 hypometric lines (3 are -2) and 13 hypermetric lines.[83]

---

[80] See discussion in section IV.E concerning tone and style.

[81] See above, p. 6. For other remarks about 1593, see also Bédier, *Ombre* (1913), xxiii; Bédier, "Tradition manuscrite"; Delbouille, *Lai d'Aristote*, 6–13; Gougenheim, *Trois Aveugles*, xv, 34, 38, 47, 207, 209; Lee, *Auberee*, 56; Ménard, *Fabliaux*, 160–61 ("Compte tenu de ces inexactitudes, il n'est pas possible d'éditer E [1593] ou F, si on veut éviter de multiplier les corrections!"); Rychner, *Contribution*, 1: 47–53, 139–40.

[82] Verses added are 1 after 184, 220, 222, 297; 2 after 8, 34, 94, 130, 194, 202, 234, 316, 368; 4 after 296, 361, 388; 6 after 382; omitted lines: 35–36, 61–62, 97–98, 105–10, 131–32, 143–44, 151–52, 157–58, 161–66, 171–72, 183, 187–92, 203–204, 217–18, 225–26, 229–30, 239–40, 265–66, 279–82, 285–86, 297, 299–300, 305–310, 313–14, 319–20, 335–38, 341–46, 349–52, 357–58, 363–64, 369–70, 379–80, 383–86, 389–98, 400–403, 406, 408.

[83] Hypometric verses (including hiatus) are: 3, 17, 29, 30, 36, 51, 57, 64, 76, 89, 115, 132,

The text of *E* shows its closest relationship to *C* in the order of the *sens croire pleurer* (see Textual Note to 270–312). Another illustration of this relationship between *E* and *C* is in the pattern of lines 335–60 and 296*cd* (see notes to 335–60 and 270–312). The text of *E* shows a relationship to *A* in the absence of lines 61–62 and 391–98. *E* shows a relationship to *D* at line 10 and in line 377. These relationships are discussed in detail in the Textual Notes to the lines mentioned, particularly in notes to lines 335–60 and 270–312.

As mentioned in the section on the *Chastoiement, Trois Savoirs,* and the *Donnei,* ms *E* has a couplet, 234*ab,* that is very close to one in the *Chastoiement A.* The lines in the *Chastoiement A* 3473–74 are:

> Quer quant en l'eve m'auras cuit
> Tu en metereis bien tels uit.

and in *E* 234*ab*:

> Bien savez quant je ceré cuit
> En vo bouche en porroit tex uit.

In the *Chastoiement B* 2545–46 the lines are:

> Et si jo sui en rost bien quit,
> Dunc serrai jo sec e petit

In the *Trois Savoirs* 82–84:

> Mout i averez un mees petit
> Poi vaille por en seau quire
> Encore en rost serroi pire

In the *Donnei* 1004–1108:

> Mut i avret un mes petit
> [Mut] poi vail jo pur en pot quire
> Uncore en rost serreie pire;
> Ki sur espei ou en pot me met
> Petit i avra morselet

In the *Oiselet B* 234–37:

> En moi povre repast avrez
> Car je sui lasches et petis
> Ja n'en croistera vostre pris
> Se vos ociez tele rien.

An analysis of the lines unique to *E* shows that most of them have parallels in lines in the *Chastoiement, Trois Savoirs,* and the *Donnei.*[84] This finding

---

134, 184*a,* 198, 210, 219, 220, 241, 246, 259, 262, 263, 268, 293, 316*a,* 317, 324, 331 (-2), 332, 353 (-2), 360, 374, 377 (-2), 382*e.* Hypermetric verses are: 19, 97, 118, 133, 203, 207, 224, 228 (+2), 301, 283, 287, 271, 388.

[84] The following list gives the lines in *E* that have analogous lines in the *Chastoiement* (ed. Hilka), *Trois Savoirs,* or *Donnei:* 184*a* = *Donnei* 26–28: Ke mut est fel quer de vilein, E la sue vie est maudite, Quant en joie ne se delite; 194*ab* = *Donnei* 945–47: Estreitement se purpensa

suggests that *E* is closer to texts that can be considered sources than any other manuscript of the *Oiselet*, and that these origins are the poems stemming from the *Disciplina*: the *Chastoiement*, *Trois Savoirs*, and the *Donnei*.[85]

These observations suggest the following hypothesis about the origin and evolution of the *Oiselet* poems: that the short version of the *Oiselet* in *E* represents a redaction of the poem closest to the *Disciplina*, and that *C* represents an expanded version of this redaction. Longer versions of the poem omit the most explicit allusions to the *Disciplina* poems, like the lines *E* 234*ab*, *E* 388*abcd*, and *E* 184*a*. Such explicit details as catching the bird with *glu* and the three truths being worth more than *trei gras veel* (*Chastoiement A* 3491) that are directly traceable to the Latin *Disciplina* (*Ostendam tibi tres sapiencie manieras quas maioris facies quam trium vitulorum carnes*) did not occur in the *Oiselet* manuscripts. (The use of *glu* in *D* is an exception.) Also not used in the *Lai de l'Oiselet* is the name of the precious stone (*jacintus* in the *Chastoiement A* comes directly from the *Disciplina*). By not using such explicit details, the *Oiselet* poems effectively removed or blurred the traces of their origins so that *E* alone with lines like 234*ab* seems to be a "missing link" with the *Disciplina*.

As interesting as ms *E* is in providing clues to the origin and amplification of the *Oiselet* poems, it must be rejected as a candidate for base manuscript. It is the most defective and carelessly written of the five manuscripts, and, with *C*, it represents the minority version (*croire pleurer*) of the story. Comparisons of *C* and *E* reveal that they are closely related. In most instances *C* resembles an amplified version of *E*, but there are instances where *E* has passages not present in *C*. Specific details that elaborate these conclusions can be found in the Textual Notes to lines 10, 61–62, 270–312, 335–60, 377, 391–98.

In printing the diplomatic/synoptic texts of the *Oiselet*, manuscript *E* is placed first, followed by *C*, *A*, and *D*. This order reflects the relative states of the poem in the five manuscripts that preserve it, from the shortest (*E*) to the longest (*D*) and preserves the two groups of text, *EC* and *ABD*.

Sovent, quantes feiz i ala, Coment preist il cel oisel; 234*ab* = *Chastoiement A* 3473–74: Quer quant en l'eve m'avras cuit Tu en metreies bien teus uit; 296*a-d* = use of *gabez* in *Trois Savoirs* 232–33 and *Donnei* 1156–57; 361*a-d* = *Chastoiement A* 3525–28: Quant li vilains a ce oï, Ses dous poinz ensemble feri, Des oilz plore et del cuer sospire, Son piz bat et ses cheveus tire; *Trois Savoirs* 155–58: Quant ceo oie lui fous vileins Tire cheveuz e tort ses meins A terre chiet e round son piz Lieve noise e braeiz e criz; *Donnei* 1087–90: Quant ço oï li fol vileins, Trait ses chevols e tort ses meins; A terre chet e bat sun piz, Si leve noisse e plurs e criz; *E* 381*a*, 382*ab* = *Chastoiement A* 3535–36: Ja t'apris je que fous sereies, Se totes paroles creeies; *Trois Savoirs* 185–86: Ne vous di jeo primes saunz respit Ne creez pas qantqe l'en dit; *Donnei* 119–20: Je vus di primes en respit Pas ne creiez quanque l'em dit; 388*a-d* = *Disciplina* (Heidelberg, p. 33, lines 11–12): quoniam dolore nichil erit recuperabile; *Chastoiement A* 3400–02: Quant la toue chose perdras, Quer bien seiz que par doloser Ne porreies rien recovrer; *Trois Savoirs* 215: Son travaille piert saunz recoverir; *Donnei* 1149: Sun travail perd sanz recovrer; and 1160: Trop creire en haste est folie.

[85] See section IV.C for a discussion of the *Chastoiement*, *Trois Savoirs*, and *Donnei des Amants*.

4. Ms A[86]

Manuscript A has a text of 390 verses. It omits 30 verses in B and adds ten.[87] The language of A is quite correct as most of the editors of works in this famous collection agree. Except for the absence of lines 39–50, 61–62, and 391–98, A would make an excellent base manuscript for an edition of the *Oiselet*. A transcription of A was printed by Weeks,[88] and I include my own transcription of A in this edition.

Twenty-two of the lines absent in A are descriptive: 39–50 amplify the description of the garden, 61–62 describe the tree, and 391–98 give the final words of admonition by the bird to the villein. Since $BCDE$ retain 39–50 and BCD retain 61–62 and 391–98, these lines must be considered representative parts of the poem, and their absence in A eliminates this manuscript as the choice of base manuscript.

In discussing a choice between A and B as base manuscript, one must of course acknowledge the long editorial history of these two manuscripts and the *Lai de l'Ombre*. In opting first for A and then for B, Bédier has left a wealth of discussion about these manuscripts.[89] On the other hand, Delbouille, who edited the *Lai d'Aristote*, and who could have used either 837 or 1104, chose instead 19152 for his edition.[90] The arguments by Bédier for and against A and B as base for an edition of the *Lai de l'Ombre*, however, are not so helpful because of the large omissions of text in A in the case of the *Oiselet*.[91] The most recent edition of the *Ombre*[92] used B, but that was because no edition of B with variants existed, whereas there are many of A.

By excluding A as base manuscript for an edition of the *Oiselet*, it is understood that what A omitted are not lacunae that could be filled in from other manuscripts, but deliberately omitted passages. The passage 39–50 may have been left out as excessive verbiage in A, since the garden is amply described in the passages preceding and following 39–50, or A might have objected to the allusion to *nigromance* (49), since A also does not have the detail that *air* and water surround the garden, but that *trees* and water do so (19). The

---

[86] See above, pp. 3–4.

[87] Verses eliminated are 39–50, 61–62, 221–22, 317–18, 369–70, 391–98, 400, 406; verses added are 2 after 10, 182, 220, 316, and 368.

[88] The following are mistakes in Weeks's edition: lines 41 and 318 *fut* — ms has *fu*; 79 *mavis* — ms has *mauuis*; 270 *ainc* — ms has *qu'ainz*; 310 *volontiers* — ms has *volentiers*. Weeks transcribes final *-x* as *-us* in *mieus* 123, 170, 180, 181, 182, 255, 278, *Dieus* 140, 141, 143, 147, *conoiteus* 149. In 79 Weeks has *rousingnol* where ms has *roxingnol*. In 160 Weeks gives *envieus*, but ms can also be read *enuieus*, which seems to fit the context better. In 113 *par coustume*, the ms omits the horizontal stroke through the shaft of p. Reading should be *p[ar] c.* In 163 ms has *cours*, but *tours* or *tors* (= towers) would be better, as Weeks points out in a footnote.

[89] For discussions of the differences between A and B, see Bédier, *Lai de l'Ombre* and "La Tradition manuscrite du *Lai de l'Ombre*"; Dees, "Considérations théoriques"; and Whitehead and Pickford, "The Introduction to the *Lai de l'Ombre*."

[90] Delbouille, *Aristote*. The *Conte du Mantel* is also in 837 and 1104, but Wulff chose 1104 partly because it was a newly discovered manuscript at the time.

[91] There are fewer differences between A and B in the *Lai de l'Oiselet* in terms of omission of text.

[92] Winters, *Lai de l'Ombre* (1986).

couplet 61–62 is descriptive of the foliage of the tree that shades the fountain. There is some general confusion in the description of this tree: since it is a pine (71), the allusion to its foliage being particularly thick in May (61–63) seems somewhat contradictory to the fact that it always has foliage (68). Although pines do put forth new shoots in spring, they are not dramatically thicker, as the deciduous trees are. Since all the manuscripts have these somewhat contradictory statements about the tree, there seems to be a symbolic use of the imagery of the tree in these passages rather than dendrological imprecision! The absence of 61–62 in *AE* could therefore be due either to the perception that this couplet draws attention to the contradictions in the details of the tree or to the fact that it was a later insertion by a poet or scribe indifferent to any but the symbolic interpretations in the descriptions of the tree. Another possible explanation is that lines 61–62 could have been omitted from *A* from either the bottom of the first column or the top of the second column of page 45 of the manuscript.

Lines 391–98 also might have been considered to be excess verbiage by the scribe of *A*. By ending the bird's final speech with line 390, the scribe of *A* has omitted a somewhat convoluted passage. In this instance, omission by *A* of these lines could be considered an improvement, but the presence of these lines in *BCD* (and the passage 388a-d in *E*) indicates that for all the other manuscripts something further was said beyond 390, and so *A* again is not representative in omitting 391–98.

5. Ms *B*[93]

Ms *B* has been chosen as the base manuscript as the most representative of the five preserving the *Lai de l'Oiselet* and, except for *A*, as the most correct of the five. The following figures give a summary of the lines either added (+) to *B* or omitted (−) from *B* by the other manuscripts, and the number of lines they have in common with *B*:

E	+40	*C*	+22	*A*	+10	*D*	+116
	−108		−22		−30		−20
	302		388		380		390

The greatest difference, of course, among the five manuscripts is their division into two groups, *EC* and *ABD*, according to the ordering of the first two sens as *croire pleurer* (*EC*) and *pleurer croire* (*ABD*) in the passage 270–312. Of the three manuscripts preserving the version *pleurer croire*, *A* has been eliminated for consideration as base because of its omission of 30 lines, and *D* primarily for its eccentric addition of 116 lines, almost all of which are unique to *D*.

A possible objection to *B* as representative of the *Oiselet* poem involves several unique lines and usages in *B*. There are seven unique lines in *B* (10, 154, 168, 220, 296, 400, and 406), and two major passages with unique usages, in lines 151–68 and 399–410. The passage 151–68 is a very complex one where

---

[93] See above, p. 4.

the bird sets forth in its song ideas about God and love, and the passage 399–410 describes the effects of the bird's disappearance on the garden and the villein. In the passage 151–68, all the manuscripts have some unique interpretations as well as additions and omissions, but *B* stands very much alone in some of its interpretations. The same observation holds for the passage 399–410. The Textual Notes to these lines elaborate these problems in detail.

There is no denying that some of the unique interpretations in *B* challenge the notion that it is the most representative of the five manuscripts, but, compared to *A* or *D*, it remains the only acceptable candidate for a base manuscript. Only an eclectic edition, using *A* as base with the missing lines supplied from the other manuscripts, is a possibility, but such a text is artificial and exists only hypothetically, whereas the presentation of a base is less the denial of the virtues of the other manuscripts than a point of departure for a perspective on them.

B. Conclusions

The following list of observations sets forth some of the conclusions about the origins of the *Oiselet* poem and the relationships of the five manuscripts to each other:

(1) If the source of the poem of the *Oiselet* is ultimately the exemplum in the *Disciplina clericalis*, then *E* preserves a primitive version of the *Oiselet*, whose intermediate versions were the *Chastoiement* and very likely the *Donnei des Amants* and/or the *Trois Savoirs*.

(2) The version in *C* is an expanded version of *E*. Its version, however, preserves only four (10*ab* and 296*cd*) lines of the 40 lines in *E* and not in *B*, and thus "erases" or does not transmit those lines that indicate origins or sources, like, most explicitly, *E* 234*ab*.

(3) *E* is the shortest version of the *Oiselet*, but this does not preclude the possibility that *E* omitted lines in some passages (see Textual Notes to lines 335–60 and 399–410).

(4) The texts in *ABD* descend from a redaction that reversed the sens *croire pleurer* to *pleurer croire*. This reversal is not characteristic of the *Disciplina* versions of the *Oiselet* and may be due to the emphasis placed on the sens *pleurer* within the text of the *Oiselet* poem itself.

(5) The texts in *A* and *B* are very close, having 380 lines in common. If it had not omitted major passages present in three or four of the other manuscripts, *A* probably would have been chosen as base manuscript. Although *D* has 390 lines in common with *B*, it nevertheless differs more qualitatively than any other manuscript with its eccentric addition of 116 verses and the number of faulty or otherwise bad lines.

(6) A text of the *Oiselet* with *B* as base adheres to the notion that the text presented is at least one that actually exists, and that it better represents the poem than an eclectic text based on *A* with lines filled in from the other manuscripts.

(7) The *Oiselet*, in the final analysis, is an excellent candidate to illustrate

Paul Zumthor's idea of "mouvance,"[94] with each manuscript having a slightly different version of the story to tell or emphasis to make. For this reason, transcriptions of all the manuscripts are given for the reader to make his choices in various passages if he so wishes.

C. Editorial Principles

The present edition uses ms *B* as base manuscript with a list of rejected readings. The texts of the other manuscripts are given in full in diplomatic and synoptic texts in order to facilitate comparisons with *B*. Line numbers in the right-hand margins indicate the numbering of the individual manuscripts. Line numbers to the left of the texts of *E*, *C*, *A*, and *D* are those of *B*. Folio and column indications are also given for all manuscripts in the left-hand margins. The presentation of the diplomatic/synoptic texts in the order *ECAD* preserves the two groupings of text according to the order of the three sens — *EC* (*croire pleurer*) and *AD* (*pleurer croire*) — and places the shortest text first (*E*) and the longest last (*D*).

In general, the attitude toward the base manuscript has been conservative. Recommendations concerning the solution of abbreviations, treatment of hiatus, etc., have been followed particularly according to suggestions of the Société des Anciens Textes (*Romania*, 52 [1926]: 243–49) and of William Roach in his edition of the Continuations (*Continuations*, 1: xlii-xliii).

Comments on the syntax, rhyme, morphology, semantics, proverbs, and scribal practices of *B* are to be found in the Textual Notes. The text is too short to draw generalized conclusions about the language of the author. Particular Textual Notes draw attention to complex passages where the patterns of lines reveal relationships among the manuscripts (Textual Notes to 10, 39–50, 151–68, 178–83, 187–92, 220–23, 270–312, 331, 316, 335–60, 377, 382–98, 399–410).

The following specific principles have been followed in editing ms *B*:

(1) *B* is emended only where there are real errors of grammar or sense or when the readings can be shown to have been produced by mistake due to copying errors such as dittography, haplology, etc. All emendations are recorded and discussed when necessary in the Textual Notes.

(2) The readings of *B* are retained even in those cases where the readings of other manuscripts might be perceived as "better" or as preserving a so-called "original" reading, unless they are due to real error as described above. All such passages are discussed at length in the Textual Notes.

The two-line capitals of the text of *B* indicate logical divisions of the story. For divisions of the story according to the various manuscripts, see the sections dealing with manuscript descriptions (II and V).

The diplomatic and synoptic texts of *E*, *C*, *A*, and *D* have not been punctu-

---

[94] Zumthor, *Essai de poétique médiévale*, 65–75.

ated, but words have been separated, abbreviations solved, the apostrophe used to separate words, and capitals used at the beginnings of the lines in order to facilitate the reading of these texts. Hypo- and hypermetric lines are listed in the footnotes to sections II and V of the Introduction where the manuscripts are described in detail. Expunctuations and other anomalies have been reproduced in the diplomatic texts as indications of the extent of scribal inattention or carelessness.

The edition is completed by a Glossary which assumes knowledge of modern French. The Glossary gives a summary of forms of irregular verbs and of many regular verbs. Inclusion of words in the Glossary is based on peculiarities of orthography, meaning, or usage.

APPENDIX

SUMMARY OF ANALOGUES AND SOURCES OF THE *LAI DE L'OISELET*

When Gaston Paris referred to the *Lai de l'Oiselet* as a "joli récit indien" in *Romania*, 25 (1896): 540, and as a "charmant conte indien" in his *Littérature française au moyen âge* (§ 77) (where he also placed it among the "fableaux"), and to the oriental origins of the story throughout the Introduction to his edition of the *Lai de l'Oiselet*, he set the stage for a full-scale inquiry into these so-called Indian origins and into the idea of genre. The summary included in this Appendix represents a reexamination in the light of recent scholarship of the sources and analogues that Gaston Paris mentions in his study of the *Oiselet*. Various motif indexes, like those of Stith Thompson, and the work of folklorists and translators of oriental works that has appeared in the hundred years since Gaston Paris's edition have facilitated such an inquiry.

My conclusion is that the *Oiselet* has only vague similarities with stories in the oldest collections, like the *Buddhist Birth Stories*, the *Panchatantra*, and the classic collections of fables, and that the source of the story cannot be traced any further back than the *Barlaam and Josaphat*.

My summary as presented here is by no means definitive, since there are endless collections of stories in other languages that I have not analyzed, but I do hope that it can at least be considered a new point of departure.

The works mentioned here by author, editor, translator, or brief title, are all given in full in the Bibliography.

Motif Indexes and General Reference Works: Stith Thompson, vol. 4, K604, *The three teachings of the bird (fox)*; J.21.12 *Rue not a thing that is past*; J.21.13, *Never believe what is beyond belief*; J.21.14, *Never try to reach the unattainable*; vol. 6, Index, *Bird*; Antti Aarne's *Types of the Folktale* (trans. Stith Thompson), no. 150, *Advice of the Fox*; Tubach, *Index Exemplorum*, no. 322, *Archer and Nightingale*; and Keller, *Motif-Index of Medieval Spanish Exempla*.

Fable editions consulted: Ben Perry, *Aesopica*, which is also published in the Loeb Classical Library as *Babrius and Phaedrus*. Perry lists 725 fables with cross-references to standard fable collections like Halm and Chambry, to Stith Thompson, and to the fables of La Fontaine.

The most complete study of the *Barlaam* texts is in the three volumes of Sonet.

> I. *Barlaam versions of the Oiselet story.* (1) Bird is a nightingale, (2) man is a hunter or fowler, (3) release occurs *after* sens are given, (4) stone is a pearl as big as an ostrich (chicken, goose) egg, and (5) *pleurer* precedes *croire*.

A. *Barlaam texts*
   1. *Barlaam* — Greek. Boissonade, 4: 79–81; Woodward and Mat-
      ingly, Loeb ed., 134–39; Migne, *PG*, 96: cols. 941–44.
   2. *Barlaam* — Latin. A sixteenth-century Latin translation in Migne,
      PG, 96: cols. 942–43, and *PL*, 73: cols. 479–80.
   3. *Barlaam* — Old French Prose. Mills, 62–63.
   4. *Barlaam* — French Verse. Gui de Cambrai. Appel, 67–70; Zot-
      tenberg and Meyer, 60–62.
   5. *Legenda Aurea*. Graesse, 815–16; trans. Eng. Ryan and Rip-
      purger, 725–26.
   6. *Barlaam* — Italian. [Botari], 37–38.
   7. *Barlaam* — Old Spanish. Keller and Linker, 92–94, 380–82.
   8. *Barlaam* — Caxton's. Joseph Jacobs, Appendix X, 13–14; Ellis,
      1: 91–93; Lenaghan, 201–203.
   9. *Barlaam* — Japanese. trans. Matsubara, 206–207.
B. *Barlaam-type texts*
   1. *Fables*, Odo of Cheriton. Hervieux, 4: 252; Ben Perry, *Aesopica*,
      no. 627, pp. 643–44 and Loeb Classical Library, no. 627, pp.
      551–52; John C. Jacobs, trans., pp. 160–61.
   2. *Gesta Romanorum*. Oesterley, 554–56; Swan (trans. Eng.),
      318–19.
C. *Mixed Barlaam texts* (Up to two elements differ from five *Barlaam*
   elements)
   1. *Baralâm* — Ethiopic text. (1) bird is not a nightingale (3) release
      in two stages. Budge, 2: 63–65.
   2. *Balavariani* — Georgian. (3) release *before* sens are given. Lang,
      96–97.
   3. *Bilawhar* — Arabic. (1) bird is a sparrow (2) man is not a hunter
      or fowler. Gimaret, 108–109.
   4. *Exempla, Vitry*. (2) man is not a hunter or fowler. Crane, 10–11
      (Eng. trans., 144–45).
   5. *Cauallero Zifar*. (1) bird is a calandria (lark) (5) order of sens
      is *croire pleurer*. Wagner, 259–62. González Muela, 236–39.
      Olsen, 76–77; Eng. trans., Nelson, 156–57.
   6. *Laughable Stories* — Syriac. (1) bird is a sparrow (3) mixed re-
      lease (third sens not given) (4) precious stone is "beyond price."
      Budge, 93.
   7. *Exempla of the rabbis*. (1) bird is not a nightingale (4) precious
      stone is worth more than a thousand dinars. Gaster, 149–50.
   8. *Mille et un contes*. (1) bird is a sparrow (4) precious stone is worth
      more than the taxes of Egypt and Syria. Basset, 2: 269–77.

II. *Disciplina clericalis* versions of the *Oiselet* story. (1) Bird is not named,
    (2) man is a rustic, laborer, or villein, (3) bird is released *before* the sens
    are given, (4) stone is a hyacinth or just a precious stone with weight
    in ounces, (5) *croire* precedes *pleurer*.

A. *Disciplina clericalis*
  1. Latin texts
    a. Hilka, Heidelberg, 1911, 33–34, and vol. 1, Helsingfors, 1911, 30–31. Repr. in González Palencia, 58–59, and translated into Spanish in González Palencia, 152–54; Eng. trans. of Hilka text in Jones and Keller, 86–87.
  2. Old French text — prose texts
    a. Labouderie, 167–69.
    b. Hilka, 2: 26.
  3. Old French texts — verse = *Chastoiement d'un père à son fils*
    a. Méon (1808), 2: 140–43.
    b. Labouderie, 397–403.
    c. Hilka texts:
      (1) *A*, 3: 57–60.
      (2) *B*, 3: 119–21.
      (3) *Harley* (*h*), 3: 153–54.
    d. Montgomery, 136–40.
  4. *Old English Disciplina* (fifteenth century) ed. Hulme (no. 17, pp. 47–48).
B. *Disciplina*-type versions
  1. *Donnei des Amants*. G. Paris, *Donnei*, 516–20.
  2. *Trois Savoirs*. P. Meyer, 217–21; Wolfgang, *Trois Savoirs*.
  3. *Churl and Bird*, Lydgate. MacCracken, 468–566; Hammond, 104–10.
  4. Steinhöwel's *Aesop* (1477). Oesterley, 312–13.
  5. *Esopo*, 1489 (Old Spanish). González Palencia, 223–25.
C. *Disciplina* versions — mixed (up to two elements differ from the five *Disciplina* elements)
  1. *Libro de los exenplos*. (1) bird is a nightingale, (3) release *after* sens are given. González Palencia, 152–54; Gayangos, 460; Keller, 110–11.
  2. *Récits d'un ménestrel de Reims*. (1) bird is a *masenge* (titmouse), (4) stone is as big as an *oeuf de geline* (chicken egg). Wailly, 237–39.
  3. Julien Macho — French *Aesop* text. (1) bird is a nightingale, (4) stone is a diamond as big as an ostrich egg. Tyroller, 242–43; Ruelle, *Isopets*, 237–39.
  4. Caxton's *Aesop*. (1) bird is a nightingale, (4) stone is a diamond. Joseph Jacobs, 2: 269–71, and 1929, 138–39; Lenaghan, 201–203.
  5. Japanese "Aesop's" fable. (3) release *after* sens are given. Trans. Matsubara, 204–205.

III. No direct *Oiselet* analogue
  A. Indirect analogue
    1. *Buddhist Birth Stories* or Jātaka tales. Rhys Davids, no. 16, The Cunning Deer; no. 31, On Mercy to Animals; no. 33, Sad Quarrel of the Quails; no. 36, The Wise Birds and the Fools.

2. *Panchatantra*. Edgerton, Ryder. Book 2, The Winning of Friends.

3. *Kalilah and Dimnah* or *Fables of Bidpai*. (1) The Grateful Pigeons, (2) The Ring Dove

   a. Syriac Text, trans. Eng. *Kalilah and Dimnah*. Keith Falconer, (1) 212–13, (2) 109–28.

   b. Spanish text, *Libro de Calila e Digna*. Keller and Linker, (1) 344–46, (2) 165–70. Trans. Eng. *Kalīlah and Dimnah*. Irving, trans. (1) 182–83, (2) 72–74. Cacho Blecua and Lacarra, eds., (1) 334–36, (2) 202–205.

   c. Arabic text, trans. French — *Kalilah et Dimna*. Miquel, (1) 271–73, (2) 133–55.

B. No *Oiselet* analogues

1. *Seven Sages* or *Book of Sindibad*, ed. Misrahi.

   a. Spanish — *Libro de los Engaños*, Keller.

   b. Trans. Eng. *Book of the Wiles of Women*, Keller.

2. *Libro de los Gatos*, Keller. Contains 75 fables of Odo of Cheriton; the *Oiselet* is no. 77.

3. *Conde Lucanor*. Knust, Blecua. Trans. Eng., York.

4. *Thousand and One Nights*. Not found in Burton. Basset's collection is called the *Mille et un Contes*, and has a *Barlaam*-type text of the story. May be in other collections, although Motif Indexes do not indicate this.

IV. *Fables*

A. The *Lai de l'Oiselet* appears in so-called Aesopic fable collections, such as Ben Perry's *Aesopica* (no. 627, pp. 643–44) which is conveniently printed in *Babrius and Phaedrus* (Loeb Classical Library, also no. 627, pp. 551–52). This fable is a *Barlaam*-type story which Perry took from the fables of Odo of Cheriton. The fable in the collection of Cheriton (ed. Hervieux) is essentially the same as the exemplum of Vitry (ed. Crane), the story in the *Gesta Romanorum* (ed. Oesterley), and in the *Legenda Aurea* (ed. Graesse). The Aesopic fable of the *Disciplina*-type is in Steinhöwel's *Aesop*, Julien Macho's *Esope*, and Caxton's *Aesop* (bird is a nightingale and the stone a diamond in Macho and Caxton). How the "Aesopic" fable appears in any modern collection of fables seems to be a function of its source in a *Barlaam* or *Disciplina*-type exemplum. Popular collections of fables may omit the reference to the precious stone (cf. Joseph Jacobs, 1929, 138–39).

B. *Oiselet*-type fables

1. Babrius no. 53 (Loeb edition), 69–71 (also Halm 271 and Chambry 230): "The Three True Statements."

2. Fable no. 610 (Loeb edition), 544, "The Fox and the Ferryman" (from Odo of Cheriton).

3. Fable no. 687 (Loeb edition), 584–85, "The Wolf and the Fer-

ryman." (Marie de France, no. 78, ed. Warnke, *De Lupo et Nauta*; ed. Roquefort, 2: no. 79. Roquefort says, footnote, p. 324, that this fable has the same subject as the *Oiselet*.)

4. Fable no. 668 (Loeb edition), 576–77, "The Three Wishes" (La Fontaine, Bk. 7, no. 5, "Les Souhaits").

5. Fable 39 (Loeb edition), 428, "The Wise Swallow" (also Halm 417, Chambry 349, La Fontaine, Bk. 1, no. 8, "L'Hirondelle et les Petits Oiseaux").

6. Babrius no. 124 (Loeb edition), 161–63, "How the Fowler Served His Guest."

7. Fable 576 (Loeb edition), 531–32, "The Fowler and Birds" (*Romulus*, Bk. 4, no. 7).

8. Fable 4 (Loeb edition), 422–43, "The Hawk and the Nightingale" (Halm 9; Hesiod, *Works and Days*, lines 202–12; Marie de France, no. 67, *De accipitre et philomela*; La Fontaine, Bk. 9, no. 18, "Le Milan et le Rossignol").

9. La Fontaine, *Fables*, Bk. 8, no. 27, "Le Loup et le Chasseur."

BIBLIOGRAPHY

ABBREVIATIONS

CFMA   Classiques Françaises du Moyen Age
PRF   Publications Romanes et Françaises
PUB   Presses Universitaires de Bruxelles
PUF   Presses Universitaires de France
PUG   Presses Universitaires de Grenoble
SATF   Société des Anciens Textes Français
TLF   Textes Littéraires Français

ALTER, JEAN V. *Les origines de la satire anti-bourgeoise en France, moyen âge — XVIe siècle.* Geneva: Droz, 1966.

APPEL, CARL, ed. *Gui von Cambrai. Balaham und Josaphas, nach den Handschriften von Paris und Monte Cassino.* Halle: Niemeyer, 1907.

ARMSTRONG, EDWARD C., ed. *The French Metrical Versions of Barlaam and Josaphat.* Princeton: Princeton University Press; and Paris: Champion, 1922. (Elliott Monographs, 10.)

————. *The Medieval French Roman d'Alexandre.* Vol. 7, *Version of Alexandre de Paris. Variants and Notes to Branch IV.* Intro. Bateman Edwards and Alfred Foulet. Princeton: Princeton University Press, 1955. (Elliott Monographs, 41.)

————, D. L. BUFFUM, BATEMAN EDWARDS, and L. F. H. LOWE, eds. *The Medieval French Roman d'Alexandre.* Vol. 2, *Version of Alexandre de Paris. Text.* Princeton: Princeton University Press, Paris: PUF, 1973. (Elliott Monographs, 37.)

AURNER, NELLIE SLAYTON. *Caxton, Mirrour of Fifteenth-Century Letters.* Boston and New York: Houghton Mifflin Co., 1926.

BAADER, HORST. *Die Lais.* Frankfurt: Klostermann, 1966.

BADEL, PIERRE-YVES. *Introduction à la vie littéraire du moyen âge.* Paris: Bordas, 1969.

BAIRD, J. L., and JOHN R. KANE, eds. and trans. *Rossignol, An Edition and Translation.* With an Introductory Essay on the Nightingale Tradition. Kent, Ohio: Kent State University Press, 1978.

[BARBAZAN, ETIENNE, ed.] *Le Castoiement, ou instruction du père à son fils, ouvrage moral en vers composé dans le treizième siècle.* . . . Lauzanne [sic] and Paris, 1760.

[BARBAZAN, ETIENNE, ed.] *Fabliaux et Contes des poètes françois des XII, XIII, XIV et XVᵉ siécles,* tirés des meilleurs auteurs. 3 vols. Paris and Amsterdam, 1756.

BARTSCH, KARL, ed. *Altfranzösische Romanzen und Pastourellen.* Leipzig: Vogel, 1870.

BASSET, RENÉ, ed. and trans. *Mille et un Contes, récits et légendes arabes.* 3 vols. Paris: Librairie orientale et américaine, 1924–26.

BASTIN, JULIA, ed. *Recueil général des Isopets.* 3 vols. Paris: SATF, 1929, 1930, 1982. Vol. 3 ed. by Pierre Ruelle.

BAUM, RICHARD. "Eine neue Etymologie von frz. *lai* und apr. *lais.* Zugleich: Ein Plädoyer für die Zusammenarbeit von Sprach-und Literaturwissenschaft." *Beiträge zum Romanischen Mittelalter,* ed. Kurt Baldinger. (*Zeitschrift für romanische Philologie,* Sonderbd.) Tübingen: Niemeyer, 1977, 17–78.

————. *Recherches sur les oeuvres attribuées à Marie de France*. Heidelberg: Winter, 1968.

————. "Les Troubadours et les lais." *Zeitschrift für romanische Philologie*, 85 (1969): 1–44.

BÉDIER, JOSEPH. *Les Fabliaux, études de littérature populaire et d'histoire littéraire du moyen âge*. 6th ed. Paris: Champion, 1925, 1969.

————, ed. *Le Lai de l'Ombre*. Paris: SATF, 1913.

————. "La Tradition manuscrite du *Lai de l'Ombre*, Réflexions sur l'art d'éditer les anciens textes." *Romania*, 54 (1928): 161–96; 321–56. (Repr. Paris: Champion, 1929.)

BENFEY, THEODOR. *Pantschatantra, fünf Bücher indischer Fabeln, Märchen und Erzählungen*, vol. I. Leipzig: Brodhaus, 1859.

BERNARDI, FRANCA DE, ed. "Il *Lai* di *Gugemer* di Maria di Francia," in *Omaggio a Camillo Guerrieri-Crocetti*. Genoa: Bozzi, 1971, pp. 181–250. (Studi e testi Romanzi e Mediolatini, 2.)

BLECUA, JOSÉ MANUEL, ed. *Don Juan Manuel. El Conde Lucanor, O, Libro de los Enxiemplos del Conde Lucanor et de Patronio*. Madrid: Castalia, 1969, 1979.

BLOCH, R. HOWARD. "Le Mantel mautaillié des fabliaux, comique et fétichisme." *Poétique*, 14 (1983): 181–98.

BOASE, ROGER. *The Origin and Meaning of Courtly Love*. Manchester: Manchester University Press, 1977.

BOER, C. DE, ed. *Chrétien de Troyes. Philomena, conte raconté d'après Ovide*. Paris, 1909. (Repr. Slatkine, 1974.)

BOETHIUS. *The Theological Tractates and The Consolation of Philosophy*. H. F. Stewart, E. K. Rand, and S. J. Tester, eds. and trans. Cambridge: Harvard University Press, 1918, 1978. (Loeb Classical Library, 74.)

BOISSONADE, J., Fr. ed. *Anecdota Graeca, e codicibus Regiis*. 5 vols. Paris, 1829–33, vol. 4: 79–81. (Repr. Hildesheim: Olms, 1962.)

BOLTON, W. F. "Parable, Allegory and Romance in the Legend of *Barlaam and Josaphat*." *Traditio*, 14 (1958): 359–66.

BOOGAARD, NICO H. J. VAN DEN. "Le Récit bref au Moyen Age," pp. 7–15 in *Epopée Animale* (see).

BOSSUAT, ROBERT, ed. *Alain de Lille. Anticlaudianus*. Paris: Vrin, 1955. (Textes Philosophiques du moyen âge, 1.)

[BOTTARI] *Storia de'SS. Barlaam e Giosaffate* (1734). 2nd ed. Rome: Mordacchini, 1816.

BREMOND, CLAUDE, JACQUES LEGOFF and JEAN-CLAUDE SCHMITT. *L' "Exemplum."* Fasc. 40, in L. Genicot, dir. *Typologie des sources du moyen âge occidental*. Turnhout, Belgium: Brepols, 1982.

BRERETON, GEORGINE E. "A Thirteenth-Century List of French Lays and Other Narrative Poems." *The Modern Language Review*, 45 (1950): 40–45.

BRUNET, JACQUES-CHARLES. *Manuel du Libraire et de l'Amateur de livres*. "Aesopus." Vol. I. Paris: Didot, 1860.

BRUNOT, FERDINAND. *Histoire de la langue française des origines à 1900*. Vol. I, *De l'époque latine à la Renaissance*. 3rd ed. Paris: Colin, 1924.

BUDGE, ERNEST A. WALLIS, ed. *Baralâm and Yĕwâsĕf*, being the Ethiopic version of a Christianized Recension of the Buddhist legend of the Buddha and the Bodhisattva. 2 vols. Cambridge: The University Press, 1923. (Repr. AMS, 1976.)

————. *The Laughable Stories collected by Mâr Gregory John Bar-Hebraeus (1264-1286)*. The Syriac text edited with an English translation. London: Luzac and Co., 1897.

BURGESS, GLYN S. *Marie de France, an Analytical Bibliography*. London: Grant & Cutler, Ltd., 1977.

Butler's Lives of the Saints, ed. and rev. Herbert Thurston and Donald Attwater. Vol. IV. "SS. Barlaam and Josaphat," pp. 432–33. New York: Kenedy & Sons, 1956.

CACHO BLECUA, JUAN MANUEL and MARÍA JESÚS LACARRA, eds. *Calila e Dimna*. Madrid: Castalia, 1984.

CAMPBELL, MARIE. "The Three Teachings of the Bird," in *Studies in Biblical and Jewish Folklore*, R. Patai, F. L. Utley, and D. Noy, eds. Bloomington, Ind.: Indiana University Press, 1960, pp. 97–107.

Catalogue des Manuscrits français. Ancien fonds. Bibliothèque Impériale — Département des Manuscrits. 5 vols. Paris: Firmin Didot, 1868–1902.

Catalogue Général des Manuscrits français. Bibliothèque Nationale. Anciens Petits Fonds français, by Henri Omont. 3 vols. Paris: Leroux, 1897–1902.

Catalogue Général des Manuscrits français. Bibliothèque Nationale. Nouvelles acquisitions françaises, by Henri Omont. 4 vols. Paris: Leroux, 1899–1918.

CHAMBRY, EMILE, ed. *Esope. Fables*. Collection des Universités de France. Assoc. Guillaume Budé. Paris: Les Belles Lettres, 1927.

CHANDLER, ALBERT R. "The Nightingale in Greek and Latin Poetry." *The Classical Journal*, 30 (1934): 78–84.

CHAUVIN, VICTOR. *Bibliographie des Ouvrages arabes ou relatifs aux arabes publiés dans l'Europe chrétienne de 1810 à 1885*. 12 vols. in 5 tomes (1–3, 4–6, 7–10, 11, 12). Liège and Leipzig, 1892–1922.

COMPARETTI, DOMENICO. *Virgilio nel medio evo*. 2nd ed. Florence, 1896. Trans. E. F. M. Benecke, 1908. (Repr. Archon Books, 1966.)

CONSTANS, LÉOPOLD, ed. *Benoît de Sainte-Maure. Roman de Troie*. 6 vols. Paris: SATF, 1904–12.

————. *Le Roman de Thèbes*. 2 vols. Paris: SATF, 1890.

COUTON, GEORGES, ed. *La Fontaine. Fables choisies, mises en vers*. Paris: Garnier, 1962.

CRANE, THOMAS FREDERICK, ed. *The Exempla of Jacques de Vitry*. The Folklore Society, 26, 1890. (Repr. Kraus, 1967.)

CURTIUS, E. R. *European Literature and the Latin Middle Ages*, trans. W. R. Trask. New York: Bollingen, 1953.

DALY, LLOYD W., trans. *Aesop without Morals*. New York: Yoseloff, 1961.

DANOS, JOSEPH R. *A Concordance to the Roman de la Rose of Guillaume de Lorris*. North Carolina Studies in the Romance Languages and Literatures, Texts, Studies, Transactions, 3. Chapel Hill, N.C.: University of North Carolina, 1975.

DAVIDS, T. W. RHYS, trans. *Buddhist Birth Stories, or, Jātaka Tales, the Oldest Collection of Folk-lore Extant, being the Jātakatthavaṇṇanā*. Vol. I, Translation (from Pāli). London: Trübner, 1880.

DAY, DENNIS MICHAEL. "A Structural Analysis of the Syntagmatic Organization of the So-Called Breton Lais: Towards the Definition of a Literary Set." Diss., University of Wisconsin-Madison, 1975.

DEES, A. "Considérations théoriques sur la tradition manuscrite du *Lai de l'Ombre*." *Neophilologus*, 60 (1976): 481–504.

DELAISSÉ, L. M. J. "Edition et Codicologie." *Scriptorium*, 7 (1953): 125–131.

DELBOUILLE, MAURICE, ed. *Henri d'Andeli. Le Lai d'Aristote*. Bibliothèque de la Faculté de Philosophie et Lettres de l'Université de Liège, 123. Paris, 1951.

DELISLE, LÉOPOLD. *Mélanges de Paléographie et de Bibliographie*. Paris: Champion, 1880.

DE RIQUER, MARTÍN. "La 'aventure,' el 'lai' y el 'conte' en María de Francia." *Filologia romanza*, 2 (1955): 1–19.

DONOVAN, MORTIMER J. *The Breton Lai: a Guide to Varieties*. Notre Dame, 1969.

DRAGONETTI, ROGER. *La Technique poétique des trouvères dans la chanson courtoise: Contribution à l'étude de la rhétorique médiévale.* Bruges: De Tempel, 1960.

DRONKE, PETER. *Medieval Latin and the Rise of European Love-Lyric.* 2 vols. 2nd ed. Oxford: At the Clarendon Press, 1968.

DUBIN, NATHANIEL EDWARD. "The Parodic Lays: A Critical Edition." Diss., University of Washington, 1974.

DUBUIS, ROGER. *Les Cent Nouvelles Nouvelles et la tradition de la nouvelle en France au moyen âge.* Grenoble: PUG, 1973.

DUCAY, ESPERANZA, trans. *Disciplina Clericalis. Pedro Alfonso.* Notas de María Jesús Lacarra. Saragossa: Guara Editorial, 1980. (La Nueva Biblioteca de Autores Aragoneses.)

DU MÉRIL, EDÉLESTAND PONTUS, ed. *Floire et Blanceflor, poèmes du XIIIe siècle.* Paris: Jannet, 1856.

DUVAL, JOHN, trans. *Cuckolds, Clerics, and Countrymen: Medieval French Fabliaux.* Fayetteville, Ark.: University of Arkansas Press, 1982.

EDGERTON, FRANKLIN, trans. *The Panchatantra.* Trans. from the Sanscrit. London: George Allen and Unwin, 1965.

ELLIS, F. S., ed. *The Golden Legend or Lives of the Saints as Englished by William Caxton.* 3 vols. (7 vols. in 3). London: Dent, 1900. (Repr. AMS, 1973.)

ELWERT, W. THEODOR. *Traité de Versification française des origines à nos jours.* (Bibliothèque française et romane, Série A. Manuels et études linguistiques, 8.) Paris: Klincksieck, 1965.

EMDEN, W. G. VAN. Cr. rev. of *Die 'Lais.' Zur Structur der dichterischen Einbildungskraft der Marie de France,* by Kurt Ringger. (Beihefte zur *Zeitschrift für romanische Philologie,* 137. Tübingen: Niemeyer, 1973), in *French Studies,* 32 (1978): 56–57.

EMPSON, WILLIAM. *Some Versions of Pastoral.* London: Chatto and Windus, 1935.

Epopée Animale, Fable et Fabliau. Mediaevalia, 78. *Marche Romane,* 28 (1978) (Actes du Colloque de la Société Internationale Renardienne, Amsterdam, 21–24 octobre 1977).

ESPINER-SCOTT, JANET GIRVAN. *Claude Fauchet, sa vie, son oeuvre.* Paris: Droz, 1938.

EWERT, ALFRED, ed. *Marie de France. Lais.* Oxford: Blackwell, 1947, 1952.

FARAL, EDMOND. *Les Arts poétiques du XIIe et du XIIIe siècle: Recherches et documents sur la technique littéraire du moyen âge.* Paris, 1924. (Repr. 1962.)

——. *Le Manuscrit 19152 du fonds français de la Bibliothèque Nationale.* Paris: Droz, 1934.

——. *Recherches sur les Sources latines des contes et romans courtois du moyen âge.* Paris: Champion, 1913. (Repr. AMS, 1975.)

FLEMING, JOHN V. *The Roman de la Rose. A Study in Allegory and Iconography.* Princeton: Princeton University Press, 1969.

FOERSTER, WENDELIN. *Kristian von Troyes. Erec und Enide.* 2nd ed. Halle (Saale): Niemeyer, 1909.

FOUCHÉ, PIERRE. *Le Verbe français. Etude morphologique.* 2nd ed. Paris: Klincksieck, 1967, 1981. (Tradition de l'Humanisme, 4.)

FOULET, ALFRED and MARY BLAKELY SPEER. *On Editing Old French Texts.* Lawrence, Kansas: Regents Press of Kansas, 1979.

FOULET, LUCIEN. *The Continuations of the Old French Perceval of Chrétien de Troyes,* ed. William Roach, vol. 3, part 2, *The Glossary of the First Continuation.* Philadelphia: American Philosophical Society, 1955.

——. "Marie de France et les lais bretons." *Zeitschrift für romanische Philologie,* 29 (1905): 19–56; 293–322.

———. *Petite Syntaxe de l'ancien français.* 3rd ed. Paris: Champion, 1966. (CFMA, 21, 2e série: Manuels.)

FOURRIER, ANTHIME. *Le Courant réaliste dans le roman courtois en France au moyen-âge.* Vol. I, *Les Débuts* (XIIe siècle). Paris: Nizet, 1960.

FRAPPIER, JEAN. *Amour Courtois et Table Ronde.* (PRF, 126.) Geneva: Droz, 1973.

———. " 'D'amors,' 'par amors.' " *Romania,* 88 (1967): 433–74.

———. "La brisure du couplet dans *Erec et Enide.*" *Romania,* 86 (1965): 1–21.

———. "Remarques sur la structure du lai, essai de définition et de classement." *Littérature narrative d'Imagination.* Paris: PUF, 1961, pp. 23–39.

GASTER, MOSES, ed. *The Exempla of the Rabbis.* New York: KTAV Pub., Inc., 1924, 1968.

GAYANGOS, PASCUAL DE, ed. *El Libro de los Enxemplos.* (Biblioteca de Autores Españoles, vol. 51.) Madrid, 1860, pp. 443–542.

GENICOT, L., dir. *Typologie des sources du Moyen Age occidental.* Turnhout, Belgium: Brepols, 1972 –.

GENNRICH, FRIEDRICH. *Die altfranzösische Rotrouenge.* Halle: Niemeyer, 1925.

GIAMATTI, A. BARTLETT. *The Earthly Paradise and the Renaissance Epic.* Princeton: Princeton University Press, 1966.

GILDEA, JOSEPH, O.S.A., ed. *Partonopeu de Blois.* 2 vols. (in 3 parts). Villanova, Pa.: Villanova University Press, 1967–70.

GIMARET, DANIEL, ed. *Le livre de Bilawhar et Bûdâsf,* selon la version arabe ismaélienne. (Hautes études islamiques et orientales d'Histoire comparée, 3.) Geneva and Paris: Droz, 1971.

GODEFROY, FRÉDÉRIC. *Dictionnaire de l'ancienne langue française et de tous ses dialectes du IXe au XVe siècle.* 10 vols. Paris, 1880–1902. (Repr. Kraus, 1969.)

GOLDIN, FREDERICK. *The Mirror of Narcissus in the Courtly Love Lyric.* Ithaca, N.Y.: Cornell University Press, 1967.

GONZÁLEZ MUELA, JOAQUIN, ed. *Libro del Caballero Zifar.* Madrid: Castalia, 1982.

GONZÁLEZ PALENCIA, ANGEL, ed. and trans. *Pedro Alfonso. Disciplina clericalis.* Edición y traducción del texto latino. Madrid-Granada: Instituto Miguel Asín, 1948.

GOSSEN, CHARLES THÉODORE. *Grammaire de l'ancien picard.* 2nd ed. Paris: Klincksieck, 1970. (Bibliothèque Française et Romane, Série A: Manuels et Etudes linguistiques, 19.)

GOSSMAN, LIONEL. *Medievalism and the Ideologies of the Enlightenment, The World and Work of La Curne de Sainte-Palaye.* Baltimore, Md.: The Johns Hopkins Press, 1968.

GOUGENHEIM, GEORGES, ed. *Cortebarbe. Les Trois aveugles de Compiègne, fabliau du XIIIe siècle.* Paris: Champion, 1932. (CFMA, 72.)

GRAESSE, J. G. TH., ed. *Jacobi a Voragine. Legenda Aurea. Vulgo Historia Lombaridica Dicta.* Ad optimorum Librorum fidem. Dresden and Leipzig: Impensis Librariae Arnoldiane, 1846.

GRAF, ARTURO. *Miti, leggende e superstizioni del medio evo.* 2 vols. Turin: Loescher, 1892–93.

GRIGSBY, JOHN L. "Narrative in Three Garbs: *roman courtois, lai, chanson de toile.*" *Romance Philology,* 34 (Special Issue, 1981): 73–87.

GRIMES, E. MARGARET, ed. *The Lays of Desiré, Graelent and Melion,* edition of the texts with an introduction. New York, 1928. (Repr. Slatkine, 1976.)

GRUBMÜLLER, KLAUS. *Meister Esopus. Untersuchungen zu Geschichte und Funktion der Fabel im Mittelalter.* Zurich and Munich: Artemis, 1977.

GUIETTE, ROBERT. "Introduction." *Fabliaux et Contes.* Paris: Stock Plus, 1960, 1981.

GUNN, ALAN M. F. *The Mirror of Love.* Lubbock, Tex.: Texas Tech Press, 1952.

HALM, CHARLES (CAROLI HALMII), ed. *Fabulae Aesopicae Collectae*. Leipzig: Teubner, 1852.

HAMMOND, ELEANOR PRESCOTT. *English Verse between Chaucer and Surrey*. New York: Octagon Books, 1965.

HASSELL, JAMES WOODROW, JR., ed. *Middle French Proverbs, Sentences, and Proverbial Phrases*. Toronto: Pontifical Institute of Mediaeval Studies, 1982.

HENSEL, WERNER. "Die Vögel in der provenzalischen und nordfranzösischen Lyrik des Mittelalters." *Romanische Forschungen*, 26 (1909): 584–670.

HERVIEUX, LÉOPOLD, ed. *Les Fabulistes Latins*. 4 vols. Paris: Firmin-Didot, 1893–1896.

HESIOD. *The Homeric Hymns and Homerica*. Trans. H. G. Evelyn-White. Cambridge: Harvard University Press, 1914, 1982. (Loeb Classical Library, 57.)

HILKA, ALFONS and WERNER SÖDERHJELM, eds. *Die Disciplina Clericalis des Petrus Alfonsi*. Heidelberg: Winter, 1911. (Sammlung mittellateinischer Texte, 1.)

———. *Petri Alfonsi. Disciplina Clericalis. I. Lateinischer Text*. Acta Societatis Scientiarum Fennicae, tome 38, no. 4. Helsingfors, 1911. II. *Französischer Prosatext*, tome 38, no. 5. Helsingfors, 1912. III. *Französische Versbearbeitungen*, tome 49, no. 4. Helsingfors, 1922.

HOEPFFNER, ERNEST. "La Tradition manuscrite des *Lais* de Marie de France." *Neophilologus*, 12 (1926–27): 1–10, 85–96.

———, ed. *Les Lais de Marie de France*. Paris: Nizet, 1971.

HUBAUX, JEAN and MAXIME LEROY. *Le Mythe du Phénix dans les littératures grecque et latine*. Paris, 1939. (Bibliothèque de la Faculté de Philosophie et Lettres de l'Université de Liège, 82.)

HULME, WILLIAM HENRY, ed. *Peter Alphonse's Disciplina Clericalis (English Translation) from the Fifteenth Century Worcester Cathedral Manuscript F.172*. Cleveland: Western Reserve University Bulletin, vol. 22, no. 3, 1919.

HUMPHRIES, ROLFE, trans. *Ovid. The Art of Love*. Bloomington, Ind.: Indiana University Press, 1957, 1970.

HUNT, TONY. "Eine bisher unberücksichtigte Handschrift des *Barlaam et Josaphat* ('version champenoise')," in *Beiträge zum romanischen Mittelalter*, ed. Kurt Baldinger. Tübingen: Niemeyer, 1977, pp. 217–29. (*Zeitschrift für romanische Philologie* Sonderbd.)

IMBS, PAUL. *Les Propositions temporelles en ancien français*. Paris: Société d'Editions, Les Belles Lettres, 1956.

IRVING, THOMAS BALLANTINE, trans. *Kalilah and Dimnah*, an English version of Bidpai's Fables based on ancient Arabic and Spanish manuscripts. Newark, Del.: Juan de la Cuesta, 1980.

JACOBS, JOHN C., trans. *The Fables of Odo of Cheriton*. Syracuse, N.Y.: Syracuse University Press, 1985.

JACOBS, JOSEPH. *Arabian Nights* (see Lane).

———. *Barlaam and Josaphat. English Lives of Buddha*. London: Nutt, 1896. (Bibliothèque de Carabas, 10.)

———. *The Earliest English Version of the Fables of Bidpai, 'The Morall Philosophie of Doni' by Sir Thomas North*. London: Nutt, 1888.

———. *The Fables of Aesop, as first printed by William Caxton in 1484 with those of Avian, Alfonso and Poggio*. 2 vols. London: Nutt, 1889.

———. *The Fables of Aesop, Selected, Told Anew and Their History Traced*. New York: Macmillan, 1894, 1929.

JAUSS, HANS-ROBERT. "Littérature médiévale et théorie des genres." *Poétique*, 1 (1970): 79–101.

Jodogne, Omer. "Le Fabliau." Fasc. 13, in L. Genicot, *Typologie* (see Genicot), 1975.

Johnston, Oliver M. "The Description of the emir's orchard in *Floire et Blancheflor.*" *Zeitschrift für romanische Philologie,* 32 (1908): 705–10.

———. "The Story of the Blue Bird and the lay of Yonec." *Studi Medievali,* 2 (1906–1907): 1–10.

Jones, Joseph Ramon and John Esten Keller, trans. *The Scholar's Guide,* a Translation of the Twelfth-Century *Disciplina Clericalis* of Pedro Alfonso. Toronto: Pontifical Institute, 1969.

Jubinal, Achille, ed. *Li Fablel dou Dieu d'Amours.* Paris: Techener, 1834.

Kahlert, Shirley Ann. "The Breton Lay and Generic Drift: A Study of Texts and Contexts." Diss., University of California at Los Angeles, 1981.

Kazhdan, Alexander. "Where, when, and by whom was the Greek *Barlaam and Joasaph* not written." (Unpub. chapter, 1985, Festschrift for Gerhardt Wirth.)

Keidel, George C. "The History of French Fable Manuscripts." *Publications of the Modern Language Association,* 24 (1909): 207–19.

———. *Romance and Other Studies.* No. 2, *A Manual of Aesopic Fable Literature. First fasc. (of 3), for the period ending A.D. 1500.* Baltimore, Md.: Freidenwald, 1896.

Keith-Falconer, Ion G. N., trans. *Kalīlah and Dimnah, or the Fables of Bidpai, an English translation of the later Syriac version.* Cambridge: University of Cambridge, 1885. (Repr. Amsterdam: Philo Press, 1970.)

Keller, John Esten, trans. *The Book of the Wiles of Woman.* Chapel Hill, N.C.: University of North Carolina Press, 1956.

———, ed. *El Libro de los Engaños.* Chapel Hill, N.C.: University of North Carolina Press, 1959.

———. *El Libro de los exenplos por a.b.c.* Clásicos Hispánicos, ser. 2, 5. Madrid: Consejo Superior de Investigaciónes científicas, 1961 (1960).

———. *El Libro de los Gatos.* Clásicos Hispánicos, ser. 2, 4. Madrid: Consejo Superior de Investigaciónes científicas, 1958.

———. *Motif-Index of Mediaeval Spanish Exempla.* Knoxville, Tenn.: University of Tennessee Press, 1949.

Keller, John Esten and Robert White Linker, eds. *Barlaam e Josafat.* Clásicos Hispánicos, ser. 2, 21. Madrid: Consejo Superior de Investigaciónes científicas, 1979.

———. *El Libro de Calila e Digna.* Clásicos Hispánicos, ser. 2, 13. Madrid: Consejo Superior de Investigaciónes científicas, 1967.

Kelly, Douglas. *Medieval Imagination.* Madison: University of Wisconsin Press, 1978.

Kibler, William W. *An Introduction to Old French.* New York: Modern Language Association of America, 1984.

Knust, Hermann. "Steinhöwels Aesop." *Zeitschrift für deutsche Philologie,* 19 (1887): 197–218.

——— and Adolf Birch-Hirschfeld, eds. *Juan Manuel. El Libro de los Enxiemplos del Conde Lucanor et de Patronio.* Leipzig: Seele, 1900.

Koch, John, ed. *Chardry's Josaphaz, set Dormanz und petit Plet.* Heilbronn: Henninger, 1879. (Altfranzösische Bibliothek, 1.)

Körting, Gustav. *Lateinisch-Romanisches Wörterbuch.* 3rd ed. New York: Stechert, 1923.

Kroll, Renate. *Der narrative Lai als eigenständige Gattung in der Literatur des Mittelalters: zum Structurprinzip der 'Aventure' in den Lais.* Tübingen: Niemeyer, 1984. (Beihefte zur *Zeitschrift für romanische Philologie,* 201.)

KUHN, ERNST. "Barlaam und Joasaph. Eine bibliographisch-literargeschichtliche Studie." *Abhandlungen der philosophisch-philologischen Classe der königlich bayerischen Akademie der Wissenschaften (München)*. Band 20 (1897): 1–88.

[LABOUDERIE, J., ed.] *Disciplina Clericalis, auctore Petro Alphonsi*. Pars Prima; *Discipline de clergie*, trad. de l'Ouvrage de Pierre Alphonse, Première Partie; *Le Chastoiement d'un Père à son fils*, trad. en vers français de l'ouvrage de Pierre Alphonse, Seconde Partie. Mélanges publiés par la Société des Bibliophiles Français, 3. Paris: Didot, 1824. (Repr. Slatkine, 1970.)

LA FONTAINE: see Couton.

LANE, EDWARD WILLIAM, trans. *The Thousand and One Nights; or, Arabian Nights' Entertainments*. Intro. by Joseph Jacobs. 6 vols. Vol. 1, 1896. London and Philadelphia: Gibbings and Lippincott, 1896.

LANG, DAVID MARSHALL, trans. *The Balavariani (Barlaam and Josaphat): A Tale from the Christian East Translated from the Old Georgian*. Berkeley and Los Angeles: University of California Press, 1966.

LÅNGFORS, ARTHUR. "Le Dit des Quatre Rois, Notes sur le ms. fr. 25545 de la Bibliothèque Nationale." *Romania*, 44 (1915–17): 87–91.

———. *Les Incipit des poèmes français antérieurs au XVIe siècle*. Paris: Champion, 1917.

LANGLOIS, ERNEST. *Origines et sources du Roman de la Rose*. Paris: Thorin, 1891.

———. *Recueil d'arts de seconde rhétorique*. Paris: Imprimerie Nationale, 1902.

———, ed. *Le Roman de La Rose*. 5 vols. Paris: SATF, 1914–24.

LANLY, ANDRÉ, trans. *Guillaume de Lorris et Jean de Meun. Le Roman de la Rose*. Vol. 1 (ll. 1–4028). Paris: Champion, 1971.

LAZAR, MOSHÉ. *Amour courtois et "fin' amors" dans la littérature du XIIe siècle*. Paris: Klincksieck, 1964.

LECLANCHE, JEAN-LUC, ed. *Le Conte de Floire et Blancheflor*. Paris: Champion, 1983. (CFMA, 105.)

LE CLERC, VICTOR. "Fabliaux." *Histoire Littéraire de la France*, 23 (1856): 69–215.

LECOY, FÉLIX, ed. *Le Chevalier au barisel, conte pieux du XIIIe siècle*. Paris: Champion, 1973. (CFMA, 82.)

———. "Le dit de l'espervier." *Romania*, 69 (1946–47): 528–34; 70 (1948–49): 408–409.

———. *Guillaume de Lorris et Jean de Meun. Le Roman de la Rose*. 3 vols. Paris: Champion, 1965–1970. (CFMA, 92, 95, 98.)

———. *Jean Renart. Le lai de l'Ombre*. Paris: Champion, 1979. (CFMA, 104.)

———. Cr. rev. of Jean Sonet. *Barlaam et Josaphat*, vol. 1. in *Romania*, 71 (1950): 403–408.

———. "Variations sur le texte du *Lai de l'Ombre*," *Romania*, 103 (1982): 433–69.

LEE, CHARMAINE. "Il giardino rinsecchito: per una rilettura del 'Lai de l'Oiselet.'" *Medioevo Romanzo*, 5 (1978): 66–84.

———, ed. *Les Remaniements d'Auberee, Etude et textes*. Naples: Liguori, 1983. (Romanica Neapolitana, 2.)

———, ANNA RICCADONNA, ALBERTO LIMENTANI, and ALDO MIOTTO. *Prospettive sui fabliaux*. Padua: Liviana, 1976.

LE GRAND [D'AUSSY, LE P. PIERRE-JEAN-BAPTISTE, S.J.], trans. *Fabliaux ou Contes du XIIe et du XIIIe siècle, Fables et Romans du XIIIe, Traduits ou extraits d'après plusieurs manuscrits du tems*. 3 vols., 1779; vol. 4, 1781: *Contes Dévots, fables et Romans Anciens: pour servir de suite aux Fabliaux*; 5 vols., 1781: *Nouvelle édition, augmentée d'une Dissertation sur les Troubadours*. Paris: Eugène Onfroy, Libraire, Quai des Augustins, 1781; 3rd ed., 5 vols. Paris: Renouard, 1829.

LEGRY-ROSIER, J. "Manuscrits de contes et de Fabliaux." *Bulletin d'Information de l'Institut de Recherche et d'Histoire des Textes*, no. 4, 1955 (1956): 37–47.

LEJEUNE, RITA, ed. *Renaut de Beaujeu. Le Lai d'Ignaure ou Lai du prisonnier*. Brussels and Liège: Vaillant-Carmanne, 1938.

LENAGHAN, R. T., ed. *Caxton's Aesop*. Cambridge: Harvard University Press, 1967.

LE ROUX DE LINCY, ed. *Le livre des proverbes français*. 2nd ed. 2 vols. Paris: Delahays, 1859.

LEWIS, C. S. *The Allegory of Love*. Oxford: Oxford University Press, 1936, 1969.

LODS, JEANNE, ed. *Les Lais de Marie de France*. Paris: Champion, 1959. (CFMA, 87.)

LOOMIS, ROGER SHERMAN. *Arthurian Tradition and Chrétien de Troyes*. New York: Columbia University Press, 1949.

LOUANDRE, CHARLES. *Chefs-d'oeuvre des conteurs français avant La Fontaine, 1050–1650*. Paris: Charpentier, 1873.

———. "Les Vieux Conteurs français." *Revue des deux mondes*, 2nd ser., 107 (1873): 433–41.

LYDGATE, JOHN. *The Churl and the Bird translated from the French. Printed by William Caxton about 1478*. Facsimile from the original type. Cambridge: Cambridge University Press, 1906.

MACCRACKEN, HENRY NOBLE, ed. *The Minor Poems of John Lydgate*. Vol. 2, *Secular Poems*. London, 1934. (Early English Text Society, Old Ser., 192.)

MARCHELLO-NIZIA, CHRISTIANE. *Histoire de la langue française aux XIVe et XVe siècles*. Paris: Bordas, 1979.

MARTIN, MARY LOU, trans. *The Fables of Marie de France, an English translation*. Birmingham, Ala.: Summa Publications, 1984.

MASAI, FRANÇOIS "Principes et conventions de l'édition diplomatique." *Scriptorium*, 4 (1950): 177–93.

MASON, EUGENE, trans. "The lay of the little Bird," in *Aucassin et Nicolette and Other Mediaeval Romances and Legends*. London and Toronto: Dent; New York: Dutton, 1910, 1925, pp. 67–74.

MATSUBARA, HIDÉICHI. "Un conte japonais parallèle au *Lai de l'Oiselet*," in *Jean Misrahi Memorial Volume. Studies in Medieval Literature*. Ed. Hans R. Runte, Henri Niedzielski, and William L. Hendrickson. Columbia, S.C.: French Literature Publications Company, 1977, pp. 197–209.

MÉNARD, PHILIPPE. *Les Fabliaux, contes à rire du moyen âge*. Paris: PUF, 1983. (Littératures modernes, 32.)

———. *Les Lais de Marie de France. Contes d'Amour et d'Aventure*. Paris: PUF, 1979. (Littératures modernes, 29.)

———. *Manuel du français du moyen âge*. Vol. 1, *Syntaxe de l'ancien français*. Bordeaux: Sobodi, 1973.

———. *Le Rire et le sourire dans le roman courtois en France au moyen âge (1150–1250)*. Geneva: Droz, 1969. (PRF, 105.)

———, ed. *Fabliaux français du moyen âge*. Vol. 1. Geneva: Droz, 1979. (TLF, 270.)

MÉON, [DOMINIQUE-MARTIN], ed. *Fabliaux et Contes des Poètes François des XI, XII, XIII, XIV et XVe siècles, tirés des meilleurs Auteurs, publiés par Barbazan*. 4 vols. Paris: B. Warée, 1808. (Repr. Slatkine, 1973.)

MERCATANTI, CATERINA LAVAGNA. "Il *lai di Lanval*," in *Omaggio a Camillo Guerrieri-Crocetti*. Genoa: Bozzi, 1971, pp. 353–414. (Studi e testi Romanzi e Mediolatini, 2.)

MEYER, PAUL. "Fragments d'une ancienne traduction française de *Barlaam et Joasaph* faite sur le texte grec au commencement du treizième siècle." *Bibliothèque de l'Ecole des Chartes*, 6th ser., vol. 2 (1866): 313–30.

———. "Notice du MS. 25970 de la Bibliothèque Phillipps (Cheltenham)." *Romania*, 37 (1908): 209–35.

————. "Notice d'un manuscrit appartenant à M. Le Comte d'Ashburnham." *Bulletin de la Société des Anciens Textes français*, 1887: 82–103.

————. "Vente des manuscrits de la famille Savile." *Bibliothèque de l'Ecole des Chartes*, 5th ser., vol. 2 (1861): 272–80.

MEYER-LÜBKE, W. *Romanisches Etymologisches Wörterbuch*. Heidelberg: Winter, 1935.

MICKEL, EMANUEL J., JR. *Marie de France*. New York: Twayne, 1974. (TWAS, 306.)

MIGNE, J.-P., ed. *Patrologiae, cursus completus . . . Patrologia Latina*. 221 vols. Paris, 1844–90.

————. *Patrologiae, cursus completus . . . Series Graeca*. 161 vols. Paris, 1857–66. Indexes. 2 vols. Paris, 1883–1912.

MIHM, MADELYN TIMMEL, ed. *The Songe d'Enfer of Raoul de Houdenc*. Tübingen: Niemeyer, 1984. (Beihefte, *Zeitschrift für romanische Philologie*, 190.)

MILLS, LEONARD R., ed. *L'Histoire de Barlaam et Josaphat, version champenoise*. Geneva: Droz, 1973. (TLF, 201.)

MIQUEL, ANDRÉ, trans. *Le Livre de Kalila et Dimna, ou Fables de Bidpaï*. Paris: Klincksieck, 1957.

MISRAHI, JEAN, ed. *Le Roman des Sept Sages*. Paris: Droz, 1938.

MONTAIGLON, ANATOLE DE and GASTON RAYNAUD, eds. *Recueil général et complet des fabliaux des XIIIe et XIVe siècles*. 6 vols. Paris: Librairie des bibliophiles, 1872–90.

MONTGOMERY, EDWARD D., JR., ed. *Le Chastoiement d'un père à son fils*. Chapel Hill, N.C.: University of North Carolina Press, 1971.

MORAWSKI, JOSEPH, ed. *Proverbes français antérieurs au XVe siècle*. Paris: Champion, 1925. (CFMA, 47.)

MOREL-FATIO, A., ed. "El Libro de exenplos por A.B.C. de Clemente Sanchez, Archidiacre de Valderas." *Romania*, 7 (1878): 481–526.

MUSCATINE, CHARLES. *Chaucer and the French Tradition*. Berkeley: University of California Press, 1957.

NELSON, CHARLES L., trans. *The Book of the Knight Zifar*. Lexington: University Press of Kentucky, 1983.

NOOMEN, WILLEM and NICO VAN DEN BOOGAARD, eds. *Nouveau recueil complet des Fabliaux (NRCF)*. 10 vols. Assen/Maastricht, The Netherlands: Van Gorcum, 1983– . (vol. 1, 1983, vol. 2, 1984, vol. 3, 1986, vol. 4, 1988.)

NYKROG, PER. *Les Fabliaux*. New ed. Geneva: Droz, 1973. (PRF, 123.)

NYROP, KR. *Grammaire historique de la langue française*. 6 vols. Copenhagen: Glydendal, vol. 1, 5th ed., 1935; vol. 2, 5th ed., 1968; vol. 3, 2nd ed., 1936; vol. 5, 1925; vol. 6, 1930. (Repr. Slatkine, 1979.)

OESTERLEY, HERMANN, ed. *Gesta Romanorum*. Berlin: Weidmannsche, 1872.

————. *Steinhöwels Aesop*. Stuttgart, 1873. (Litterarischen Vereins, 117.)

O'GORMAN, RICHARD, ed. *Les Braies au Cordelier, Anonymous Fabliau of the Thirteenth Century*. Birmingham, Ala.: Summa Publications, Inc., 1983.

OLSEN, MARILYN A., ed. *Libro del Cauallero Çifar*. Madison, Wisc.: Hispanic Seminary of Medieval Studies, 1984.

OMONT, HENRI. *Fabliaux, dits et contes en vers français du XIIIe siècle*, fac-similé du manuscrit français 837 de la Bibliothèque Nationale, publié sous les auspices de l'Institut de France. Paris: Leroux, 1932.

ORR, JOHN, ed. *Jehan Renart. Le Lai de l'Ombre*. Edinburgh: At the University Press, 1948.

PAINTER, GEORGE D. *William Caxton*. London: Chatto and Windus, 1976.

PARIS, GASTON, ed. "Le Donnei des Amants." *Romania*, 25 (1896): 497–541.

————. "Le lai de l'épervier." *Romania*, 7 (1878): 1–21; "Un lai d'amours," 407–15.

———. *Le lai de l'Oiselet*, poème français du XIIIe siècle, publié d'après les cinq manuscrits de la Bibliothèque nationale, et accompagné d'une introduction. Paris: Typographie Georges Chamerot, 1884. (Imprimé pour le mariage Depret-Bixio, 19 Avril 1884.)

———. "Lais inédits, de Tyolet, de Guingamor, de Doon, du Lecheor et de Tydorel." *Romania*, 8 (1879): 29–72.

———. *Légendes du Moyen âge*, Roncevaux, Le Paradis de la reine Sibylle, La légende du Tannhäuser, Le Juif errant, Le Lai de l'Oiselet. Paris: Hachette, 1903.

———. *La Littérature française au moyen âge (XIe-XIVe siècle)*. 5th ed. Paris: Hachette, 1914. (1st ed. 1888, 2nd ed. 1890, 3rd ed. 1905, 4th ed. 1909.) (AMS, repr. 1975.)

———. *Poèmes et Légendes du Moyen-Age*. Paris: Société d'édition artistique, [1900].

PARIS, PAULIN. "Lais." "Dits." *Histoire Littéraire de la France*, 23 (1856): 61–68; 266–86.

———. *Les Manuscrits françois de la Bibliothèque du Roi*. 7 vols. Paris: Techener, 1836–48.

PARRY, JOHN JAY, trans. *Andreas Capellanus. The Art of Courtly Love*. New York: W. W. Norton, 1969. (Columbia University Press, 1941.)

PATCH, HOWARD ROLLIN. *The Other World according to Descriptions in Medieval Literature*. Cambridge: Harvard University Press, 1950.

PAUPHILET, ALBERT. *Poètes et romanciers du moyen âge*. Paris: Gallimard, 1952.

PAYEN, JEAN CHARLES. *Le Lai Narratif*. Fasc. 13, in L. Genicot, dir., *Typologie* (see Genicot). Turnhout, Belgium: Brepols, 1975.

———. *Le Motif du repentir dans la littérature française médiévale*. Geneva: Droz, 1967. (PRF, 98.)

———. "A Semiological Study of Guillaume de Lorris." *Yale French Studies*, 51 (1974): 170–84.

PEETERS, PAUL, S.J. "La première traduction latine de *Barlaam et Joasaph* et son original grec." *Analecta Bollandiana*, 49 (1931): 276–312.

PELAN, MARGARET M., ed. *Floire et Blancheflor*. Paris: Société d'Edition, Les Belles Lettres, 1937.

PELAN, MARGARET M. and N. C. W. SPENCE, eds. *Narcisus, poème du XIIe siècle*. Paris: Société d'Editions, Les Belles Lettres, 1964.

PERRY, BEN EDWIN, ed. *Aesopica*. vol. 1. Urbana, Ill.: University of Illinois Press, 1952.

———. *Babrius and Phaedrus*. Cambridge and London: Harvard and Heinemann, 1965, 1984. (Loeb Classical Library, 436.)

PICKENS, RUPERT T. "*Estoire, lai*, and Romance: Chrétien's *Erec et Enide* and *Cligés*." *Romanic Review*, 66 (1975): 247–62.

PIEHLER, PAUL. *The Visionary Landscape, A Study in Medieval Allegory*. Montréal: McGill-Queen's University Press, 1971.

POIRION, DANIEL, ed. *Guillaume de Lorris et Jean de Meun. Le Roman de la Rose*. Paris: Garnier-Flammarion, 1974.

———. *Le Merveilleux dans la littérature française du moyen âge*. Paris: PUF, 1982. (Que sais-je? no. 1938.)

———. *Le Poète et le Prince, l'évolution du lyrisme courtois de Guillaume de Machaut à Charles d'Orléans*. Paris: PUF, 1965.

———. *Le Roman de la Rose*. Paris: Hatier, 1973. (Connaissance des Lettres, 64.)

POPE, MILDRED K. *From Latin to Modern French*. rev. ed. Manchester: Manchester University Press, 1952, 1966.

POTELLE, MICHEL. "Le conte de l'oiselet dans le *Donnei des Amanz*," in *Mélanges offerts à Rita Lejeune*. Vol. 2. Gembloux, Belgium: Duculot, 1969, pp. 1299–1307.

PROPP, VLADIMIR. *Morphologie du conte*. Paris: Seuil, 1970.

RABY, F. J. E. *A History of Secular Latin Poetry*. 2 vols. Oxford, 1934.

RAYNAUD, GASTON, ed. "La Chastelaine de Vergi." *Romania*, 21 (1892): 145–93.

———. *La Chastelaine de Vergi, poème du XIIIe siècle*. 4th ed. rev. by Lucien Foulet, 1963. (CFMA, 1, 1892.)

REID, T. B. W., ed. *Twelve Fabliaux. From Ms. F. Fr. 19152 of the Bibliothèque Nationale*. Manchester: Manchester University Press, 1958.

RIBARD, JACQUES, ed. *Jean de Condé. La Messe des Oiseaux et le dit des Jacobins et des fremeneurs*. Geneva and Paris: Droz, 1970. (TLF, 170.)

———. "Des lais au XIVe siècle? Jean de Condé," in *Mélanges de langue et de littérature du moyen âge et de la Renaissance offerts à Jean Frappier*. Vol. 2. Geneva: Droz, 1970, pp. 945–55.

RINGGER, KURT. *Die Lais*. Tübingen: Niemeyer, 1973. (Beihefte, *Zeitschrift für romanische Philologie*, 137.)

ROACH, WILLIAM, ed. *The Continuations of the Old French Perceval of Chrétien de Troyes*. 5 vols. Philadelphia: The American Philosophical Society, 1949–1983.

ROBERTSON, D. W. "The Doctrine of Charity in Mediaeval Literary Gardens." *Speculum*, 26 (1951): 24–49.

——— and BERNARD F. HUPPÉ. *Fruyt and Chaf: Studies in Chaucer's Allegories*. Princeton: Princeton University Press, 1963.

ROQUEFORT, B. DE, ed. *Poésies de Marie de France, poète anglo-normand du XIIIe siècle*. Vol. 2. Paris: Chasseriau, 1820.

ROQUES, MARIO, ed. *Les Romans de Chrétien de Troyes*. Vol. 1, *Erec et Enide*; vol. 4, *Le Chevalier au Lion (Yvain)*. Paris: Champion, 1952–60, 1963–65. (CFMA, 80, 89.)

ROSS, WERNER. "Rose und Nachtigall: Ein Beitrag zur Metaphorik und Mythologie des Mittelalters." *Romanische Forschungen*, 67 (1955): 55–82.

RUELLE, PIERRE: see Bastin.

RYAN, GRANGER and HELMUT RIPPERGER, trans. *The Golden Legend of Jacobus de Voragine*. 2 vols. London, New York, and Toronto: Longmans, Green, 1941.

RYCHNER, JEAN, ed. *Contribution à l'étude des Fabliaux*. 2 vols. Geneva: Droz, 1960.

———. "La critique textuelle de la Branche III (Martin) du *Roman de Renart* et l'édition des textes littéraires français du moyen âge." *Bulletin d'information de l'Institut de recherche et d'histoire des textes*, 15 (1967–68): 121–36.

———. "Les Fabliaux: genre, styles, publics." *Littérature narrative d'Imagination*. Paris: PUF, 1961, pp. 41–54.

———. *Les Lais de Marie de France*. Paris: Champion, 1966. (CFMA, 93.)

——— and PAUL AEBISCHER, eds. *Marie de France. Le lai de Lanval*. Geneva: Droz, 1958. (TLF, 77.)

——— and ALBERT HENRY, eds. *Le Lais Villon et les poèmes variés*. 2 vols. Geneva: Droz, 1977. (TLF, 239, 240.)

RYDER, ARTHUR W., trans. *The Panchatantra, translated from the Sanscrit*. Chicago: University of Chicago Press, 1956, 1964.

SCHENCK, MARY JANE STEARNS. *The Fabliaux, Tales of Wit and Deception*. Amsterdam and Philadelphia: John Benjamins, 1987. (Purdue University Monographs in Romance Languages, 24.)

SCHULTZ-GORA, O., ed. *Zwei altfranzösische Dichtungen. La Chastelaine de Saint Gille, Du Chevalier au Barisel*. Halle: Niemeyer, 1919.

SCHWAN, EDUARD and DIETRICH BEHRENS. *Grammaire de l'ancien français*, trans. Oscar Bloch. 4th ed. Leipzig: Reisland, 1932.

SCHWARZBAUM, HAIM. "International folklore motifs in Petrus Alfonsi's *Disciplina Clericalis*." *Sefarad*, 21 (1961): 267–99 (Exempla I–VI); 22 (1962): 17–59 (Exempla

VII–XXVI); 22 (1962): 321–44 (Exempla XXVII–XXXIV); 23 (1963): 54–73 (additions and commentary).

SEMPOUX, A. *La Nouvelle.* Fasc. 9, in L. Genicot, dir., *Typologie* (see Genicot), 1973.

SIENAERT, EDGARD. *Les lais de Marie de France, du conte merveilleux à la nouvelle psychologique.* Paris: Champion, 1978.

SONET, JEAN, ed. *Le Roman de Barlaam et Josaphat.* 3 vols. Paris: Vrin, 1949–52. (Bibliothèque de la Faculté de Philosophie et Lettres de Namur, 6, 7, 9.)

SOURIAU, ETIENNE. *Les deux cent mille situations dramatiques.* Paris: Flammarion, 1950.

SPARGO, JOHN WEBSTER. *Virgil the Necromancer, Studies in Virgilian Legends.* Cambridge: Harvard University Press, 1934.

STEVENS, JOHN. *Medieval Romance, Themes and Approaches.* New York: Norton, 1973, 1974.

STUIP, RENÉ, ed. *La Chastelaine de Vergi,* Edition critique du ms. B.N. f. fr. 375 avec Introduction, Notes, Glossaire et Index, suivie de l'édition diplomatique de tous les manuscrits connus du XIIIe et du XIVe siècle. The Hague and Paris: Mouton, 1970.

SUCHIER, HERMANN, ed. *Aucassin et Nicolette, texte critique accompagné de paradigmes et d'un lexique.* 7th ed., ed. and trans. Albert Counson. Paderborn: Schoeningh; Paris: Gamber, 1909.

SWAN, CHARLES, trans. *Gesta Romanorum,* reviewed and corrected by Wynnard Hooper. London: Bell, 1888.

SWEETSER, FRANKLIN P., ed. *Blancandin et l'Orgueilleuse d'amour.* Geneva: Droz; Paris: Minard, 1964. (TLF, 112.)

————. *Les Cent Nouvelles Nouvelles.* Geneva: Droz; Paris: Minard, 1966. (TLF, 127.)

THIRY-STASSIN, MARTINE and MADELEINE TYSSENS, eds. *Narcisse: conte ovidien français du XIIe siècle.* Paris: Société d'Editions, Les Belles Lettres, 1976.

THOMPSON, STITH. *Motif-Index of Folk-Literature.* 6 vols. Bloomington: University of Indiana Press, 1955–58.

————. *The Types of the Folktale. A Classification and Bibliography. Antti Aarne's Verzeichnis der Märchentypen.* Helsinki: Academia Scientiarum Fennica, 1961. (FF Communications, 184.)

THOSS, DAGMAR. *Studien zum locus amoenus im Mittelalter.* Vienna and Stuttgart: Braumüller, 1972. (Wiener romanistische Arbeiten, 10.)

TOBIN, PRUDENCE MARY O'HARA, ed. *Les Lais anonymes des XIIe et XIIIe siècles,* édition critique de quelques lais bretons. Geneva: Droz, 1976. (PRF, 143.)

TOBLER, ADOLF. *Mélanges de grammaire française.* 2nd ed. Trans. Max Kuttner and Léopold Sudre. Paris: Picard, 1905.

————, ed. *Li Proverbe au Vilain.* Leipzig: Hirzel, 1895.

————. *Le Vers français, ancien et moderne.* Trans. Karl Breul and Léopold Sudre. Paris, 1885. (Repr. Slatkine, 1972.)

———— and ERHARD LOMMATZSCH. *Altfranzösisches Wörterbuch.* Wiesbaden, 1925– (to vol. 10, 1976, "tympanistes").

TOPSFIELD, LESLIE T. *Troubadours and Love.* Cambridge: Cambridge University Press, 1975.

TUBACH, FREDERIC C. *Index Exemplorum, A Handbook of Medieval Religious Tales.* Helsinki: Academia Scientiarum Fennica, 1969. (FF Communications, 204.)

TYROLLER, FRANZ. *Die Fabel von dem Mann und dem Vogel in ihrer Verbreitung in der Weltliteratur.* Berlin: Felber, 1912. (Literarhistorische Forschungen, 51.)

ULRICH, J. "Die altfranzösische Sprichwörtersammlung. *Proverbes ruraux et vulgaux.* (B.N. 25545)." *Zeitschrift für französische Sprache und Litteratur,* 24 (1902): 1–35.

VERHULSDONCK, J. TH. "Le Ms. B.N. 25.545." *Marche Romane*, 28 (1978): 193–97.

VERMETTE, ROSALIE ANN. "THE CHAMPENOIS VERSION OF THE *Barlaam et Josaphat*: A Study in Textual Transmission." Diss., University of Iowa, 1975.

VIELLIARD, FRANÇOISE. *Manuscrits français du Moyen Age.* Bibliotheca Bodmeriana. Catalogues, 2. Cologny-Geneva: Fondation Martin Bodmer, 1975.

VINAVER, EUGÈNE. "Principles of Textual Emendation." *Studies in French Language and Mediaeval Literature presented to Mildred K. Pope.* Manchester, 1939, pp. 351–69.

VON WARTBURG, W. *Französisches Etymologisches Wörterbuch.* 18 vols. and suppl. 1928–76.

WACKER, GERTRUD. *Über das Verhältnis von Dialekt und Schriftsprache im Altfranzösischen.* Halle: Niemeyer, 1916. (Beiträge zur Geschichte der romanischen Sprachen und Literaturen, 11.)

WAGNER, CHARLES PHILIP, ed. *El Libro del Cauallero Zifar.* Ann Arbor: University of Michigan, 1929.

WAILLY, NATALIS DE, ed. *Récits d'un ménestrel de Reims au treizième siècle.* Paris: Renouard, 1876.

WARD, H. L. D. and J. A. HERBERT. *Catalogue of Romances in the Department of MSS in the British Museum.* 3 vols. London: The Trustees, 1883–1910.

WARNKE, KARL, ed. *Die Fabeln der Marie de France.* Halle: Niemeyer, 1898. (Bibliotheca Normannica, 6.) (Repr. Slatkine, 1974.)

———. *Die Lais der Marie de France.* Halle: Niemeyer, 1900. (Bibliotheca Normannica, 3.)

WATSON, PAUL F. *The Garden of Love in Tuscan Art of the Early Renaissance.* Philadelphia: The Art Alliance Press, 1979.

WAY, G. L., trans. *Fabliaux or Tales, abridged from French Manuscripts of the XIIth and XIIIth Centuries by M. Le Grand,* selected and translated into English verse, with a Preface, Notes, and Appendix by the late G. Ellis. A new ed. corrected. 3 vols. (in one). London: Rodwell, 1815.

WEEKS, RAYMOND, ed. "Le lai de l'Oiselet," in *Medieval Studies in Memory of Gertrude Schoepperle Loomis.* Paris: Champion, and New York: Columbia University Press, 1927, pp. 341–53.

WELTER, J.-TH. *L'Exemplum dans la littérature religieuse et didactique du moyen âge.* Paris and Toulouse: Occitania, 1927. (Repr. AMS, 1973.)

WHITEHEAD, F. and C. E. PICKFORD. "The Introduction to the *Lai de l'Ombre*: Sixty Years Later." *Romania*, 94 (1973): 145–56.

WILHELM, JAMES J. *The Cruelest Month. Spring, Nature, and Love in Classical and Medieval Lyrics.* New Haven and London: Yale University Press, 1965.

WILLIAMS, CLEM C., JR. "The Genre and Art of the Old French Fabliaux, a preface to the Study of Chaucer's Tales of the Fabliau Type." Diss., Yale University, 1961.

WILSON, GEOFFREY. *A Medievalist in the Eighteenth Century. Le Grand d'Aussy and the Fabliaux ou Contes.* The Hague: Nijhoff, 1975.

WINTERS, MARGARET E., ed. *Jean Renart. The Lai de l'Ombre.* Birmingham, Alabama: Summa Publications, Inc., 1986.

WOLFF, R. L. "The Apology of Aristides, A Reexamination." *Harvard Theological Review*, 30 (1937): 233–47.

———. "Barlaam and Joasaph." *Harvard Theological Review*, 32 (1939): 131–39.

WOLFGANG, LENORA D. "The *Trois Savoirs* in Phillipps Manuscript 25970," in *Continuations: Essays in Honor of John L. Grigsby.* Ed. Norris J. Lacy and Gloria Torrini-Roblin. Birmingham, Ala: Summa Publications, Inc., 1989, pp. 307–18.

Woodward, Rev. G. R., H. Mattingly, and D. M. Lang, trans. *St. John Damascene. Barlaam and Joasaph.* new ed. Cambridge and London: Harvard and Heinemann, 1914, 1983. (Loeb Classical Library, 34.)

Wulff, F.-A., ed. "Le Conte du *Mantel.*" *Romania,* 14 (1885): 343–80.

Zenker, Rudolf, ed. "Der Lai de l'Epine." *Zeitschrift für romanische Philologie,* 17 (1893): 233–55.

Zotenberg, Hermann and Paul Meyer, eds. *Barlaam und Josaphat, französisches Gedicht des dreizehnten Jahrhunderts von Gui de Cambrai.* Stuttgart, 1864. (Bibliothek des litterarischen Vereins, 75.)

Zumthor, Paul. "La brièveté comme forme," in *La Nouvelle.* Montréal: Plato Academic Press, 1983. (Actes du Colloque International de Montréal. McGill University, 14–16 octobre 1982), pp. 3–8.

———. *Essai de poétique médiévale.* Paris: Seuil, 1972.

———. *Langue et techniques poétiques à l'époque romane (XIe–XIIIe siècles).* Paris: Klincksieck, 1963.

LE LAI DE L'OISELET

[77a] Il avint jadis a un tans,
    Bien a passé plus de cent ans,
Qu'il estoit uns riches vilains;
De son·non ne sui pas certains,   4
Mes riches ert de grant maniere,
De bois, de prez, et de riviere,
Et de qanqu'afiert a preudome.
Se dire vos en voil la some,   8
Il avoit un manoir si bel
En tot le monde n'ot itel
Ne si gent, ne si delitable.
Le conter vos sembleroit fable.   12
Or vos en dirai la façon:
77b   Je ne cuit que jamés face on
Tel donjon, ne si riche tor;
Une riviere cort entor,   16
Qui enclooit tot le porpris,
Et un vergier qui fu de pris
I avoit d'eve et d'air enclos.
Cil qui le fist ne fu pas fos,   20
Ainz fu uns chevaliers gentis;
Apres le pere l'ot li fis,
Qui le vendi a ce vilain;
Einsi ala de main en main: 24
Bien savez que par mauvés oir
Dechieent viles et manoir.

  Li vergiers fu biaus a devise:
    Herbes i ot de mainte guise,   28
Que je ne sai mie nomer;
Mes se le voir en veil conter,
Il i avoit roses et flors,
Qui jetoient molt granz odors,   32
Et espices de tel maniere
Que une ame gisent em biere
Qui malade fust et enferme,
S'en alast toute saine et ferme   36
Por tant que el vergier geüst
Tant c'une nuit passee fust.
De bones herbes fu garnis;

Et li praiaus fu si honis   40
Qu'il n'i avoit ne mont ne val;
Et li arbre tuit parigal
Estoient d'un grant contremont:
Si bel vergier n'avoit el mont.   44
Ja cel fruit ne demandissiez
Que vos trover n'i peüssiez,
Et si i estoit en tout tans.
Cil qui le fist fu molt sachans;   48
Il fu tot fet par nigromance,
Laienz avoit mainte provance.
Li vergiers fu et biaus et lons;
Il estoit a compa[s] reons;   52
Enmi avoit une fontainne,
77c   Qui bele estoit et clere et sainne,
Si sordoit a si grant randon
Com s'ele bousist a bandon,   56
Et si estoit froide com marbre.
Ombre li fesoit un bel arbre,
Dont les branches s'en estendoient,
Qui sagement duites estoient.   60
Fueilles i avoit a plenté:
Entor le plus bel jor d'esté,
Quant ce venoit el mois de mai,
N'i peüssiez choisir le rai   64
Du soleil, si estoit ramuz;
Molt par doit estre chier tenuz,
Et si estoit de tel nature
Que la fueille tot tens li dure: 68
Vent ne tempeste tant s'esforce,
N'en abat ne fueille n'escorce.

Li pins fu deliteus et biaus,
   Chanter i venoit uns oisiaus   72
Deus foiz le jor, et plus noiant.
Et si sachiez a escïant,
Qu'il i venoit la matinee
Et l'autre foiz a la vespree.   76
Li oiseaus fu et biaus et genz:
Molt seroit granz destruiemenz
Qui vos en diroit la façon:
Il estoit mendres d'un pinçon,   80
Un poi graindre du roëtel,
Si chantoit si bien et si bel
Rossignol, melle ne mauvis
Ne l'estornel, ce m'est avis,   84

Chant d'aloe ne de kalandre
N'est pas si plesant a entendre
Comme li suens, bien le sachiez.
Li oiseaus fu bien afaitiez   88
A dire lais et noveaus sons
Et rotrüenges et chançons;
Gigue ne harpe ne vïele
N'i vausist pas une cenele.   92
Du chant avoit une merveille,
77d   Onques n'oïtes sa pareille:
Car tel vertu avoit li chans,
Ja nus hom ne fust si dolans,   96
Por que l'oisel chanter oïst,
Que maintenant ne s'esjoïst
Et oublïast sa grant dolor.
Et s'il n'eüst pensé d'amor,   100
Si fust il maintenant espris,
Et cuidast estre de tel pris
Come est empereres ou rois,
Mes qu'il fust vilains ou borjois;   104
Et s'il eüst cent anz passez,
Et du siecle ne fust finez,
S'il oïst de l'oisel le chant
Qui ne semblast de maintenant   108
Qu'il fust meschins et damoisiaus,
Et si cuidast estre si biaus,
Qu'il fust amez de damoiseles
De meschines et de puceles.   112
Et une autre merveille i ot,
Que li vergiers durer ne pot
Se tant non que li oiseillons
I venist chanter ses doz sons: 116
Car du chant issoit li humors
Qui en vertu tenoit les flors;
Se li oiseaus en fust alez
Cheüe fu[st] sa grant biautez;   120
Maintenant li vergiers sechast,
Et la fontainne restanchast,
Qui par l'oisel sont en vertu.

Li vilains cui li estres fu   124
     Venoit chascun jor par costume
Por oïr cele soautume
A la fonta[inn]e souz le pin.
Par une ma[tine]e i vint   128
Son vis la[va] en la fontainne,

Et li oiseaus a grant alainne
Qui ert sor le pin li chantoit
Un son qui deliteus estoit: 132
78a   Li lais fu molt biaus a entendre,
77d   Essample i porroit on aprendre,
78a   Dont miex en vaudroit en la fin.
Li oiseaus dit en son latin: 136
"Entendez," fet il, "a mon lai,
Et chevalier et clerc et lai,
Qui vos entremetez d'amors
Et qui en sentez les dolors;   140
Et a vos le di ge, puceles,
Qui estes avenanz et beles,
Et le siecle volez avoir:
Je vos di et creant por voir   144
Vos devez Dieu amer avant,
La loi tenir et son commant,
Volentiers alez au mostier,
Et si oëz le Dieu mestier: 148
Car du servise Deu oïr
Ne puet nului mal avenir;
Et par verité le recort,
Diex et amis sont d'un acort,   152
Et bone amor ne het il mie,
C'on demainne sanz vilennie.
Diex escoute bele proiere,
Aumosne ne met pas ariere;   156
Diex covoite toute largesce,
N'i a nule mauvese teche.
Diex si aimme honor et bonté,
Si aimme amor et loiauté.   160
Li aver sont li envïeus,
Li tenant et li covoiteus,
Et li vilain sont li mauvais,
Et li felon sont li punais.   164
Mes seul cortoisie et honor
Et loiauté maintient amor.
Et se vos a ce vos tenez,
Dieu et s'amor emporterez."   168
Ce dit li oiseaus en son chant,
Et quant vit le vilain seant
Desouz le pin qui l'esgardoit,
Qui fel et enuieus estoit,   172
Si li chante en autre maniere:
78b   "Et car lai ton corre, riviere!
Donjon, periz; meson, car chiez!

Matisiez, flors; herbes, sechiez!   176
Arbres, car lessiez le porter!
Ci me soloient escouter
Gentis dames et chevaliers
Qui la fontaine avoient chier,   180
Et plus longuement en vivoient,
Et miex par amors en amoient,
Maintenoient chevalerie.
Or m'ot cil vilains plains d'envie,   184
Qui miex aimme assez le denier
Qu'i[l] ne face le donoier;
Puis que mes chans li fu faillis
Fu il a covoitier sougis.   188
Cil me soloient escouter
Por deduire et por deporter,
Et por lor cors miex aaisier;
Et cist i vient por miex mengier!"   192

Quant ce ot dit, si s'en vola,
   Et li vilains qui remest la
Pense, se il le pöuet prendre,
[A]ssez tost le porroit chier vendre;   196
Et se vendre ne le pooit,
En jaiole le meteroit,
Si l'i chanteroit tart et tempre.
Son engin prent et si l'atempre,   200
Et esgarde, enquiert et porvoit
Tant que les branches aperçoit,
La ou se seoit plus souvent.
Il fet laz et si les i tent,   204
Molt a bien sa chose atempree.
Et quant ce vint a la vespree,
Que cil oiseaus el vergier vint
Tantost est asis sor le pin;   208
Il fu pris erroment au las.
Li chaitis, li dolenz. Li las
Monte amont, l'oiselet aert.
"Tel loier a qui vilain sert,"   212
Fet li oiseaus, "ce m'est avis.
78c   Mal avez fet qui m'avez pris,
Qu'en moi a povre reançon."
   —"Ainz en avré mainte chançon!   216
Or me chanterez plus sovent:
Servi m'avez a vo talent,
Or servirez a ma partie
Et ferez a ma commandie."   220

—"J'en ai le pior a moi pris.
Je seul avoir a mon devis
Et bois et rivieres et prez:
Or sui en jeole enserrez,   224
Or mais n'avré deduit ne joie;
Je soloie vivre de proie,
Or me donra l'en a mengier
Si comme en fet a prisonnier.   228
Lessiez moi aler, biaus amis,
Et bien soiez seürs et fis
Ja em prison ne chanterai."
    —"Par foi, et je vos mengerai!   232
Ja par autre tor n'en irez."
    —"En moi povre repast avrez,
Car je sui lasches et petis:
Ja n'en croistera vostre pris   236
Se vos ocïez tele rien.
Lessiez m'aler, si ferez bien,
Pechié feroiz se m'ocïez."
    —"Certes por noient emparlez,   240
Car com plus proiez en seroie,
Sachiez que je mains en feroie."
    —"Certes," fet li oiseaus, "c'est drois,
Car ainsi l'aporte la lois: 244
Douce reson vilain aïre,
Grant pieç'a que l'ai oï dire.
Mes je vos mostre une autre chose:
Besoins fet fere mainte chose.   248
Ma force ne m'i puet tenser;
Mes se vos me lessiez aler,
De trois sens vos feroie sage
Q'ains ne sot [hons] de vo lignage,   252
Si vos porroient molt valoir."
78d   —"Se seürté em puis avoir,"
Fet li vilains, "tost le ferai."
    —"Tele fïance comme j'ai,"   256
Fet li oiseaus, "je vos creant."
Et cil le lesse aler atant.

L i oiseaus sor le pin s'en vole,
  Qui eschapez fu par parole.   260
Il fu laiz et touz hericiez,
Car laidement fu manoiez:
Tenuz ot esté contre lainne;
A son bec sa plume remainne   264
Et rasiet au miex que il puet.

Li vilains, cui savoir estuet
Les trois sens, semont que il die.
Li oiseaus fu plains de voisdie,   268
Si dit: "Se tu bien i entens,
Aprendre i puez un molt biau sens:
Ne pleure ce c'onques n'eüs."
Li vilains fu molt irascus,   272
Puis respondi par felonnie:
"Tu m'as ta fïance mentie:
Trois sens tu me deüs aprendre,
Si com tu me feïs entendre,   276
Q'ains ne sot hons de mon lignage;
Mes de ce est toz li monz sage;
Nus n'est si fox n'onques ne fu
Qui plorast ce que n'ot eü.   280
Tu m'as si largement menti."
Et li oisiaus li respondi:
"Volez vos que jel vos redie
Si que vos ne l'oblïez mie?   284
Vos entendez tant a pledier
Que peor ai de l'oblïer:
Je cuit que ja nu retendrez."
—"Je le sai miex que vos assez,"   288
Fet li vilains, "de grant pieç'a.
Dahez ait qui gre vos savra
D'aprendre ce dont en est sages!
Je ne sui mie si sauvages,   292
Par mon chief, com vos me tenez.
79a Por ce, se tu m'es eschapez,
Que sor toi n'ai mes nul pooir,
Or le metrai en nonchaloir,   296
Si ne m'alez mie gabant,
Bien sai cestui! Dites avant."
—"Entent a moi," fet li oiseaus,
"Li autres est et bons et beaus: 300
Ne croire qanque tu oz dire."
Li vilains fronce le nes d'ire,
Et dit: "Je le savoie bien!"
—"Biaus amis, donques le retien,   304
Gardez que vos ne l'oblïez!"
—"Or sui je molt bien assenez,"
Fet li vilains, "por sens aprendre.
Le musage me fez entendre,   308
Qui ce me rueves detenir.
Je te voudroie ja tenir!
Mes se tenoies mes covens,

Tu m'aprendroies le tierz sens.   312
Dites qex il est, je l'orrai."
—"Entent i bien, et jel dirai:
Li tierz est tiex, qui le saroit
Jamés povres hons ne seroit."   316
Et quant li vilains l'entendi,
Molt durement s'en esjoï,
Et dit: "Cestui m'estuet savoir,
Car volentiers tent a avoir."   320
Qui li veïst l'oisel coitier!
"Il est," fet il, "tens de mengier;
Aprenez le moi erroment."
Et quant li oiseillons l'entent,   324
Si dit: "Je te chastoi, vilains:
Que ce que tu tiens en tes mains,
Ne le giete jus a tes piez."
Lors fu li vilains corouciez;   328
Et quant il s'est teüz grant pose,
Si dit: "N'estoit ce autre chose?
Ce sont ci paroles d'enfant,
Que je sai bien a escïant.   332
Tiex est au siecle soufroitos
79b Qui ausi bien le set con vos.
Menti m'avez et engingnié:
De qanque m'avez ensaingnié   336
Estoie je sages devant."
Li oiseaus respont a itant:
"Par foi, se tu ces sens seüsses,
Lessié pas aler ne m'eüsses   340
Quant tu me tenis a tes mains."
—"Voir avez dit," fet li vilains.
Li oiseaus qui fu engingneus
Li dist: "Cist vaut les autres deus,   344
Et puis aprés des autres cent."
Li vilains li respont: "Comment?"
—"Comment? Je te di, malostru,
Tu ne sez que t'est avenu,   348
Car se tu m'eüsses tüé,
Si com tu eüs empensé,
Jamés jor ne fust, par mes euz,
Qu'il ne t'en fust durement mieuz."   352
—"Ha! por Deu, que sez tu donc fere?"
—"Haï! fel vilain deputere,
Il a en mon cors une pierre
Qui tant est precïeuse et chiere,   356
Bien est de trois onces pesant.

La vertu de li est si grant
Qui en son demainne l'aroit
Ja chose ne demanderoit   360
Que maintenant ne li fust preste."
Qant li vilains entendi ceste,
Si tort ses poinz, si ront ses dras,
Si se claimme chaitis et las,   364
A ses ongles son vis despiece.
Li oiseaus en fet grant leesce,
Qui de sor le pin l'esgardoit.
Il a tant atendu qu'il voit   368
Qu'il a toz ses dras despeciez,
Et qu'il s'est en mainz leus bleciez.
Puis li a dit: "Chaitis vilains,
Quant tu me tenis en tes mains,   372
G'iere plus legiers d'un moisson,
De mesenge, ne de pinçon;
Ne pesoie pas demie once."
Cil qui de felonnie gronce   376
Li dit: "Certes vos dites voir."
—"Vilains, or puez tu bien savoir
Que de la pierre t'ai menti."
—"Or le sai ge," fet il, "de fi;   380
Mes certes avant le cuidai."
—"Vilains, orendroit proverai
Des trois choses que nes savoies,
Et de ce que tu nes disoies: 384
'Nus n'est si fox, ne onc ne fu,
Qui plorast ce que n'ot eü';
Meintenant, ce m'est vis, ploras
Ce q'ains n'eüs, ne ja n'avras!   388
Des trois sens estes abosmez:
Biaus amis, si les retenez;
Il fet bon aprendre bon mot:
C'on dit que cil n'entent qui ot,   392
Et tex parole par grant sens
Qui poi a en lui de porpens;
Tex parole de cortoisie
Qui ne la savroit fere mie;   396
Et tex cuide estre bien senez
Qui a folie est assenez."

Quant ce ot dit, si s'en vola,
C'onques puis el vergier n'entra,   400
Et de tel eür s'en ala
Li vergiers failli et secha,

79c (margin at line 374)

N'onques puis li oiseaus ne vint:
Les fueilles cheïrent du pin,   404
Et la fontainne restancha;
N'i vint plus nus, ne habita.
Li vilains perdi son deduit.
Or sachent bien, toutes et tuit,   408
Li proverbes dit en apert:
Cil qui tot covoite tout pert.

Rejected Readings of *B*

Title Cest le lay de loiselet — 33 de grant m. — 34 Qui — 73 Trois f. le
j. et p. noient (-1) — 74 escient (-1) — 104 ou cortois — 106 Que —
107 Cil — 116 c. les d. — 121 le vergier — 123 Et p. loisel est en — 124
Li oiseaus qui el vergier fu — 133–34 *Inv.* — 185 Que — 189 Ci — 196
t. li p. — 197 Et ce v. — 198 En la j. le metroit — 199 Si li tendroit et
main et — 205 atrempee — 206 Q. ce vint a la matinee — 213 o. vos ma-
vez pris — 214 f. ce mest avis — 238 L. mester si — 245 Toute r. — 267
sens comment que — 283 q. je v. — 292 Ne je ne sui m. sauvages — 332
a escient (-1) — 340 Lessier — 357 est demie once p. — 392 que qui nen-
tent et ot — *Explicit* Explicit les lays de breteigne

DIPLOMATIC TEXTS

E	C
E	**C**
B. N. f. fr. 1593 (E)	B. N. f. fr. 25545 (C)
Le lay de l'oiselet	Li laiz de l'oiselet

172b	1	[I] avint jadiz a un tens		*(151a)*	1	[I] avint jadis a un temps	
	2	Bien a passe plus de cent ans			2	Bien a passe plus de cent ans	
	3	Qu'il fu uns riches vilains			3	Qu'il estoit uns riches vilains	
	4	De son non ne sui pas certains	4		4	De son non ne suis pas certains	4
		•				•	
		•				•	
	5	Mes riches fu de grant meniere			5	Mais riches iert de grant maniere	
	6	De prez de bois et de riviere			6	De prez de bois et de riviere	
	7	De quanque il affiert a riche home		*151b*	7	De tout ce qu'afiert a riche homme	
	8	Se dire vous an vuel la somme	8		8	Se dire vous en veil la somme	8
		Et le voir vous an vuel conter				•	
		A paines trouvast l'en son per				•	
	9	Il avoit un menoir tant bel			9	Il avoit un manoir si bel	
	10	Qu'a bourc n'a vile n'a chastel	12		10	N'a borc n'a vile n'a chastel	
		•				Et se je vos en veil conter	
		•				En tout le monde n'ot son per	12
	11	N'ot si bel ne si delitable			11	Ne si bel ne si delitable	
	12	Dou conte vous sambleroit fable			12	Li contes vos sambleroit fable	
	13	Qui vous an diroit la facon			13	Qui vos en diroit la facon	
	14	Je ne cuit que jamais fasce hom	16		14	Je ne cuit que jamais face on	16
	15	Tel donjon ne si riche tor			15	Tel donjon ne si riche tour	
	16	La riviere couroit entor			16	La riviere court tut entour	
		•				•	
		•				•	
	17	Qui anclot tot le porpris			17	Qui tout enclooit le pourpris	
	18	Et s'i ot un vergier de pris	20		18	Dedens ot vergier de pris	20
	19	Qui d'eve clere estoit entor clos			19	Qui d'yaue et d'air estoit enclos	
	20	Cil qui le fist ne fu pas fos			20	Cil qui le fist ne fu pas fos	

DIPLOMATIC TEXTS

A
B. N. f. fr. 837 (A)
Le Lay de l'oiselet

D
B. N. f. fr. 24432 (D)
Ci commance le dit de l'oiselet et du vilain

		A					D	
45a	1	Il avint jadis a un tans			(*42a*)	1	Il avint jadis en un temps	
	2	Bien a passe plus de cent ans				2	Bien a passe quatre cens ans	
	3	Qu'il estoit uns riches vilains					•	
	4	De son non ne sui pas certains	4				•	
		•					Que il estoit uns riches hom	
		•					Je ne se pas nommer son non	4
	5	Mes riches ert de grant maniere				5	Mes il estoit de grant maniere	
	6	De prez de bois et de riviere				6	De pres de bois et de riviere	
	7	Et de quanqu'afiert a riche homme				7	Et de quanqu'afiert a riche homme	
	8	Se dire vous en vueil la somme	8			8	De ce vous veil dire la somme	8
		•					Avoit de ce ne faut pas dire	
		•					Liez hons estoit sanz nesun ire	
	9	Il avoit un manoir si bel				9	Il avoit un manoir si bel	
	10	A borc n'a vile n'a chastel				10	En bourc n'en ville n'en chastel	12
		Se le voir vous en vueil conter					Se le voir vous en weil conter	
		En tout le monde n'ot son per	12	*42b*			En tout le monde n'ot son per	
	11	Ne si gent ne si delitable				11	Ne si biau ne si delitable	
	12	Certes il vous sambleroit fable				12	Li contes vous en sembleroit fable	16
	13	Qui vous en diroit la facon				13	Qui vous en diroit la facon	
	14	Je cuit que james ne face on	16			14	Je ne cuit que ainz face hom	
	15	Tel donjon ne si haute tor				15	Tel donjon ne si riche tour	
	16	Quar riviere coroit entor				16	Escoutez seigneur par amour	20
		•					Entour couroit une riviere	
		•					Belle et clere de grant maniere	
	17	Qui enclooit tout le porpris				17	Qui enclooit tout le porpris	
	18	Et li vergiers qui fu de pris	20			18	Et un vergier qui fu de pris	24
	19	Estoit d'arbres et d'eve enclos				19	I avoit d'arbres d'iaue enclos	
	20	Cil qui le fist ne fu pas fols				20	Cilz qui le fist ne fu pas fols	

E				C		
21	Ainz fu uns chevaliers gentiz			21	Ains fu uns chevaliers gentis	
22	Apres le pere l'ot li filz	24		22	Apres le pere l'ot li fis	24
23	Si le vendi a un vilain			23	Puis le vendi a cel vilain	
24	Ansis ala de main en main			24	Ainsis ala de main en main	
25	Bien savez que par mauvais oir			25	Bien savez que par malvais hoir	
26	Dechieent viles et menoir	28		26	Dechieent viles et manoir	28
	•				•	
	•				•	
27	Li vergiers fu biaus a devise			27	[L]i vergiers fu biax a devise	
28	Arbres i ot de mainte guise			28	Herbes y ot de mainte guise	
29	Que je ne sai pas nommer			29	Que je ne sai mie nommer	
30	Mais se voir en vuel conter	32		30	Mais je vos puis por voir conter	32
31	Il i avoit roses et flors			31	Qu'il y avoit roses et flors	
32	Et espices de tex odours			32	Qui getoient mout grans odors	
33	Et herbes de tele maniere			33	Et espices de tel maniere	
34	S'une ame i gisoit en litiere	36		34	Que s'une arme geust an litiere	36
	•			35	Qui malade fust et anferme	
	•			36	S'en alast tout sainne et ferme	
	Qui fust malades et enfox				•	
	Si ce relevast il tox				•	
37	Pour itant com jardin geust			37	Por tant qu'en cel vergier geust	
38	Tant c'unne nuiz passee fust	40		38	Tant c'unne nuit passee i fust	40
39	De chieres herbes ert garniz			39	Et de ses herbes fust garnis	
40	Et li vergiers ert si honiz			40	[E]t li praiaus fu si onnis	
41	Que il n'i a ne mont ne val			41	Qui n'y avoit ne mont ne val	
42	Tuit li arbre sont parigal	44		42	Et li arbre tuit parigal	44
43	Si c'en revont tot contremont			43	Estoient d'un grant contremont	
44	Il n'ot si bel vergier el mont			44	Il n'ot si bel vergier ou mont	
45	Ja de fruit n'i demandissiez			45	De cel fruit ne demandissiez	
46	Que vous trouver n'i peussiez	48		46	Que vos trover n'i pouissiez	48
47	• • • • • • • • • • • •			47	Et si duroit en tous les tens	
48	Cil qui le fist fu molt saichant			48	Cilz qui le fist fu mout sachans	
49	Il fu touz faiz par nigromance			49	Il fu tos fais par nigromance	
50	Il i avoit mainte prouvance	52		50	S'i faisoit on mainte esprovance	52

172c (left margin, line 39)
151c (right margin, line 41)

A

21	Ainz fu uns chevaliers gentiz	
22	Apres le pere l'ot li filz	24
23	Qui le vendi a cel vilain	
24	Ainsi ala de main en main	
25	Bien savez que par mauves oir	
26	Dechieent viles et manoir	28
	•	
	•	
27	Li vergiers fu biaus a devise	
28	Herbes i ot de mainte guise	
29	Que je ne sai mie nommer	
30	Se le voir vous en vueil conter	32
31	Il i avoit fueilles et flors	
32	Qui getoient molt granz odors	
33	Et espices de tel maniere	
34	C'une ame gisant en litiere	36
35	Qui malade fust et enferme	
36	S'en alast toute saine et ferme	
	•	
	•	
37	Por tant que el vergier geust	
38	Tant c'une nuit passee fust	40
	•	
	•	
	•	
	•	
	•	
	•	42c
	•	
	•	
	•	
	•	
	•	

D

21	Ce fu uns chevaliers gentils	
22	Apres le pere l'ot li fils	28
23	Qui le vendi a un vilain	
24	Ainsi ala de main en main	
25	Vous savez bien que par mal hoir	
26	Se dechieent maint bel avoir	32
	Et mainte terre et mainte rente	
	Par le surcrois de male vente	
27	Li vergiers fu biaus a devise	
28	Arbres i ot de mainte guisse	36
29	Que je ne se mie nommer	
30	Mes por voir vous puis raconter	
31	Qu'il y avoit roses et flours	
32	Qui jetoient moult grans odours	40
33	Et espices de tel maniere	
34	Que dame gisans en litiere	
35	Qui malade fust et enferme	
36	S'en iroit toute saine et ferme	44
	•	
	•	
37	Por tant que u vergier geust	
38	Et c'une nuit estre i peust	
39	De chieres herbes fu garnis	
40	Et li preaus fu si omnis	48
41	Qu'il n'i avoit ne mont ne val	
42	Et li arbre tuit parigal	
43	Estoient d'un grant contremont	
44	Plus bel vergier n'avoit u mont	52
45	Ja tel fruit n'i demandissiez	
46	Que vous trouver n'i peussiez	
47	Ainsi estoient il tous temps	
48	Cilz qui le fist fu moult sachans	56
49	Il fu tous fais par nigremance	
50	Leans avoit mainte provance	

	E			C	
	E			**C**	
51	Li vergiers fu biaus et lons		51	[L]i vergiers fu et lez et lons	
52	Toz fu faiz a compas reons		52	Et a compas tout en reont	
53	S'ot en un lieu une fontaine		53	Et emmi ot une fontainne	
54	Qui tant par est et clere et saine	56	54	Dont l'iaue estoit et clere et sainne	56
55	S'i sourdoit a si grant randon		55	Si sourdoit a si grant randon	
56	Com c'ile bouist a boillon		56	Com c'ele boulist de randon	
57	Si fu plus froides que maubres		57	S'iert ele plus froide que marbres	
58	Umbres li fait uns molt biaus aubres	60	58	Ombre li fist li plus biax arbres	60
	•			•	
	•			•	
59	Dont les branches ans atochoient		59	Dont les branches lez s'estendoient	
60	Que sagement duites estoient		60	Qui sagement duites estoient	
	•		61	Foilles y avoit a plante	
	•		62	En tout le plus lonc jor d'este	64
63	Car enz ou plus lonc jor de may		63	Que l'en dist ens ou mois de may	
64	N'i poist passer li rai	64	64	Ne peussent choisir le ray	
65	Du soloil si est il ramuz		65	Dou souloil si estoit rammus	
66	Il doit bien estre chier tenuz		66	Mout devoit estre chier tenus	68
67	Car il est de tele nature		67	Et si estoit de tel nature	
68	Que touz tens la fuelle li dure	68	68	Qu'an tous tens sa foille li dure	
69	Vans ne orages tant efforce		69	Vens ne orez tant ait grant force	
70	N'en abat fuelle ne escorce		70	N'en abat jus foille n'escorce	72
71	Li pinz fu delitouz et biaus		71	[L]i pins fu delitous et biaus	
72	Et chanter i suit uns oisiaus	72	72	Chanter y venoit uns oisiaus	
73	Deus fois le jour et plus niant		73	Deus fois le jor et puis niant	
74	Et sachiez bien a esciant		74	Et si sachiez a esciant	76
76	Qu'il venoit a la vespree		75	Qu'il y venoit la matinee	
75	Et le main a la matinee	76	76	Et puis apres a la vespree	
77	Icil oisiaus u est si gens		151d 77	Li oisiax fu mervilles gens	
78	Trop seroit grans destruiemenz		78	Ce seroit grans detriemens	80
79	Qui vous an diroit la facon		79	Se vos disoie sa facon	
80	Il estoit maindres d'un moisson	80	80	Il estoit menres d'un moisson	

A

	51	Li vergiers fu et biaus et lons	
	52	Il estoit a compas roons	
	53	Enmi estoit une fontaine	
	54	Qui molt estoit et clere et saine	44
	55	Et sordoit de si grant randon	
	56	Com s'ele boillist a bandon	
	57	Et s'estoit froide comme marbre	
	58	Ombre li fesoit un bel arbre	48
		•	
		•	
	59	Dont les branches bel s'estendoient	
	60	Qui sagement duites estoient	
		•	
		•	
45b	63	Quant ce venoit el mois de may	
	64	N'i peussiez choisir le ray	52
	65	Du soleil tant par ert ramus	
	66	Molt par doit estre chier tenus	
	67	Quar il est de tele nature	
	68	Que toz tens sa fueille li dure	56
	69	Vens ne orez tant ait de force	
	70	N'en abat fueille ne escorce	
	71	Li pins ert deliteus et biaus	
	72	Chanter i venoit uns oisiaus	60
	73	Deus foiz le jor et plus noiant	
	74	Et bien sachiez a esciant	
	75	Qu'il i venoit la matinee	
	76	Et puis le soir a la vespree	64
	77	Li oisiaus fu merveilles genz	
	78	Molt seroit granz detrimenz	
	79	Qui vous en diroit la façon	
	80	Il ert plus petiz d'un moisson	68 *42d*

D

51	Li vergiers ert et biaus et lons	
52	A compas tous fais et reons	60
53	Enmi avoit une fontaine	
54	Dont l'iaue estoit et clere et saine	
55	Et sourdoit a si grant rendon	
56	Com s'el venist par comduison	64
57	Si estoit plus froide que marbre	
58	Ombre li faissoit un bel arbre	
	Que la gent apeloient pin	
	Tous temps ert vert soir et matin	68
59	Dont les branches loins s'estendoient	
60	Qui noblement duites estoient	
61	Fueilles i avoit a plente	
62	En tout le plus bel jor d'este	72
63	Quant ce vient ens u mois de may	
64	N'i peussiez choissir le ray	
65	Du solleil tant estoit ramus	
66	Moult devoit estre chier tenus	76
67	Car il estoit de tel nature	
68	Que sa verdeur tous temps li dure	
69	Vent ne tempeste tant soit forte	
70	N'en abat fueille ni escorce	80
71	Li pins fu deliteus et biaus	
72	Chanter i venoit uns oissiax	
73	Deus fois le jour et plus noient	
74	Et bien sachiez a escient	84
75	Qu'il i venoit la matinee	
76	Et l'autre fois a la vespree	
77	Li oissiaus fu et biaus et gens	
78	Moult seroit grans detriemens	88
79	Qui vous en diroit la façon	
80	Il estoit mendres d'un pincon	

	E	
	E	
	81 Un pou graindes d'un roietel	
	82 Si chantoit si bien et si bel	
172d	83 Chans d'aloue ne de maviz	
	84 Ne de melle ce m'est avis	84
	85 Ne de loigceing ne de kalende	
	86 N'estoit si plesans a entandre	
	87 Com est li siens bien le sachiez	
	88 Et si par est si afaitiez	88
	89 De diz dire et de biaus sons	
	90 D[e] retrouanges de chancons	
	91 Guine ne harpe ne viele	
	92 Ne vausist pas une cinele	92
	•	
	•	
	93 En son chant ot une mervelle	
	94 Ainz nunz hom ne vit sa parelle	
	Que ja nuns tant dolans ne fust	
	Ne tant ou sieccle este eust	96
	95 S'il oist de l'oiselet le chant	
	96 Si fust il jones et joians	
	•	
	•	
	100 Et s'en eust pance d'amors	
	99 Si n'eust il au cuer dolors	100
	101 Et en fust maintenant espris	
	102 Et cuidast estre de tel pris	
	103 Com est empereres ou rois	
	104 Mes qu'il fust vilains ou bourjois	104
	•	
	•	
	•	
	•	

C

C		
81 Et fu plus grans d'un roietel	
82 Si chantoit si bien et si bel	84
83 Lorsignot melle ne mauvis	
84 Ne l'estornel se m'est avis	
85 Chans d'aloe ne de kalendre	
86 N'estoit si plaisans a entendre	88
87 Com iert li siens bien le sachiez	
88 Et si estoit si affaitiez	
89 De dire lais et noviax sons	
90 De rotruhenges et chancons	92
91 Gygue ne harpe ne viele	
92 Ne vaucissent une cynele	
•	
•	
93 Car ens el chant ot tel mervoille	
94 Qu'ains nus hom n'oy sa paroille	96
•	
•	
95 Et tel vertus avoit li chans	
96 Que nuns hom ne fust si dolans	
97 Pour coi l'oisel chanter oist	
98 Maintenant ne s'en resjoist	100
99 Et oubliast ses grans dolors	
100 Et si represist ses amors	
101 Maintenant fust d'amors soupris	
102 Et cuidast estre de tel pris	104
103 Com est empereres ou rois	
104 Mais qu'il fust vilains ou borjois	
105 Et c'il eust cent ans passez	
106 Et en cest siecle fust remez	108
107 S'oist de l'osillon le chant	
108 Si cuidast il tout maintenant	

A

81	Un petit graindre d'un roitel	
82	Si chantoit si bien et si bel	
	•	
	•	
85	Chans d'aloe ne de chalendre	
86	N'est pas si plesanz a entendre	72
87	Comme est li siens bien le sachiez	
88	Li oisiaus fu bien afetiez	
89	A dire lais et noviaus sons	
90	Et rotruenges et chancons	76
91	Gigue ne harpe ne viele	
92	N'i vousist pas une cenele	
83	Roxingnol melle ne mauvis	
84	Ne l'estormiaus ce m'est avis	80
93	El chant avoit une merveille	
94	Que nus hom n'oi sa pareille	
	•	
	•	
95	Quar tel vertu avoit li chanz	
96	Ja ne fust nus hom si dolanz	84
97	Se l'oiselet chanter oist	
98	Que maintenant ne s'esjoist	
99	Et oubliast ses granz dolors	
100	Et s'ainc n'eust parle d'amors	88
101	S'en fust il maintenant espris	
102	Et cuidast estre de tel pris	
103	Comme est empereres ou rois	
104	Mes qu'il fust vilains ou cortois	92
105	Et si eust cent anz passez	
106	Si fust il au siecle remez	
107	S'il oist de l'oisel le chant	
108	Se il samblast il maintenant	96

D

81	Un pou graindres d'un linotel	
82	Si chantoit si bien et si bel	92
83	Rosingnol melle ne mauvis	
84	·Ni estornel ce m'est avis	
85	Chant d'aloe ne de kalendre	
86	N'est pas si plesans a entendre	96
87	Com est li siens bien le sachiez	
88	Li oissiaus fu si afaitiez	
89	A dire lays et nouvias sons	
90	Que rotruanges ne chancons	100
91	Guige ne harpe ne viele	
92	. . . .	
	•	
	•	
93	El chant avoit une merveille	
94	Onques n'oistez sa pareille	104
	•	
	•	
95	Car tel vertu avoit le chant	
96	Que ja hons ne fust si dolant	
97	Mes que l'oissel chanter oist	
98	Que maintenant ne c'esjoist	108
99	Et qu'il n'oubliast sa doulour	
100	Et s'il n'eust pense d'amour	
101	S'en fust il maintenant espris	
102	Et cuidast estre de tel pris	112
103	Com est empereres et roys	
104	Fust ou vilain ou bourjois	
105	Et s'il eust cent ans passes	
106	Et fust du siecle trespasses	116
107	Pour qu'oist de l'oisel le chant	
108	Si li semblast il maintenant	

E   C

.   .
.   .
.   .
.   .
.   .
.   .
.   .
.   .
.   .
.   .
.   .
.   .
.   .
.   .
.   .

111	Et estre amez de dames beles		111	Estre ammerres de dammes beles	
112	De meschines ou de pucelles		112	De meschines et de puceles	112
113	Et une autre merveille i ot		113	[M]ais une autre mervoille y ost	
114	Que li vergiers durer ne pot	108	114	Que li vergiers durer ne post	
115	Fors tant com li oisillons	152a	115	Se tant non que li oisillons	
116	I venoit chanter ces douz sons		116	Y venoit chanter les dous sons	116
117	Car dou con issoit fors l'amours		117	Car de chant usent li ammeur	
118	Qui en vertu i tenoit les flors	112	118	Qui en vertu tiennent les fleurs	
120	Et le vergier et tot le mez		120	Les autres et trestout le mez	
119	Et se li oisiaus fust remez		119	Et se le oisiax fust remez	120

.   .
.   .

121	Maintenant li vergiers cichast		121	Maintenant li vergiers sechast	
122	Et la fontaine i atanchast	116	122	Et la fontaingne restanchast	
123	Qui par l'oisel fu en vertu		123	Qui por l'oisel sont en vertu	
124	Li vilains cui li estres fu		124	[L]i vilains cui li estres fu	124
125	Souvent i venoit par coustume		125	Y venoit deus fois par coustume	
126	Pour oir cele souuenture	120	126	Por oir cele souatume	

A

		A	
	109	Qu'il fust meschins et damoisiaus	
	110	Et si cuidast bien li dansiaus	
		•	
		•	
		•	
		•	
		•	
		•	
		•	
		•	
		•	
		•	
		•	
		•	
	111	Qu'il fust amez de damoiseles	
	112	De meschines et de puceles	100
45c	113	Et un autre merveille i ot	
	114	Que li vergiers durer ne pot	
	115	Desi la que li oiseillons	
	116	I venist chanter ses douz sons	104
	117	Quar du chant issent les amors	
	118	Qui en vertu tienent les flors	
	120	Et li arbres et toz li mez	
	119	Mes que li oisiaus fust remez	108
		•	
		•	
	121	Maintenant li vergiers sechast	
	122	Et la fontaine restanchast	
	123	Qui par l'oisel sont en vertu	
	124	Li vilains cui li estres fu	112
	125	I vient chascun jor p[ar] coustume	
	126	Por oir cele souatume	

D

	D		
109	Qu'il fust meschins et jouvenciaus		
110	Et si cuidast estre ausi biaus	120	
	Com fu li biaus parthenopiex		
	Ou nercisus qui a ces ieus		
	Por sa biaute rega[r]da tant		
	En l'iaue qui estoit courant	124	
	Qu'il en mourut ce fu sanz doute		
	Que la veue li failli toute		
	Por sa tres grant biaute mirer		
	Mourut sus l'iaue en regarder	128	
	Aussi seroit vis au viellart		*43a*
	Se il ouoit icel bel art		
	De cel oissel et ce chant cler		
	Qu'il peust a ceus resembler	132	
111	Et qu'il fust amez de danzelles		
112	Et de dames et de pucelles		
113	Une autre grant merveille i ot		
114	Que li vergiers ouvre ne pot	136	
115	Se tant non com li oisillons		
116	I venoit chanter les dous sons		
117	Car du chant issoit les amours		
118	Qui en vertu tenoit les flours	140	
120	Et li arbres et tous les cymes		
119	Et se li oissillon meismes		
	S'en fust alez ne tant ne quant		
	Si veissiez vertu moult grant	144	
121	Maintenant li arbres sechast		
122	Et la fontaine s'estanchast		
123	Qui par l'oissel iert en vertu		
124	Li vilains qui li arstre fu	148	
125	Venoit chascun par coustume		
126	Por flerier celle souastune		

	E			C	
128	Une matinee s'an vint		127	A la fontainne sor le pin	
127	A la fontaine lez le pin		128	Par une matinee vint	128
129	Son vis lava a la fontaine		129	Son vis lava a la fonteinne	
173a 130	Et li oisiaus a longue alaine	124	130	Et li oisiax a haute alainne	
	•			•	
	•			•	
	Deseure l'aubre li chanta			Qui sor le pin haut li chanta	
	Qui deliteuz li sambla			Un lait qui delitous chant a	132
	•			•	
	•			•	
133	Qui molt ert plaisans a a entendre		133	Li lais fu mout bons a entendre	
134	Exemple i puet on aprendre	128	134	Exemples y porroit on prendre	
135	De grant bien se vient en la fin		135	Dont on vaurroit miex en la fin	
136	Li oisiaus dit en son latin		136	[L]i oisiax dist en son latin:	136
137	Entendez trestuit a mon lai		137	Entendez fait il a mon lai	
138	Vous chevalier et cler et lai	132	138	Et chevalier et clerc et lai	
139	Qui vous antremetez d'amours		139	Qui vos entremetez d'amors	
140	Et qui en soffrez les dolours		140	Et qui en souffrez les dolors	140
141	Et vous dames et damoiseles		141	Et a vos le di dammoiseles	
142	Qui estes avena[n]s et beles	136	142	Qui iestes avenans et beles	
	•			•	
	•			•	
	•			•	
	•			•	
146	En verte vous ai et couvent		145	Que vos amez deu tout avant	
145	Vous devez dieu amer avant		146	Tenez sa loi et son commant	144
147	Volantierz alez au moustier		147	S'alez volentiers au monstier	
148	Pour escouter le dieu mestier	140	148	Et si oiez le dieu mestier	
149	Car dou servise dieu oir		149	Car dou servise deu oir	
150	Ne vous puet il nul mal venir		150	Ne puet a nelui mal venir	148
	•		151	Et por verite vos racort	
	•		152	Diex et amors sont d'un acort	

	A			D	
	A			**D**	
127	A la fontaine souz le pint		127	A la fontaine souz le pin	
128	Par une matinee i vint	116	128	Vint li vilains un bon matin	152
129	Son vis laver a la fontaine		129	Son vis lava a la fontaine	
130	Et li oisiaus a longue alaine		130	Et li oissel a haute alaine	
131	Qui desus le pint li chantoit			•	
132	Un chant qui deliteus estoit	120		•	
	•			•	
	•			•	
	•			Chantoit sus le pin doucement	
	•			Un lay d'amours jolivement	156
133	Li lais ert molt bons a entendre		133	Ce lay est moult bon a entendre	
134	Example i porroit on bien prendre		134	Bonne essemple i pouroit on prendre	
135	Dont miex l'en seroit en la fin		135	Dont miex en seroit en la fin	
136	Li oisiaus dist en son latin	124	136	Li oissiaus dist en son latin	160
137	Or entendez tuit a mon lai		137	Entendez tretuit a mon lay	
138	Et chevalier et clerc et lai		138	Et chevalier et clerc et lay	
139	Qui vous entremetez d'amors		139	Qui vous entendez en amours	
140	Et qui en souffrez les dolors	128	140	Et qui en souffrez les doulours	164
141	Et a vous le di je puceles		141	Et a vous le di ge pucelles	
142	Qui estes avenanz et beles		142	Qui estez avenans et belles	
143	Qui le siecle volez avoir	*43b*	143	Qui le siecle voulez avoir	
144	Je vous di vraiement por voir	132	144	Je vous di et creant pour voir	168
	•			Que je vous dire une note	
	•			Qui ne doit pas estre frivole	
145	Vous devez dieu amer avant		145	Vous devez dieu amer avant	
146	Tenir la loi et son commant		146	Tenir la loy et son commant	172
147	Volentiers aler au moustier		147	Voulentiers aler au moustier	
148	Et si escoutez le mestier	136	148	Souvent oir le dieu mestier	
149	Quar du service dieu oir		149	Car du servise dieu oir	
150	Ne vous peut il nus maus venir		150	Ne puet nuli [me]savenir	176
151	Et par verite vous recort		151	Et pour verite vous recort	
152	Diex et amors sont d'un acort	140	152	Dieu et amour sont d'un acort	

	E			C	
153	Dieux donne senz et cortoisie			•	
154	Et fine amour ne le het mie	144		•	
	•		*152b*	Dex aimme sens et honorance	
	•			Amors l'a pas en viltance	152
	•		159	Dex het orgueil et faucete	
	•		160	Et amors aimme loiaute	
155	Dieus escoute bele proiere		155	Dex escoute bele proiere	
156	Fine amour ne met pas ariere		156	Amors ne la met pas arriere	156
	•		157	Dex couvoite sor tous largesce	
	•		158	Il n'i a nule male teche	
159	Dieus het orguel et faucete			•	
160	Et amours les tient en vi[l]te	148		•	
	•			•	
	•			•	
	•		161	Li aver sont li envious	
	•		162	Et li tenant li couvoitous	160
	•		163	Et li felon sont li malvais	
	•		164	Et li vilain sont li pugnais	
	•		165	Sens et cortoisie et honnors	
	•		166	Et loiaute contient amors	164
167	Se vous a ce vous acordez		167	Et se vos a ce vos tenez	
168	Dieu et le siecle avoir poez		168	Deu et le siecle avoir pouez	
	•			•	
	•			•	
	•			•	
	•			•	
	•			•	
	•			•	
	•			•	
	•			•	
169	Ce dit li oisiaus en son chant		169	Ce dist li oisiaus an son chant	
	•			•	

	A			D	
		A			**D**
153	Diex aime honor et cortoisie		153	Dieu aimme sans et courtoisie	
154	Et bone amor ne het il mie		154	Bonne amour ne het il mie	180
	•			•	
	•			•	
	•			•	
	•			•	
155	Diex escoute bele proiere		155	Diex aimme moult belle priere	
156	Amors ne le met mie arriere	144	156	Amours ne la met pas arriere	
157	Diex covoite sor tout larguece		157	Dieus couvoite sus tous largesce	
158	Il n'a nule mauvese teche		158	Il n'i a nulle male teiche	184
159	Diex aime et honor et bonte		159	Diex ainme et honneur et bonte	
160	Et amors aime leaute	148	160	Et amours ainme loiaute	
	•			Loyaute est dieus et amours	
	•			Loial amour sert dieu tozjors	188
162	Li aver sont li covoitex		161	Li aver sont li envieus	
161	Et li tenant li enviex		162	Et li tenant li couvoiteus	
45d 163	Et li vilain sont li mauvais		163	Et li vilain sont li mauves	
164	Et li felon sont li pusnais	152	164	Et li felon sont li punes	192
165	Mes sens cortoisie et honor		165	Sans courtoissie et sans honnour	
166	Et leaute maintient amor		166	Et loiaute maintient amour	
167	Et se vous a ce vous tenez		167	Et ce vous a ce vous tenez	
168	Dieu et le siecle avoir poez	156	168	Dieu et le siecle avoir pouez	196
	•			Si vous en rendra la merite	
	•			De vos pechiez serez tuit quite	
	•			Car se vivez en tel maniere	
	•			Vostre penance ere legiere	200
	•			Or escoutez le chant du lay	
	•			Ce que il dit en son dous lay	
	•			Au vilain que il vit venir	
	•			Qui au vergier s'aloit seir	204
169	Ce dist li oisiaus en son chant		43c 169	Ce dit li oissiaus en son chant	
	•			Ce que avez oi devant	

E			C		
	E			**C**	
170	Quant il vit le vilain seant	152	170	[E]t quant voit le vilain seant	168
	•			•	
	•			•	
	•			•	
	•		171	Qui desous l'arbre l'escoutoit	
	•		172	Qui fel et couvoitous estoit	
173	Si coumanca d'autre rimeniere		173	Dont rechanta d'autre maniere	
174	Cor laisse ton courre riviere		174	Car laisse ton corre riviere	172
175	Donjons perrins tors car dechiez		175	Donjons manoirs tors car dechiez	
176	Matissiez flors herbes sichiez	156	176	Matissiez flors herbes sechiez	
177	Arbre lassiez vostre porter		177	Arbre car laissiez le porter	
178	Ci se soloient deporter		178	Ci se souloient deporter	176
179	Gentiz dames et chevalier		179	Gentis dames et chevalier	
180	Qui tant avoient mon chant chier	160	180	Qui la fontainne avoient chier	
181	Et an mon chant se deportoient		181	Qui an mon chant se delitoient	
182	Et par amours miex en amoient		182	Et par ammors miex en amoient	180
	•			Si en fesoient les largesces	
	•			Les cortoisies le prouesces	
184	Or m'oit cil vilains plains d'envie		183	Maintenoient chevalerie	
	Qu'ainz n'ama joie en sa vie	164	184	Or m'a cil vilains plains d'envie	184
173b 185	Il ameroit miex un denier		185	Qui aimme assez miex le denier	
186	Qu'il ne feroit son donoier		186	Qu'il ne face le donoier	
	•			•	
	•			•	
	•		*152c* 189	Cil me venoient escouter	
	•		190	Por deduire et por miex ammer	188
	•			•	
	•			•	
	•		192	Mais cist i vient por miex mengier	
	•		191	Por miex boire et por gloutoier	
	•			•	
	•			•	

	A			D	
	A			**D**	
170	Et quant vit le vilain seant		170	Et quant vit le vilain venant	
	•			Si commanca plus haut son chant	208
	•			Desouz le pin fu li vilains	
	•			Qui estoit de mauvestie plains	
171	Desouz le pint qui l'escoutoit		171	Par desous le pin se seoit	
172	Qui fel et enuieus estoit	160	172	Fel enuieus cruieus estoit	212
173	Si a chante d'autre maniere		173	Dont chanta en autre maniere	
174	Quar lesse ton corre riviere		174	Car lesse ton courre en riviere	
175	Donjons peris cours quar dechiez		175	Donjons periz court car dechiez	
176	Matissiez flors arbres sechiez	164	176	Fleurs mortissiez herbes sechiez	216
177	Arbre quar lesse ton porter		177	Arbres car lessiez le porter	
178	Ci me soloient escouter		178	Ceus me souloient escouter	
179	Clerc et dames et chevalier		179	Gentilz dames et chevalier	
180	Qui la fontaine avoient chier	168	180	Qui le vergier avoient chier	220
181	Qui plus longuement en vivoient		181	Car plus largement en vivoient	
182	Et miex par amors en amoient		182	Et mieus par amour en en amoient	
	Si en fesoient les largueces			•	
	Les cortoisies les proeces	172		•	
183	Maintenoient chevalerie		183	Et tenoient chevalerie	
184	Or m'ot cil vilains plains d'envie		184	Or m'ot ce vilain plain d'envie	224
185	Qui miex aime assez le denier		185	Qui plus goulousse le mengier	
186	Qu'il ne face le dosnoier	176	186	Que il ne fet le dosnoier	
187	Puis que mon chant li est faillis		187	Puis que mon chant li est faillis	
188	Est il au covoitier sougis		188	Est il a couvioitier sousgis	228
189	Cil me soloient escouter		189	Ceulz le souloient escouter	
190	Por deduire et por miex amer	180	190	Pour deduit et pour miex amer	
	•			Pucelle et hommes plusours	
	•			Qui estoient surpris d'amours	232
191	Et por lor cors miex rehaitier		191	Tout pour leur cors miex aaissier	
192	Et cis i vient por miex mengier		192	Et cilz i vient pour plus mengier	
	•			Et pour plus englouter viende	
	•			Que male passion l'estande	236

E			C		
	•			•	
	•			•	
	•			•	
	•			•	
	•			•	
	•			•	
	•			•	
	•			•	
	•			•	
	•			•	
	•			•	
	•			•	
	•			•	
	•			•	
	•			•	
	•			•	
	•			•	
	•			•	
	•			•	
193	Quant ce ot dit si c'en ala		193	[Q]uant ce ot dit si s'en vola	
194	Et li vilains qui remest la	168	194	Et li vilains qui remest la	192
	Qui ades a mal engin pence			•	
	Ases tost apres se pourpance			•	
195	Que cel oiselet peust prendre		195	Pensa que c'il le pouoit prendre	
196	Auques tost le porroit chier vendre	172	196	Assez tost le porroit chier vendre	
197	Et se vendre ne le pooit		197	Et se vendre ne le pouoit	
198	En jaole le metroit		198	En jaiole l'enfermeroit	196
199	S'i chanteroit et tart et tempre		199	Se l'i chanteroit tart et tempre	
200	Ses angins conquiert et atrampre	176	200	Son affaire engingne et attempre	
201	Tant guaite li vilains et voit		201	Et quiert et agaite et porvoit	
202	Que il les branches aparcoit		202	Tant que les branches apercoit	200
	•		203	Ou cil s'aseoit plus souvent	
	•		204	Puis a fait las si les i tent	

	A			D	
	•			Et de male mort puist mourir	
	•			Dyable font ici venir	
	•			Vilains enuieus et rebours	
	•			Qui en eus n'ont joie d'amours	240
	•			Ne soulas ni envoisseure	
	•			Mais ice vilain plain d'ardure	
	•	43d		Enmeroit miex plaine escuelle	
	•			D'un blanc frommage en foisselle	244
	•			De feves ou de pois au lart	
	•			Qu'il ne feroit avoir sa part	
	•			De lais d'amours ne de chancons	
	•			Ne de gentes dames aus crins blons	248
	•			Ne que veillier ni acoler	
	•			Mes au boire et au mengier	
	•			Entendroit il moult voulentiers	
	•			La seroit preus comme levriers	252
	•			Que male mort le puisse prendre	
	•			Qui la gueule li face estandre	
193	Quant ce ot dit si s'en ala		193	Quant ce ot dit si s'en vola	
194	Et li vilains qui remest la	184	194	Et li vilains qui remaint la	256
	•			•	
	•			•	
195	Pensse se il le pooit prendre		195	Pense que s'il le pouoit prendre	
196	Assez tost le porroit chier vendre		196	Assez tost li pourroit chier vendre	
197	Et se vendre ne le pooit		197	Et se vendre ne li pouoit	
198	En jaiole le meteroit	188	198	En sa geolle le metroit	260
199	Et l'i chanteroit tart et tempre		199	Si l'i chanteroit tart et tempre	
200	Son engin a fet si l'atempre		200	Son engin atorne et tempre	
201	Et enquiert et gaite et porvoit		201	Encerche et giete et porvoit	
202	Tant que les branches apercoit	192	202	Tant que les branches apercoit	264
203	Ou il s'asseoit plus souvent		203	Ou il se seoit plus souvent	
204	Iluec fet las si les i tent		204	Il y fist las si les estant	

E

Ou li oisiaus plus souvent s'asist
Ses las a fait si les i mist   180
205 Molt a bien sa chose atrampee
206 Tant que ce vint a la vespree
207 Que li oisiaus ou jardin revint
208 Si s'ala seoir sor le pin   184
•
•
•
•
•
•
•
•

209 Maintenant si fu pris aus las
210 Li vilains li chaitis las
211 Monta amont l'oisel aert
212 Tel loier a qui vilain sert   188
213 Dit li oisiaus ce m'est avis
214 Mal avez fait qui m'avez pris
•
•
•
•
•
•
•
•
•
•
•
•

C

•
•
205 Mout a bien sa chose atrampee
206 [E]t quant ce vint a la vespree   204
207 Li oisiax ou vergier revint
208 Et quant il s'assit sor le pint
•
•
•
•
•
•
•
•

209 Tout maintenant fu pris au las
210 Li vilains li cheitis li las   208
211 Monte amont l'oisillon aert
212 [T]el loier a qui vilain sert
213 Fait li oisiax ce m'e[s]t avis
214 Mal avez fait qui m'avez pris   212
•
•
•
•
•
•
•
•
•
•
•
•

A

	•	
	•	
205	Molt a bien sa chose atempree	
206	Et quant ce vint a la vespree	196
207	Li oisiaus el jardin revint	
208	Et quant il s'assist sor le pint	
	•	
	•	
	•	
	•	
	•	
	•	
	•	
	•	
209	Si fu maintenant pris au las	
210	Li dolanz li chetiz li las	200
46a 211	Vint avant l'oiseillon aert	
212	Tel loier a qui vilain sert	
213	Fet li oisiaus ce m'est avis	
214	Mal avez fet qui m'avez pris	204
	•	
	•	
	•	
	•	
	•	
	•	
	•	
	•	
	•	
	•	
	•	

D

	•	
	•	
205	Moult a bien sa glus atempree	
206	Et quant ce vint a la vespree	268
	•	
	•	
	Que la seson vint et le temps	
	Et l'eure pour crier ces chans	
	A l'oisselet si est venus	
	Mes il s'asist droit sus la glus	272
	Car nulle chose n'en savoit	
	Du lieu qui aglue estoit	
	Ains cuidoit qu'il fust autel	
	Comme il souloit estre non el	276
209	Li oiselez fu pris au las	
210	Li maus vilains chetiz et las	
	•	
	•	
213	Estoit en aguet u pourpris	
214	Acourant vint et si l'a pris	280
44a	Or sa dist il dans oissillons	
	Or me dires vous de vos sons	
	Malesgre vostre nes devant	
	Si vous vendre prochainement	284
	La vilonie et le despit	
	Qu'autre foiz m'avez fet et dit	
	Et se ne me voulez chanter	
	Je vous cuit si bien atremper	288
	Qu'a moi n'a autre ne dires	
	Mal quant de moy departires	
	Biaus dous amis dit li oissiaus	
	De moy prendre est trop grans maus 292	

E

			C			
	E			C		
215	Si en avrez povre rancon		215	Em moi a povre raencon	
216	Ainz en avrai mainte chancon	192	216	[A]ins averai mainte chancon	
	•			•	
	•			•	
	•			Fait li vilains de ceste prise	
	•			Servit avez a vo devise	216
219	Fait li vilains plains d'anvie		219	Or servirez a ma partie	
220	C'est cheance mal partie		220	[C]este cheance est mal partie	
	•			•	
	•			•	
	Dit li oisiaux ce m'e[s]t avis			•	
221	J'en ai assez le menor pris	196	221	Fait li oisiax ce m'e[s]t avis	
222	Je suel avoir en mon devis		222	Avoir souloie a mon devis	220
	Toute la terre et le porpris			•	
	•			•	
	•			•	
223	Bos champaignes vergiers et prez		223	Champainne bois riviere et prez	
224	Or sere en jaole boute⁻	200	224	Or iere en jaiole enfermez	
	•	152d	225	Jamais n'avrai solas ne joie	
	•		226	Je souloie vivre de proie	224
227	Si me donra on a mangier		227	Or me donra on a mengier	
228	Com a un a un autre prisonnier		228	Si com on fait le prisonnier	
	•			•	
	•			•	
	•		229	Laissiez m'aler biax dous amis	
	•		230	Et bien soiez vos seurs et fis	228
231	Ja prisonniers n'i chanterai		231	Ja prisonniers ne chanterai	
232	Fait cil et je vous mangera[i]	204	232	[P]ar foi et je vos mengerai	
	•			•	
	•			•	
233	Que par autre tor n'en irez		233	Ja par autre tor n'en irez	
173c 234	En moi povre repast avrez		234	Em moi povre repast arez	232

A

215	En moi a povre raencon	
216	Ainz en orrai mainte chancon	
217	Quar molt chanterez plus sovent	
218	Servi m'avez a vo talent	208
	•	
	•	
219	Or servirez a ma partie	
220	Ceste chancons est mal partie	
	•	
	•	
	•	
	•	
	•	
	•	
	J'en ai la pior part emprise	
	Je sueil avoir a ma devise	212
223	Champaigne bois riviere et prez	
224	Or sui en jaiole enserrez	
225	James n'avrai ne bien ne joie	
226	Je soloie vivre de proie	216
227	Or me donra l'en a mengier	
228	Si comme un autre prisonier	
	•	
	•	
229	Lesse moi aler biaus amis	
230	Que bien soies seurs et fis	220
231	Ja en prison ne chanterai	
232	Par foi et je te mengerai	
	•	
	•	
233	Ja par autre tor n'en irez	
234	En moi povre repast avrez	224

D

215	Qu'en moy a povre reancon	
216	Vous demourrez en ma prison	
	•	
	•	
	•	
	•	
219	Dit li vilains toute ma vie	
220	Ceste chancon est mal partie	296
	Dist li oissiaus ce poisse moy	
	Vous me tenez ce poisse moy	
	•	
	•	
	•	
	•	
	G'en ay la pire d'assez prise	
	Je suel avoir a ma devise	300
223	Champaines rivieres et pres	
224	Or sui en geolle enfermes	
225	James n'avre deduit ne joie	
226	Je souloie vivre de proie	304
227	Or me donra on a mengier	
228	Com a un povre prisonnier	
	Li oiselles dist au vilain	
	Un mot qui ne dit pas en vain	308
229	Lesse moy aler biaus amis	
230	Car bien soiez seurs et fis	
231	Ja en prison ne chanteray	
232	Par foy et je te mengeray	312
	Dit le vilain puis que te tien	
	Des or en avant seras mien	
233	Ja par autre tour n'en irez	
234	En moy povre repast avrez	316

	E				C	
	Bien savez quant je cere cuit			•		
	En vo bouche en porroit tex wit	208		•		
235	Je sui molt laches et petiz		235	Car je suis lasches et petis	
236	Petit en croistra vostre pris		236	Ne ja n'en acroistra vo pris	
237	Se vous ociez tele rien		237	Se vos occiez tele rien	
238	Lassiez m'aler si ferez bien	212	238	Laissiez m'aler si ferez bien	236
	•		239	Pechiez ferez se m'ociez	
	•		240	Par foi por niant enparlez	
241	Car je plus les en ceroie		241	Et que plus proiez en seroie	
242	Dit li vilains mains en feroie		242	Sachiez que je mains an feroie	240
243	Par foi dit li oisiaus c'est droiz		243	[C]ertes fait il oisiax c'est drois	
244	Car ausi l'aporte la loiz	216	244	Car ainsi l'aporte la lois	
245	Douce raison vilain aire		245	Douce raisons vilain ayre	
246	Et s'ai piec'a oi dire		246	Maintes fois l'avons oy dire	244
247	Qu'en cortoisie a molt fort chose		247	Mais uns dist nons enseingne et glose	
248	Besoig fait faire mainte chose	220	248	Besoins fait faire mainte chose	
249	Bien voi je ne me puis tenser		249	Ne force ne m'i puet tenser	
250	Se laissier me volez aler		250	Mais se vos me laissiez aler	248
251	De tex trois senz vous ferai sage		251	De trois sens vos feroie sage	
252	Qu'ainz ne sot hom de vo lignage	224	252	Qu'ains ne sot hons de vo lignage	
253	Ne nuns ne le porroit savoir		253	Si vos porroient mout valoir	
254	Se je fiance an puis avoir		254	[S]e seurte em puis avoir	252
255	Dist li vilains je le ferai		255	Fait li vilains tost le ferai	
256	De tel fiance comme j'ai	228	256	Tele fiance com je ai	
257	Dist li oisiaus je vous creant		257	Fait li oisiax vos en creant	
258	Et cil le lait aler atant		258	Et cil le lait aler atant	256
	•			•	
	•			•	
259	Li oisiaus sur l'aubre vole		259	[L]i oisiax sor l'arbre s'en vole	
260	Qui achapez fu par parole	232	260	Qui eschapez fu par parole	
264	A son bec ses plumes ramaine	153a	261	Mas estoit et tous hericiez	
263	Car menez fu contre laine		262	Car laidement iert manoiez	260

	A			D	
	•			•	
	•			•	
235	Fet li oisiaus ce m'est avis		235	Dit li oyssiaus trop sui petis	
236	Ja n'en croistera vostre pris	44b	236	Ja n'en escroistra vostre pris	
237	Se vous ociez tele rien		237	Se vous occiez telle rien	
238	Lessiez me aler si ferez bien	228	238	Lessiez m'aler si feres bien	320
239	Pechie ferez se m'ociez		239	Pechie feres se m'ociez	
240	Certes por noient enparlez		240	Dit li vilains or vous tessiez	
241	Quant je plus proiez en seroie		241	Com je plus priez en seroie	
242	Certes et je mains en feroie	232	242	Sachiez que trop mains en feroie	324
243	Certes fet li oisiaus c'est voirs		243	Dit li oissiaus il est bien droiz	
244	Quar ainsi l'aporte la lois		244	Car ainsi l'aporte la loyz	
245	Douce resons vilain aire		245	Douce raison vilain aire	
246	Mainte foiz l'avez oi dire	236	246	Par maintes foiz l'ai oy dire	328
247	Mes uns diz nous enseigne et glose		247	Mes un dit nous monstre et glose	
248	Besoins fet fere mainte chose		248	Besoing fait faire mainte chose	
249	Ma force ne me puet tensser		249	Ma force ne me puet tenser	
250	Mes se vous me lessiez aler	240	250	Mes se vous me lessiez ester	332
251	De trois sens vous feroie sage		251	De trois sens vous fere ge sage	
252	Qu'ainc ne sot hom de vo lingnage		252	Tel ne set hons de vo linage	
253	Si te porroient molt valoir		253	Si vous pourroient moult valoir	
254	Se seurte en puis avoir	244	254	Se seurte en puis avoir	336
255	Fet li vilains je le ferai		255	Dit le vilain je te lerai	
256	Tele fiance comme j'ai		256	Aler tel fiance com j'ay	
257	Fet il leaument vous creant		257	Dit li vilains je te creant	
258	Et cil le lest aler atant	248	258	T'en donre ge de maintenant	340
	•			Et li vilains le lesse aler	
	•			Et cilz vet sus l'arbre monter	
259	Li oisiaus sor l'arbre s'en vole		259	Li oissiaus sus l'arbre s'en vole	
260	Qui eschapez fu par parole		260	Eschapez fu par sa parolle	344
46b 261	Il fu lais et toz hericiez		261	Touilliez fu et touz hericiez	
262	Quar laidement fu manoiez	252	262	Car laidement fu maniez	

	E	
261	Molt estoit mal et hurecie	
262	Car l'endemain fust mangie	236
	•	
	•	
267	Li vilains semont qu'il li die	
268	Les trois sens que nou lait mie	
269	Vilains fait il or i entens	
270	Apanre i porras un grant sens	240
	•	
	•	
301	Ne croire pas quanque tu ois dire	
302	Li vilains fronce le nez d'ire	
303	Puis dist je le savoie bien	
304	Biaus douz amis or les retien	244
	•	
	•	
	•	
	•	
	•	
	•	
	•	
	•	
	•	
283	Volez vous que je le vous redie	
284	Si que vous ne l'obliez mie	
	•	
	•	
173d 287	Bien sai que j'ai ne le retenrez	
288	Je le sai mieux de vous assez	248
289	Dit li vilains molt grant piec'a	
290	Dehas qui gre vous an sara	
291	D'aprendre ce dont il est sages	
292	Je ne sui mie si sauvages	252

	C	
263	Tenus ot este contre lainne	
264	A son bec sa plume ramainne	
265	Et raciet au miex que il puet	
266	Li vilains cui savoir estuet	264
267	Les trois sens le semont qu'il die	
268	[L]i oisiax fu plains de voidie	
269	Se li dist se tu bien entens	
270	Apenre porras un grant sens	268
	•	
	•	
301	Ne croi pas quanques tu ois dire	
302	Li vilains fronce le nez d'ire	
303	Et dist je le savoie bien	
304	Biax amis dont or le retien	272
	•	
	•	
	Garde que tu ne l'oblier	
	Or me puis je bien apenser	
307	Fait li vilains de sens aprendre	
308	Musage me fais a entendre	276
309	Qui ce me rueves retenir	
310	Je te vaurroie retenir	
	•	
	•	
296c̲	Bien sai quant tu m'eschaperoies	
d̲	Jamais autrui ne gaberoies	280
297a̲	Mais je m'en vois a tart ventant	
298	Cestui sai bien di l'autre avant	
299	[E]ntan i bien fait li oisiax	
300	Li autres est et bons et biax	284
271	Ne pleure pas ce qu'ains n'eus	
272	Li vilains ne fu mie mus	

A

263 Tenuz ot este contre laine
264 A son bec ses plumes ramaine
265 Et les assiet au miex qu'il puet
266 Et le vilain savoir estuet   256
267 Les trois sens se veut que li die
268 Li oisiaus fu plains de voisdie
269 Et li dist se tu bien entens
270 Aprendre i porras molt grant sens   260
     •
     •
271 Ne pleure pas ce qu'ainc n'eus
272 Li vilains ne fu mie mus
273 Ainz li a dit par felonie
274 Tu m'as ta fiance mentie   264
275 Trois sens me devoies aprendre
276 Si com tu me feis entendre
277 Qu'ainc ne sot hom de mon lingnage
278 Mes de ce est toz li mons sage   268
279 Nus n'est si fols n'onques ne fu
280 Qui plorast ce qu'ainz n'ot eu
281 Tu m'as bien largement menti
282 Et li oisiaus li respondi   272
283 Veus tu dont que jel te redie
284 Grant paor ai que ne l'oublie
285 Vous entendez tant au pledier
286 J'ai grant paor de l'oublier   276
287 Je cuit que ja nes retendrez
288 Je les sai miex de vous assez
289 Fet li vilains des grant piec'a
290 Dehez ait qui gre vous savra   280
291 D'aprendre ce dont je sui sages
292 Je ne sui mie si sauvages

D

263 Tenus ot este contre laine.
264 A son bec sa plume ramaine   348
265 Et ralie au mieus qu'il puet
266 Li vilains qui savoir voulet
267 Les trois sens le semont qu'il die
268 Li oissiaus fu plains de voidie   352
269 Si li dit se tu bien entens
270 Aprendre i porras un bon sens
     Or oez que dit li oissiaus
     Qui tant fu avenans et biaus   356   *44c*
271 Ne pleure pas ce qu'ains n'eus
272 Li vilains ne fu mie mus
273 Ainz respondi par felonnie
274 Tu as ta fiance mentie   360
275 Trois sens me devoies aprendre
276 Si comme tu me feis entendre
277 Qu'ains ne sot hons de mon lingnage
278 Mes j'en se le monde tout sage   364
279 Nus n'est si folz n'onques ne fu
280 Qu'il plorast ce qu'ains n'ot eu
281 Tu m'as moult largement menti
282 Et li oissiaus li respondi   368
283 Veulz tu dont que je le te die
284 Si que tu ne l'oublies mie
285 Tu entans itant a pledier
286 Que poour ai de l'oublier   372
287 Je cuit que ja nel retenrez
288 Je le se miex que vous d'assez
289 Dit li vilains de grant piec'a
290 Dehais qui gre vous en savra   376
291 D'aprendre ce dont il est sage
292 Je ne suis mie si sauvage

E		C	
E		**C**	
293 Com vous ici me tenez		273 Ains respondi par felonnie	
294 Pour ce que m'estes eschapez		274 Tu m'as ta fiance mentie	288
295 Et je n'ai mais sor vous pooir		275 Trois sens me devoies aprendre	
296 Dites de moi tot vo voloir	256	276 Si com tu me feis entendre	
a Bien me tenez ore pour nice		277 C'onques ne sot tous mes lignages	
b Pleust dieu je vous retenisse		278 Mais de ce est tous li mons sages	292
c Certes quant vous m'eschaperiez		279 Il n'est si fox n'onques ne fu	
d Jamais autre ne gaberiez	260	280 Qui ce plorast qu'il n'at eu	
297a Mes je m'en vois a tart vantant		153b 281 Tu m'as mout largement menti	
298 Cestui sai je dis l'autre avtant		282 [E]t li oisiax li respondi	296
•		283 Volez vos que je les redie	
•		284 Si ne les oublierez mie	
271 Ne plorer pas ce que n'as eu		285 Vos entendez tant a plaidier	
272 Li vilains ne fu mie mu	264	286 Que paour ai de l'oublier	300
273 Ainz li respont par felenie		287 Je cuit que ja nes retenrez	
274 Tu as ta fiance mentie		288 Je les sai miex de vos assez	
275 Tex trois sens me ~~feis~~ deus aprendre		289 Fait li vilains bonne piece a	
276 Si com tu me feis antandre	268	290 Dashait qui gre vos en savra	304
277 Qu'ainz ne sot hom de mon lignage		291 D'apenre ce dont il est sages	
278 Mais se c'est ore li mains sage		292 Je ne suis mie si sauvages	
•		293 Par mon chief com vos me tenez	
•		294 Mais por ce qu'estes eschapez	308
•		297 M'alez ores ainsis gabant	
•		311 Mais se vos me tenez couvant	
•		312 Vos m'aprenderez l'autre sen	
311 Mes s'or me teniez couvent		Car des deus ai ge bien l'assen	312
312 Or m'apanriez le tiers sens	272	•	
•		•	
•		296 Or le dites a vo voloir	
•		295 Car sor vos n'ai point de pouoir	
•		313 Dites quex est il si l'orrai	
•		314 Enten y bien jel te dirai	316

A

293	Par mon chief que vous me tenez	
294	Por ce se m'estes eschapez	284
295	Et si n'ai mes sor vous pooir	
296	Dites de moi vostre voloir	
	•	
	•	
	•	
	•	
297	Or ne me va mie gabant	
298	Cestui sai bien or di avant	288
299	Enten i bien dist li oisiaus	
300	Li autres est et bons et biaus	
301	Ne croire pas quanques t'os dire	
302	Li vilains fronce le nez d'ire	292
303	Et dist je le savoie bien	
304	Biaus amis donques le retien	
305	Gardez que vous ne l'oubliez	
306	Or sui je molt bien assenez	296
	•	
	•	
307	Fet li vilains por sens aprendre	
308	Musage me fez a entendre	
309	Qui ce me rueves retenir	
310	Je te voudroie ca tenir	300
	•	

46c

311	Mes se tu me tiens couvenens	
312	Tu me diroies le tiers sens	
	•	
	•	
313	Dites quels est il si l'orrai	
314	Enten i bien jel te dirai	304

D

293	Par mon chief com vous me tenez	
294	Pour ce ce m'estez eschapez	380
295	Et que sus vous n'ai mes pouoir	
296	Si dites de moi vo vouloir	
	•	
	•	
	•	
	•	
297	Or ne m'alez mie gabant	
298	Ces deus say ditez l'autre avant	384
299	Dont entans bien dit li oissiaus	
300	Li autres est bons et biaus	
301	Ne creez pas quanqu'oez dire	
302	Le vilains fronche le nes d'ire	388
303	Et dit je le savoie bien	
304	Biaus amis donques les retien	
305	Gardez que vous ne l'oubliez	
306	Or suis je bien voir asegiez	392
	•	
	•	
307	Fet li vilains pour senz aprendre	
308	Musage me faites entendre	*44d*
309	Qui ce me rouvez retenir	
310	Je vous voudroie ore tenir	396
	•	
	•	
	•	
	•	
	L'oissel dit couvent me tenez	
	Et li tiers sens aprenderez	
313	Dites quiex il est si l'orrai	
314	Entens i bien je le dirai	400

	E			**C**	
315	Li tiers est tex qui le feroit		315	[L]i tiers est tex qui le saroit	
316	Que jamais pouvres ne ceroit		316	Jamais povres hons ne seroit	
	Ne savrez demander ceste			•	
	Que maintenant ne li fust prestre	276		•	
317	Et quant li vilains l'oi		318	Mout durement s'en esjoy	
318	Molt durement c'en esjoi		317	Quant la vertu dou sen oy	320
	•			•	
	•			•	
	•		319	Et dist cestui m'estuet savoir	
	•		320	Car durement tens a l'avoir	
321	Qui li veist l'oisiau coitier		321	Qui li veist l'oisel coitier	
322	Il est fet il tens de mangier	280	322	Et dire il est tens de mengier	324
323	Aprenez le moi vistement		323	Car le me dites erranment	
324	Vilains fait il or entant		324	Et quant li oisillons l'entant	
326	Ce que tu tanras a tes mains		325	Je te chastoi cheitis vilains	
325	Ce dit ce te chastoi vilains	284	326	Que se que tu tiens en tes mains	328
327	Ne le giete pas a tes piez		327	Ne gette pas jus a tes piez	
328	Certes dit li vilains n'est riens		328	[L]i vilains fu mout correciez	
	•			•	
	•			•	
329	Quant il vit ce qui fu grief chose		*153c* 329	Quant il oit si faite ramposne	
174a 330	Si dist n'estoit ce autre chose	288	330	Se li dist n'est ce autre chose	332
332	Que vous alez devisant		331	Ce sont adavinal d'anfant	
331	Ice sont sanz d'enfant		332	Et si saches a esciant	
333	Tex est povrez et soffraiteuz		333	Tex est povres et souffraitous	
334	Qui les set ausi bien que vous	292	334	Qui les set aussi bien com vous	336
	•		335	Menti m'avez et engignie	
	•		336	De quanques tu m'as enseingnie	
	•			•	
	•			•	
	•			•	
	•				

A

315 Li tiers est tels qui le savroit
316 James povres hom ne seroit
•
•
•
•
Quant li vilains l'a entendu
Molt liez et molt joianz en fu   308
319 Et dist cestui vueil je savoir
320 Quar volentiers tent a avoir
321 Qui li veist l'oisel coitier
322 Il est fet il tens de mengier   312
323 Aprenez le moi erraument
324 Et quant li oiseillons l'entent
325 Si dist je te chastoi vilains
326 De ce que tu tiens a tes mains   316
327 Ne gete pas jus a tes piez
328 Li vilains fu molt corouciez
•
•
329 Et quant il s'est teus grant pose
330 Si dist n'estoit ce autre chose   320
331 Ce sont ci paroles d'enfant
332 Quar je sai bien a esciant
333 Teus est povres et soufretous
334 Qui ausi bien le set com vous   324
335 Menti m'avez et engingnie
336 De quanques m'avez enseignie
•
•
•
•

D

315 Li tiers est tiex qui le savroit
316 James hons povres ne seroit
•
•
317 Et quant li vilains l'entandi
318 Moult durement s'en esjoi   404
•
•
319 Et dist cestui m'estuet savoir
320 Car voulentiers tens a l'avoir
321 Qui li ouist l'oissel coitier
322 Il est dist il temps de mengier   408
323 Apren le moi tout errannment
324 Et quant li oissillons l'entent
325 Si dit je te chastoi vilains
326 Que ce que tu tiens en tes mains   412
327 Ne jete pas jus a tes piez
328 Li vilains fu moult couprouciez
De courrout ne puet mot soner
En son aler prist a porpenser   416
329 Et quant ce fu tenu grant pose
330 Et n'est ce donques autre chose
331 Ce sont enseignement d'enfant
332 Car je se ce bien a escient   420
333 Tiex est lasches et souffretous
334 Qui aussi bien le set com vous
335 Menti m'avez et engingnie
336 De quanque m'avez enseingnie   424
Menti m'avez dit li vilains
Je voudroie que en mes mains
Ge tenisce ore maintenant
De ce que me vas engingnans   428

	E			C	
	•		337	Estoie je sages devant	
	•		338	[L]i oisiax respont maintenant	340
339	Vilains se tu cestui seusses		339	Par foi se tu ses sens seusses	
340	. . . aus aler tu ne m'eusses		340	Ja laissier aler ne m'eusses	
	•			•	
	•			•	
	•			•	
	•			•	
	•			•	
	•			•	
	•			•	
	•			•	
	•			•	
	•			•	
	•		349	Car se tu m'eusses tue	
	•		350	Si com avoies ampense	344
	•		351	Jamais ne fust jors par mes iex	
	•		352	Que ne t'en fust durement miex	
353	Comment savez dont faire		353	Commant que sez tu donques faire	
354	Chetis vilains de put afaiiare	296	354	Ha vilains cheitis deputaire	348
348	Tu ne ses qu'il ne t'est avenu		348	Tu ne sez qu'il t'est avenu	
347	Il t'est formant mesavenu		347	Il t'est durement mescheu	
355	Dedans mon cors a une pierre		355	Em mon cors a une tel pierre	
356	Qui tant est precieuse et chiere	300	356	Qui tant est precieuse et chiere	352
	•		357	Bien est de trois onces pesans	
	•		358	La vertus est en li si grans	
359	Que li hom qui la porteroit		359	Qui en sa baillie l'aroit	
360	Jamais povrete n'avroit		360	Ja riens demander ne saroit	356
362	Ne ne savroit demander ceste		361	Que maintenant ne l'eust preste	
361	Qui maintenant ne li fust prestre	304	362	Et quant li vilains entant ceste	
	Quan li vilains a ce oi			•	
	Sachiez qu'il n'est pas esjoi			•	

		A				D	
	337	Estoie je sages devant			337	Estoie je sages devant	
	338	Et quant li oiseillons l'entant	328		338	Li oissiaus respont maintenant	
	339	Si dist se tu cest sens seusses			339	Par foi se tu ce sens seusses	
	340	Ja lessie aler ne m'eusses		*45a*	340	Ja lessie aler ne m'eusses	432
	341	Quant tu me tenis en tes mains			341	Quant tu me tenis en tes mains	
	342	Vous dites voir fet li vilains	332		342	Voir avez dit fet li vilains	
	344	Mes je sai bien les autres deus			344	Mes je sai bien les autres deus	
	343	Li oisiaus qui fu engingneus			343	Li oissiaus qui fu engigneus	436
	345	Li dist cis vaut des autres cent			345	Li dist cil vault des autres cent	
	346	Et li vilains li dist comment	336		346	Li vilains li enquiert comment	
	347	Comment jel dirai durfeu				•	
	348	Tu ne sez qu'il t'est avenu				•	
		•				Dit li vilains entent a moi	
		•				Que tu ne ses ne ce ne quoi	440
	349	Quar se tu m'eusses tue			349	Car se tu m'eusses tue	
	350	Si com tu eus enpensse	340		350	Si com tu l'eus empense	
	351	Ne fust james jor par mes iex			351	Il ne fust james par mes iex	
	352	Qu'a ton vivant ne t'en fust miex			352	Qu'il ne t'en fust durement miex	444
	353	Ha por dieu que sez tu donc faire			353	Li vilains dit que ces tu faire	
	354	Ahi fel vilain deputaire	344		354	Li oissiaus dit fel deputaire	
		•				•	
		•				•	
	355	Il a en mon cors une piere			355	Il a en mon cors une pierre	
	356	Qui tant est precieuse et chiere			356	Qui tant est precieuse et chiere	448
	357	Bien est de trois onces pesant			357	Bien est de trois onces pesant	
	358	La vertu de li est si grant	348		358	La vertu en par est si grant	
	359	Qui en son demaine l'avroit			359	Qui en son demaine l'aroit	
	360	James rien ne demanderoit			360	James riens ne demanderoit	452
46d	361	Que ele lues ne li fust preste			361	Que maintenant ne li fust preste	
	362	Quant li vilains entendi ceste	352		362	Quant li vilains entendi ceste	
		•				•	
		•				•	

	E			C	
	Ainz est a pou enragiez d'ire			•	
	Ses drapiaus deront et decire	308		•	
	•		363	Debat som pis deront ses dras	
	•		364	Si se claimme cheitis et las	360
365	Son vis et ces chevox depiece		365	Son vis a ses ongles depiece	
366	L'oisel en maine grant liesce		366	[L]i oisiax en fait grant leesce	
	•			•	
	•			•	
367	Qui desur l'aubre se seoit		367	Qui de sor l'arbre l'esgardoit	
368	Tant a atandu que il voit	312	368	Tant a attendu que il voit	364
	•			•	
	•			•	
	•		369	Qu'il a tous ses dras depeciez	
	•		370	Et qu'il c'est an mains lieus bleciez	
	Que touz ces dras a depecie			•	
	Et an maint leu se fu plaie			•	
	•			•	
	•			•	
371	Puis li a dit mauvais vilains		153d 371	Puis li a dist cheitis vilains	
372	Quant tu me tenis en tes mains	316	372	Quant tu me tenis en tes mains	368
373	J'estoie moine que moisson		373	J'estoie menres d'un moisson	
374	Qu'aloue ne que pincons		374	Ne que masange ne pincon	
375	Qui ne poise pas demi once		375	Qui ne poise pas demi once	
376	Cil qui de felonnie fronce	320	376	Cil qui de felonnie gronce	372
377	Par dieu vous dites voir		377	Li dist par foi vos dites voir	
378	Vilains ne pues tu tos savoir		378	Vilains or puez tu bien savoir	
	•		379	Que de la pierre t'ai menti	
	•		380	Or le sai ge fait cil de fi	376
381	Que de la pierre menti t'ai	324	381	Mais par foi devant le cuidai	
382	Voire mais devant le cuidai		382	Vilains maintenent prouverai	
	Dist li fox vilains esprovez			•	
	Vilains or t'ai mes sens provez			•	

A

- •
- •

363	Si bat sa coupe et ront ses dras	
364	Et se claime chetiz et las	
365	Son vis a ses ongles depece	
366	Li oisiaus en ot grant leece	356

- •
- •

367	Qui sus le pint le regardoit	
368	Et a tant atendu qu'il voit	

- •
- •
- •

Qu'il a tout le vis depecie
Et qu'il est en maint leu blecie

- •
- •

371	Puis li a dit chetiz vilains	
372	Quant tu me tenis en tes mains	
373	Je fui plus legiers d'un moisson	
374	Que masenge ne que pincon	364 45b
375	Qui ne poise pas demie once	
376	Cil qui de felonie fronce	
377	Li dist par foi vous dites voir	
378	Vilains dont pues tu bien savoir	368
379	Que de la pierre t'ai menti	
380	Or le sai je molt bien de fi	
381	Mes certes orains le cuidai	
382	Vilains orendroit prove t'ai	372

- •
- •

D

- •
- •

363	Ses cheveus tire et ront ces dras	
364	Si se clainme chetis et las	456

- •
- •

Depiece a ces ongles sa joe
Li oissiaus en volete et joe

367	Qui desus l'arbre se juchoit	
368	Il a tant atendu qu'il voit	460

Que li vilains c'est debatus
Si vilainnement comtenus

369	Qu'il a tous ces dras depeciez	
370	Et qu'il s'est en mains lieus bleciez	464

- •
- •

Or ouez que li oissiaus
Quant ot atendu un petit

371	Si li a dit chetis vilains	
372	Quant tu me tenis en tes mains	468
373	G'iere plus legiers d'un moissons	
374	D'une mesange ou d'un pinson	
375	Qui ne poisse pas demi once	
376	Cilz qui de felonnie gronce	472
377	Certez vous dites voir	
378	Vilains or pues tu bien savoir	
379	Que de la pierre t'ai menti	
380	Ce sai je bien dit il de fi	476
381	Mes devant certes le cuidai	
382	Vilains orendroit proverait	

- •
- •

	E			C	
	On ne doit pas tot le mont croire			•	
	Tu deis orains c'est la voire	328		•	
	•		383	Des trois sens que pas ne savoies	
	•		384	Et de ce que tu me disoies	380
	•		385	Que hons si fox onques ne fu	
	•		386	Qui ce plorast qui n'ait eu	
174b	C'onques nuns hom ne plora			•	
	Ce c'onques n'ot ne ja n'avra			•	
387	Mais orandroit tu plore as		387	Se m'est avis que or ploras	
388	Ce que onques n'ot ne ja n'avras	332	388	Se qu'ains n'eus ne ja n'avras	384
	Mauvaisement as esploitie			•	
	Folie avoiez couvoitie			•	
	Car par t'angoisse perderas			Et quant me tenis en tes las	
	Ce que ja ne recouveras	336		Ce qu'an mains eus as piez ruas	
	•		389	Des trois sens iestes abosmez	
	•		390	Biax ammis or les retenez	388
	•		391	Il fait bon aprenre bon mot	
	•		392	On dist que tex n'entent qui ot	
	•		393	Que tex parole de grans sens	
	•		394	Qui n'e[s]t pas de sage porpens	392
	•		395	Tex parole de cortoisie	
	•		396	Qu'il ne la saroit faire mie	
	•		397	Et tex cuide estre bien senez	
	•		398	Qui est a sotie atornez	396
399	Quant ce ot dit si com ala		399	[Q]uant ce ot dit si s'en vola	
	•			•	
	•		401	Et a tel heure s'en ala	
	•			•	
	•		403	Qu'ains puis ou vergier ne revint	
	•			•	

A

·

·

383 Que des trois sens pas ne savoies

384 Et de ce que tu me disoies

385 Nus n'est si fols n'onques ne fu

386 Qui plorast ce qu'ainc n'ot eu 376

·

·

387 Maintenant ce m'est vis ploras

388 Ce qu'ainc n'eus ne ja n'avras

·

·

·

·

389 Des trois sens estes abosmez

390 Biaus amis si les aprenez 380

·

·

·

·

·

·

·

399 Quant ce ot dit si s'en vola

·

401 Et a tele eure s'en ala

·

403 Qu'ainc puis el vergier ne revint

·

D

·

·

383 Des trois cens que pas ne savoies

384 Et de ce que tu me dissoies 480

385 Nus n'est si folz n'onques ne fu

386 Qu'il pleurast ce qu'ains n'ot eu

·

·

387 Maintenant ce m'est [v]is ploras

388 Ce qu'ains n'eus n'a[vra]z 484

·

·

·

·

389 Des trois sens estez [ab]osmes

390 Biaus amis or les m'aprenez

391 Il fet bon aprendre bon mot

392 L'en dit que cil n'entant qu'il n'ot 488

393 Et celle parolle a grant sens

394 Qui en a pou de pourpens

395 Tel parole de courtoissie

396 Qui ne le saroit faire mie 492

397 Et tel cuide a estre bien senez

398 Qui a folie est assenez

399 Quant ce ot dit si s'en vola

·

401 Et en telle heure s'en ala 496

·

403 Qu'ainz puis arriere ne revint

Ne nen ne set que il devint

		E					C	
	•				404	Les foilles chairent dou pint	400
	•				•	
	•				402	Li vergiers failli et secha	
405	Et la fontaine recicha			405	Et la fontainne restancha	
	•				•	
404	Les fuelles cheirent du pint			•	
407	Li vilains perdi son deduit	340	154a	407	Li vilains perdi son deduit	
	•			408	Et bien sachiez toutes et tuit	404
409	Li profetes dit en apert			409	Que li prodons dist en apert	
410	Cil qui tot couvoite tot pert			410	Cilz qui tout couvoite tout pert	
	•			Ci faut li lais de l'oiselet	
	•			Dou vilain ne donroie un pet	408
	•			Il perdi par son couvoitier	
	•			Et son deduit et son vergier	

Explicit le lai de l'oiselet   Explicit li lais de l'oiselet

A

404	Les fueilles cheirent du pint	384
	•	
402	Li vergiers chei et secha	
405	Et la fontaine restancha	
	•	
	•	
407	Li vilains perdi son deduit	
408	Bien le sachiez toutes et tuit	388
409	Li proverbes dist en apert	
410	Cil qui tout covoite tout pert	
	•	
	•	
	•	
	•	

Explicit le lai de l'oiselet

D

404	Les fueilles secherent du pin	
	Ne fu plus vert soir ne matin	500
402	Li vergiers failli et secha	
405	Et la fontaine restancha	
	•	
	•	
407	Le vilain perdi son deduit	
408	Et bien sachent toutes et tuit	504
409	Le proverbe dit en apert	
410	Cilz qui tout covoite tout pert	
	•	
	•	
	•	
	•	

Explicit le dit de l'oyselet

TEXTUAL NOTES

ABBREVIATIONS: (For items not in this list, see Bibliography.) Bédier, ed. *Chanson* = Bédier, Joseph, ed. *La chanson de Roland*. Publiée d'après le manuscrit d'Oxford et traduite. Paris: Piazza, 1937. (Repr. Union Générale d'éditions, 1982); Bloch-von Wartburg = Bloch, Oscar and Walther von Wartburg. *Dictionnaire étymologique de la langue française*. 5th ed. Paris: PUF, 1968; *Brut* = Arnold, Ivor. *Le Roman de Brut de Wace*. 2 vols. Paris: SATF, 1938–40; *Chronique métrique attribuée à Geffroy de Paris* = Diverrès, Armel. *La Chronique métrique attribuée à Geffroy de Paris*. Paris: Société d'Edition, Les Belles Lettres, 1956. (Publications de la Faculté des Lettres de l'Université de Strasbourg, 129); *Dictionnaire général* = Hatzfeld, Adolph, Arsène Darmsteter, and Antoine Thomas; *Dictionnaire général de la langue française*. 2 vols. Paris: Delagrave, 1895–1900; *Donnei* = Paris, Gaston, ed. "Le Donnei des Amants." *Romania*, 25 (1896): 497–541; F.E.W. = von Wartburg, W. *Französisiches Etymologisches Wörterbuch*. 25 vols. and suppl., 1928– ; Foerster, ed. = Foerster, Wendelin, ed. *Christian von Troyes. Sämtliche erhaltene Werke*. 1. *Cligés*, 1884. 2. *Yvain*, 1913. 3. *Erec und Enide*, 1909. Halle: Niemeyer; Foerster-Breuer = Foerster, Wendelin and Hermann Breuer. *Wörterbuch zu Kristian von Troyes' Sämtlichen Werken*. Halle (Saale): Niemeyer, 1933; God. = Godefroy, Frédéric. *Dictionnaire de l'ancienne langue française et de tous ses dialectes du IXe au XVe siècle*. 10 vols. Paris, 1880–1902. (Repr. Kraus, 1969); Greimas = Greimas, A. J. *Dictionnaire de l'ancien français*. Paris: Larousse, 1968; Henry, ed. = Henry, Albert W., ed. *Les Oeuvres d'Adenet le Roi*. tome 5, vols. 1–2, *Cleomadés*. Brussels: Editions de l'Université de Bruxelles, 1971; Hilka, ed. *Cligés* = *Kristian von Troyes. Cligés*, ed. Wendelin Foerster. 4th ed., Alfons Hilka. Halle: Niemeyer, 1921; Holden, ed. = Holden, A. J., ed. *Le Roman de Rou de Wace*. 3 vols. Paris: Picard, 1970-73. (SATF 1970); Matzke and Delbouille, eds. = Matzke, John E. and Maurice Delbouille, eds. *Le Roman du Castelain de Couci et de la Dame de Fayel par Jakemes*. Paris: SATF, 1936; Micha, ed. = Micha, Alexandre. *Les Romans de Chrétien de Troyes. II. Cligés*. Paris: Champion, 1957, 1965. (CFMA 84); *New Grove Dictionary* = *New Grove Dictionary of Music and Musicians*. 20 vols. London: Macmillan, 1980; NRCF = Noomen, Willem and Nico van den Boogaard, eds. *Nouveau recueil complet des Fabliaux*. vol. 1, 1983; vol. 2, 1984; vol. 3, 1986. Assen/Maastricht, The Netherlands: Van Gorcum; Ritchie = Ritchie, R. L. Graeme. *Recherches sur la Syntaxe de la conjonction "que" dans l'ancien français depuis les origines de la langue jusqu'au commencement du XIIIe siècle*. Paris: Champion, 1907; Roach, E., ed. = Roach, Eleanor, ed. *Le Roman de Mélusine ou Histoire de Lusignan par Coudrette*. Paris: Klincksieck, 1982; Roach, William, ed. *Perceval* = Roach, William, ed. *Le Roman de Perceval ou Le Conte du Graal*. 2nd ed. Geneva: Droz; Paris: Minard, 1959. (TLF, 71); *Roman de la Rose* = Lecoy, Félix, ed. *Guillaume de Lorris et Jean de Meun. Le Roman de la Rose*. 3 vols. Paris: Champion, 1965–1970. (CFMA 92, 95, 98); Ruelle, ed. = Ruelle, Pierre, ed. *Huon de Bordeaux*. Brussels and Paris: PUB and PUF, 1960; Sommer, ed. = Sommer, Heinrich Oskar. *The Vulgate Version of the Arthurian Romances Edited from Manuscripts in the British Museum*. 7 vols. and Index. Washington, D.C., 1908-16. (Repr. 1969); Stimming, ed. = Stimming, Albert, ed. *Der*

Festländische Bueve de Hantone. Fassung 3, vols. 1-2. Halle: Niemeyer, 1914-20. (Gesellschaft für romanische Literatur 34, 42); Tobler, *Vermischte Beiträge* = Tobler, Adolf. *Vermischte Beiträge*. vol. 5. Leipzig: Hirzel, 1912; T.-L. = Tobler, Adolf and Erhard Lommatzsch. *Altfranzösisches Wörterbuch*. Wiesbaden, 1925- . (to vol. 10, 1976, "tympanistes"); *Trois Savoirs* = Meyer, Paul. "Notice du ms. 25970 de la Bibliothèque Phillipps (Cheltenham)." *Romania*, 37 (1908): 209-35; *Vie de Saint Martin* = Söderhjelm, Werner, ed. *Das altfranzösische Martinsleben des Péan Gatineau aus Tours*. Helsingfors: Wentzel, 1899; Wagner = Wagner, Robert-Léon. *Les Phrases hypothétiques commençant par "si" dans la langue française, des origines à la fin du XVIe siècle*. Paris: Droz, 1939; Walberg, E., ed. = Walberg, E., ed. *La Vie de Saint Thomas le Martyr par Guernes de Pont-Sainte-Maxence*. Lund: Gleerup, 1922 (also in CFMA, 1936, 77).

3 *riches vilains* For this character in the fabliaux, see, for example, *Le vilain mire, NRCF*, vol. 2, no. 13, line 1; *Aloul, NRCF*, vol. 3, no. 14, line 5; *Berangier au lonc cul*, 3: 252-53 (eds. Montaiglon-Raynaud).

10 *En tot le monde n'ot itel* This line is unique in *B*. All other manuscripts have a different line 10 and a couplet 10*ab*, which is 8*ab* in *E*. Ms *D* has a couplet 10*ab* as well as a couplet after line 8. It seems likely that the couplet 10*ab* was in *B*'s copy and that *B* summarized the meaning into one line (10). In *E* the placement of the couplet makes the expression *son per* refer to the *riche home* of line 7, whereas in *ACD* the *son per* of 10*b* refers to the *manoir* of line 9. *D* also has a couplet after line 8, different from the one in *E*, but the placement of this couplet seems to suggest a relationship of *E* and *D*. (See notes to lines 377 and 215-22 for other evidence of a relationship between the texts of *E* and *D*.)

19 *d'eve et d'air enclos* In *B* and *C* this allusion to air recalls the garden in Chrétien de Troyes, *Erec* (ed. Roques, 5689-5714). All the manuscripts have water; *A* and *D* also have trees; and *E* has only water and a faulty line (+1). The wall of air in the garden recalls the legends about Virgil. See Comparetti, *Virgilio nel medio evo* (trans. Benecke), 262, 293, 347; Spargo, *Virgil the Necromancer*, 12, 22, 60-68; Loomis, *Arthurian Tradition*, 178. Merlin, in the *Vulgate Lancelot*, was enclosed by a wall of air by Niniane (Sommer, *Vulgate Version*, 2: 461).

25-26 Proverb: Le Roux de Lincy, 2: 498; Morawski no. 1590 (cf. nos. 1212, 2388); Ulrich nos. 292, 332 (Proverbs from B.N.*f.fr.* 25545).

27-38 Cf. *Alexandre* (ed. Armstrong), 7: 3310-18; *Rose* (ed. Lecoy), 1321-30.

33 *tel < grant* On the omission of the first word of a comparison, see Roach, *Continuations*, 5: n. to 42198-99. See also my note to 292. The original *grant* of line 33 may have been a dittography of *granz* in line 32.

34 *Que une ame gisent em biere* The original *Qui* of the manuscript may have been a dittography in anticipation of 35 *Qui* and so was emended to *Que*. On the word *ame* as a syllepsis for "nul homme," see Roach, *Continuations*, 5: n. to 37157; Foulet, *Syntaxe*, 276-78; Nyrop, 1: 338; Pope, 230. The word *gisent* in this line is a present participle of *gesir*.

35-36 Ms *E* has an interesting set of forms here: *enfox : tox*. *E* could be emended on the basis of *enfers* and *fers*, which are masc. nom. sing. forms of *enferme* and *ferme* used in *ABCD*. See T.-L., 3: cols. 327-28; and 3: col. 1739, lines 21-33.

39-50 This passage is absent in *A* and present in all the other manuscripts. *A* could have excised these lines as excess verbiage since the garden is amply described in 27-38 and 51-70. *A* might not have liked the reference to *nigromance* (line 49) in this section, and a clue to this attitude might be in line 19 where *A* does not have air and water enclosing the garden but trees and water and thus a less overt reference to magic and the supernatural. See above, Introduction, D. Thematic Sources: The *locus amoenus*, for a discussion of texts that have magical gardens. Cf. Roach, *Continuations*, 5: n. to 41069–1184, where a description of the practices of the scribe of *S*, who eliminates passages of description, may be like those of the scribe of *A* of the *Lai de l'Oiselet*.

40 *praiaus* God., 6: 362*b* (s.v. *prael*) and T.-L., 7: col. 1688, 28–30, cite lines 40–41 from the *Oiselet* (from Méon, 1808).

40 *honis* This word is listed in T.-L., 6: col. 1123, 18-col. 1126, 40 (s.v. *oni*). They cite this line from the *Lai de l'Oiselet* in col. 1125, lines 1–3, from the Méon ed. of Barbazan (1808, vol. 3: 116, l. 42, "onnis"). T.-L. give the definition "eben, flach, glatt," which fits perfectly for this passage. The *glossaire* of Méon-Barbazan (vol. 3, s.v. *onnis*) gives "uni, semblable." See also God., 5: 604*b*. The spellings *onnis* or *ounis* are well attested.

42 *parigal* God., 5: 771*b*, cites lines 44–46 of the *Oiselet* (from Méon, 1808) (s.v. *parivel*). Cf. T.-L., 7: cols. 268–69.

43 *grant* Used as a noun here. Cf. T.-L., 4: cols. 558–59.

52 The round garden here recalls the garden at the end of the *Rose* (ed. Lecoy), 20264–67. For a discussion, see Introduction, IV.D. For an interpretation of this symbolism, see D. W. Robertson, "The Doctrine of Charity."

60 *duites* T.-L., 2: col. 2096, cite *Cligés* (ed. Hilka) 6405 for this word, and the past participle (of *duire*) is applied to tree branches. (Cf. also *Cligés* 6417.) They also cite this line of the *Oiselet* (from Méon 1808). In Micha's edition of *Cligés* the line is 6317 (cf. also 6329), and the translation "disposer" is suggested in the glossary; in English, "arranged, trained."

61-62 This couplet, present in *BCD*, is absent in *AE*. It could have been omitted as excess verbiage since the description of the foliage of the tree contains a reference to the season in line 63. The wording is a bit confusing, as is shown by the mixture of the adjectives "long" and "beautiful" with days in May or summer. *B* solves the problem with *Entor*.

62 *Entor* T.-L., 3: col. 610, 29–33, cite examples of *entor* before expressions of time: "entur midi," "entor mïenuit," "entour le veille de Noël," "entor äust" (August). Cf. God., 3: 269 *ab*.

72 *oisiaus* See Foulet, *Glossaire* (s.v. *oisel*) on forms of this word and their usages. (See the Glossary, s.v. *oiseaus*, for all forms of the word in the *Oiselet*.)

73 *Deus* < *Trois* The context calls for the emendation here. The bird came in the morning and evening (*la matinee, a la vespree*). There is a possibility that this is a slip associated with lines like 480–81 of the *Roman de la Rose* (ed. Lecoy) where the garden is described: "Qu'il y avoit oisiaus. iii. tanz / qu'entot le reaume de France."

73-74 *noiant : escïant* < *noient : escïent* The use of *escïent* in 74 would have left the line −1. *ACE* all have correct lines as emended in *B*. Only *D* has the same error *escïent* in 74 and a line that is −1.

80-92 The size of the bird in this passage and the description of its song are very interesting. Lines 80–81 and 373–75 describe the size of the bird in terms of comparison, which is precisely the professional ornithological technique. It is described as smaller than a finch (*pinçon*, 6 inches; *ACE moisson*, sparrow, 5¾ inches) and a little larger than a wren (*roëtal*, 3¾ inches; *D linotel*, linnet or Old World finch, 5¼ inches). This form in *D* is not attested in T.-L. or God. Both give *linote*, fem. T.-L. also give *lineruel*, masc. and *linete*, fem. [5: col. 485, 44-col. 486, 6]). The comparison in *D* is also less satisfying since the range of sizes is only between 6 inches (*pinçon*) and 5¼ inches (*linotel*), whereas in *ABCE* the range is between 6 or 5¾ inches and 3¾ inches (*pinçon* or *moisson* and *roëtel*). In lines 373–75 the bird is described as lighter than a sparrow (*moisson*), a tit (*mesenge*, 5½ inches) or a finch (*pinçon*), weighing less than a half-ounce. Ms *E* uses *aloue* here (374, lark, 5½ to 7½ inches) which may be too big for the comparison (and the line is also −1). The description of the bird's size leads to the revelation that he could not possibly have a three-ounce precious stone inside him as he had said in line 357, because he is too small and did not weigh even a half-ounce.

It is to be remarked first that these comparisons work. The knowledgeable listener/ reader would appreciate the description and the precision of the comparison, except, perhaps, for *aloue* in line *E* 374 and the *linotel* of *D* 81.

The song of the bird is compared favorably to a list of famous songbirds, 83–85: *aloue* (sky or meadow lark), *maviz* (thrush), *melle* (blackbird), *rossignol* (nightingale), *estornal* (starling), *kalandre* (calandra lark).

He is prepared to sing *lais, sons, rotrüenges, chançons,* and his music puts *gigue* (*E guine,* not attested), *harpe* and *viële* (89–92) to shame (*N'i vausist pas une cenele*)!

In the *Roman de la Rose* the music of the garden is of two kinds: birdsong (699–711) and the singing of *Leesce* (727–28) and of other musicians and dancers (741–56) in the garden of *Deduit* (715–28). In the *Lai de Oiselet,* the bird does all the singing and combines all the songs both of human singers and players and of the other songbirds. Cf. the *Donnei,* where the bird says: "Tuz chanz d'oiseals sout contrefere Od sun chanter, en sa manere" (941–42). Cf. *Brut* (ed. Arnold), lines 1042–60, for a similar list of songs and instruments.

The forms of the word for nightingale in this passage (*B rossignol,* 85, *A roxingnol,* 83, *C lorsignot,* 85, *D rosignol,* 83, *E loigceing,* 85; cf. *losseignol,* T.-L., 8: col. 1492) reflect its etymology from *luscina* through a diminutive blended with *roscinia.* Cf. Nyrop, 1: 15, 207, 346, 434; Greimas; T.-L., 8: cols. 1492–96, who cite the *Oiselet* (1493, 36–41, from Méon, 1808); God., 10: 593*ab*; Pope, 30. For the motif, see Hensel, Ross, and Chandler.

81 *roëtel* God., 7: 225*c*–226*a* (s.v. *roietel*) cites the *Oiselet,* lines 80–81 (from *ms* 1593), and T.-L., 8: col. 1409, 16–20, cite lines 80–82 from the *Oiselet* (from Méon, 1808).

89 *lais* The bird singing lays and other forms of songs is a commonplace. Cf. *Rose* (ed. Lecoy), 701–708; *Donnei,* 157. The word appears three times in *B*: 89, 133, 137. *C* uses *lai* twice more in 132 and 408*a*. God., 4: 695*a* cites lines 130–35 from the *Oiselet* (from Méon, 1808, 3: 119). That a *lai* is a bird's song is discussed in many places. See esp. Baum, "Eine neue Etymologie von frz. *lai,*" and "Les Troubadours et les lais"; and *New Grove Dictionary,* 10: 364–76.

90 *rotrüenges* God., 7: 245*a* (s.v. *rotruenge*), and T.-L., 8: col. 1514, 36–38 (s.v. *rotrouenge*), cite lines 89–90 from the *Oiselet* (from *ms* 1593) for this word. On this type of song, see *New Grove Dictionary,* 16: 259–60. Gennrich, *Altfranzösische Rotrouenge,* 11, cites the *Lai de l'Oiselet* and gives the music, 47–48, to the romance from Bartsch, cited on p. 18 of the Introduction.

92 Proverb: Hassell *C* 21. God., 9: 16*b*, gives three examples of this proverbial use. Cf. *Chronique métrique attribuée à Geffroy de Paris,* 1929–30: Serreüre d'huis ne torele N'i valust pas une cenele.

93 *Du* It is tempting to emend *Du* to *El* here since all the other mss have a form of *en.*

94 *oïtes* The usual form of the pret. 5 of *ouïr* (*oïr*) is *oïstes.*

96 *nus* See note about this form in Foulet's Glossary to the First Continuation, vol. 3: pt. 2, p. 200 (s.v. *nun*); T.-L., 6: cols. 915–16; and F.E.W. 7: 233a (s.v. *nūllus*).

100 *amor* A form of this word also appears in manuscript *B* in lines 139, 153, 166, 168, 182. Line 139 has *d'amors* and 182 *par amors*. On the use of inflectional -s with these forms, see Frappier, "'D'amors,' 'Par amors,'" *Romania* 88 (1967): 433–74. See also note to 151–68 for a discussion of the use of *amor* in the *Oiselet*.

104 *borjois < cortois AB cortois, CDE borjois*. This line recalls a text like *Li Fablel dou Dieu d'Amors* (ed. Jubinal), verses 81–84: "Sous ciel n'a home, s'il les oïst canter, Tant fust vilains ne l'esteut amer; Iluec m'asis por mon cors deporter, Desus une ente ki mult fait à loer." The reading *CDE borjois* or *AB cortois* in this line seems to depend on the interpretation of the conjunction *mes que*. In *AB* the meaning is "even if," and in *CDE*, the meaning is "unless," or "except that." The interpretation of *AB* seems to be more generous, the birdsong could move the hearer to thoughts of love and to believing himself an emperor or king *even if* he were a *vilains* or a *cortois*. The interpretation in *CDE* is that the hearer would be so moved *unless* he were a *vilains* or *borjois*; i.e., these two types are excluded from being moved by love. I think the context of the *Lai de l'Oiselet* and the attitude toward the villein support the latter interpretation. The villein is not moved by love, nor could the bourgeois be, and so the exclusionary interpretation of *mes que* is applied and the emendation is made. On *mes que*, see R. L. Graeme Ritchie, *Recherches sur la syntaxe de la conjonction "que,"* 105–108.

108 *Qui = cui*, dative of the relative pronoun *qui*. Cf. Foulet, *Syntaxe*, 181 and 342–43.

111 *C* has an interesting form *ammerres*, a survival of *amátor*. T.-L., 1: col. 342, list it under the oblique form *ameor* (< *amatorem*), and so do Foerster-Breuer in the *Worterbuch zu Kristian*, 2nd ed., 12, col. 2: there is one instance in Chrétien, *Yvain* 2723 (ed. Roques, 2725). In *C* 117 the form *ammeur* (nom. pl.) has two syllables, but should normally have three. See *Aucassin et Nicolette* 40, line 35 (ed. Suchier); *Blancandin et l'Orgueilleuse* (ed. Sweetser), 4600, 5370, 5602 — all in the obl. case. The *Roman de la Rose* (ed. Lecoy) 7442 has *ameor* nom. pl.; *Chastelain de Couci* (ed. Matzke-Delbouille), 397, *ameour* (three syllables, nom. pl.); *Lai d'Aristote* (ed. Delbouille), 550, *amere* (nom. sg.). This latter agrees with ms *C* 111. The nom. and acc. cases of the Latin word give very different results in Old French: nom. *amátor* > amere (or *amérre*); acc. *amatórem* > ameor > ameëur.

116 *ses < les AE* have *ses* and *BCD les*. This is an instance where *BCD* do not pay attention to context, cf. *la jaiole* of 198.

117 *li humors* All the other manuscripts have a form of *amor* here. This passage caused many difficulties for the scribes. *D*, for example, uses a plural subject *les amours* with singular verb *issoit* in 117 and *tenoit* in 118, masc. *tous* with fem. *cimes* in 120 and *oisillon* nom. without inflectional -s. For a full discussion of why *li humors* is retained, see note to lines 151–68.

122 God., 3: 598c gives lines 118–22 of the *Lai de l'Oiselet* for the form *atanchast* in line 122 (from ms *E*, line 116; Godefroy uses old numbering 169d; newer numbering is 172d) (also s.v. *estanchier*). God. corrects 118 by omitting an *i* before *tenoit* that made the line +1. In line 119 he has *oisiaul*; the ms has *oisiaus*. Line 121 in *E* has *cichast* for *sechast B*, a form not in T.-L. or the F.E.W. In 176 *E* uses *sichiez*. The form *atanchast* shows an instance of the interchange of prefixes *es-* and *a-*. See also line 260 where *E* has *achapez* and *B eschapez*. See also note to 405.

123 The emendations here bring 124 into line with the conclusion of the poem: the bird maintains both the garden and the fountain. The scribe of *B* seems to have detached this line from the context, reading only the *fontainne* of 122 as the subject of the verb *est* in 123.

124 The scribe of *B* wrote *Li oiseaus qui el vergier fu* which I have emended to *Li vilains cui li estres fu*. This time the scribe of *B* seems to have lost the context completely and simply wrote 124 to follow 123 which was about the bird. He seems to take no notice of the change of subject here. Only *C*, in fact, makes a break in the text at line 123, leaving a space for a large capital. *ACE* have an appropriate line, but *D* has *arstre (arbre)* instead of *estres*.

126 *soautume* The usual spelling of this word is *souatume* or *soatume*. Cf. T.-L., 9: cols. 689–90, who cite this line of the *Oiselet* (from Méon, 1808). (*AC* have *souatume*, *D souastune*, *E souuenture*.)

127 A fountain under a pine tree is in *Rose* (ed. Lecoy), 1425, and *Donnei*, 460.

127–28 *pin : vint* It is not necessary to emend *B* for the eye rhyme since the final consonant is *s, r,* or *t*. Cf. Tobler, *Vers fr.*, 150–54; Nyrop, 2: 35; Pope §§ 400–402 (*-r*), 617–21 (*-s,-t*); Gildea, 2: notes to lines 43, 439–40, 594, 4672 (restoration of *-t*), 7378 (rhyme as opposed to inflection). The rhyme *pin : vint* also occurs in lines 207 : 208 and 403 : 404. The other manuscripts react in varying ways: *E* follows *B* at 127 : 128 and 207 : 208 but assonances *pint : deduit* at 404 : 407 (see note to 399–410). *C* has *pin : vint* 127–28, but has *revint : pint* for 207 : 208 and 403 : 404. *A* uses *pint* in all three cases. *D* avoids the rhyme altogether by having *pin* rhyme with *matin* (58a–b, 127–28, 404–404a; *D* omits 207–8). *D* also creates a couplet 403–403a where *revint : vint*.

127–29 Letters in square brackets are not visible in the manuscript.

133–34 *inv.* Line 133 in the manuscript is at the bottom of 77d so that the couplet is split between 77d and 78a, and 134 was copied before 133 by anticipation. For a similar use of *essample*, see *Rose* (ed. Lecoy), 1552.

137–68 These 32 lines constitute the "lai de l'oiselet" within the *Lai de l'Oiselet*. For the use of lai as birdsong, see note to line 89 and the Introduction, pp. 20–21. Cf. also the speeches of *Amors* in the *Rose* (ed. Lecoy), esp. 2071–112 and 2201–07.

140 *sentez B* alone has *sentez* and *ACDE* have *souffrez*. It is tempting to change here, but the sense of the line is maintained, and so, in accordance with the editorial policy, I do not change when there is no real error.

142 *Qui estes avenans et belles* This is a common tag line. See Roach, *Continuations*, 4: n. to 21366.

151 *par Por* would be better, but *par* often is used where *por* would be expected (cf. Kibler, 180–81).

151–68 This passage of the poem varies most in terms of vocabulary, and *B* clearly stands apart from the other manuscripts in some of these usages. In *ACDE* the message is that God and love are in accord, and if you heed what they love and hate, you will succeed. In *B* the message is that God and lovers are in accord, and if you heed what God loves and hates, you will win both Him and His love. The greatest differences in this passage are due to the use of the word *amor*. In *E* the passage has only eight lines: God is the subject up to line 159, and *amour* is the subject for one line (160). *E* uses the expression *fine amour* twice (154 and 156), and it is from *E* that G. Paris took *fine amour* for his line 156. *E* uses *amours* as subject once in this passage (160), and it is personified: *Et amours les [orguel et faucité] tient en vi[l]té*. In *CAB* the role of *amor* as subject is expanded: In *C amors* is subject in lines 152, 152b, 160, 156, 166; in *A amors* is subject in 152, 156, 160, 166; in *D* in 152, 156, 160, 160a,

160*b*. In *B*, however, there are *no instances of amor(s) subject* and *B* has very deliberately avoided personifying *amor*: in 152, *B* uses *amis* and in 156 *Aumosne*, and in 160 and 166 *amor* is object. The latter usage presents a problem of syntax. In *AC* 165-66 *amor(s)* is subject of the singular verb *maintient*; in *D* line 165 is changed so that 166 stands alone with *loiauté* as subject and *amor* as object. In *B* the interpretation is more complex because of the use of *seul* in 165. Since *B* has no other case of *amor(s)* subject in this passage, the use of *seul* is interpreted as an adverb which allows *cortoisie* to be the singular subject of *maintient* with *honor* and *loiauté* as parentheticals and *amor* as object: "But courtesy alone (and honor and fidelity) maintains love." On the uses of *seul* adverb, see Nyrop, 2: 235; Foulet, *Gloss*, s.v. *seul*; God., 7: 446*bc* (s.v. *sol*). On a singular verb with a plural subject, see Foulet, *Syntaxe*, 202-03.

The deliberate non-use of *amor(s)* as subject in *B* recalls line 117 where *B* also stands alone using *li humors*, whereas all the other manuscripts have a form of *amor(s)*. When line 117 is considered together with the passage 151-68, it becomes clear that *B* has systematically excluded personifying *amor(s)*. Not all these changes in *B*, however, result in the best lines: 154 is unique in *B*; line 153 does not follow smoothly from line 152; the repetition of *si aimme* in 159 and 160 is awkward; and line 168 in *B* does not close the passage as it began (cf. line 143). Line 162 in *B* does not have the distinctions made by *ACD*, but the chiasmus of *envieus* and *covoiteus* in *AC* further complicates or moots the distinctions being drawn in lines 161-62 in the other manuscripts.

The text of this passage in Gaston Paris illustrates how difficult it is to arrive at a satisfactory reading. The following five lines from his text show how much he altered his base manuscript *C* in order to produce what he considered to be a satisfying text. The italics indicate departure from *C*:

> Die*us* et Amors sont d'un acort.
> Die*us aime* onor et cortoisie,
> *Et fine* Amors *ne les het mie*
> Dieus het orguel et *fausseté*
> Et Amors *les tient en vilté*;   (G. P., ll. 154–58)

> C

> Diex et amors sont d'un acort.
> Diex aimme sens et honorance,
> Amors ne l'a pas en viltance
> Dex het orgueil et fauceté
> Et amors aimme loiauté;   (*C* 150–54)

In addition to altering the spellings for *Diex*, *aimme*, and *fauceté* and capitalizing *amors*, he takes *onor et cortoisie* from *A* (*A honor*) for line 155; line 156 from *E*, with changes (*E Et fine amour ne le het mie*); and *les tient en vilté* from *E* (*E* 160) for line 158.

The word *vilté* (*E* 160) undergoes some interesting shifts in this passage: it is *viltance* in *C* (152*b*) and *vilennie* in *B* (154). The word *het* also undergoes a shift: in 159 *EC* have a line with *het* and *ABD* have a line with *aim(m)e*.

In sum, there is no one entirely satisfactory reading of this passage. Although *B* has some unique usages, it is not alone in altering the passage in a deliberate attempt to interpret the message.

157 *covoite* (162 *covoiteus*) The *n* in modern French *convoiter*, *convoitise* was inserted by false analogy. See explanation in the *Dictionnaire général*, 1: 535 (s.v. *convoiter*). Gaston Paris, who uses ms *C*, slips here when he uses *n*: *ms C* has *couvoite* (157), *couvoitous* (160, 172). (Lines in G. Paris's edition are 161 and 164; he uses a different

word for his line 174. See my note to line 311.) Cf. *Rose* (ed. Lecoy), 1125–88 for the use of *largesce*.

157–58 *largesce : teche* This rhyme is cited by Gertrud Wacker, 62, from G. Paris, 1884, as "*teche : largesse.*" G. Paris, however, had normalized these lines (161–62) to *largece : tece* so that both words are Picard in form rather than mixed Picard and Francien. Ms *C* reads neither as Wacker cites it nor as G. Paris uses it; but exactly like *B. AD* have the same mix (*larguece : teche* and *largesce : teiche*), and *E* omits these lines. On these forms, see Gossen, 91, 100; Pope, § 722, 285–86; E. Roach, 89 (mix of *Picard* and *Francien* forms). Cf. *Oiselet* 365 : 366 and the rhyme *despiece : leesce*.

171 *esgardoit* Perhaps *AC escoutoit* is better, but *B* is certainly not wrong. Cf. the poem in Bartsch, Bk. 1, no. 27, pp. 22–23, where the bird is almost driven mad by the fact the villein had listened to him:

> Li rosignolez disoit:
> par un pou qu'il n'enrajoit
> du grant duel que il avoit,
> que vilains l'avoit oi.   (29–32)

Note that the villein of this *pastorelle* is under a tree. In the *Rose* (ed. Lecoy), *Dangiers* was also under a tree (3653–93). (Cf. my note to 174–92.)

172 On *enuieus* as "disagreeable," the *lectio difficilior*, see *NRCF*, 1: 320, n. to 48.1.

173 *chante* Perhaps the past tense of the other mss is better, but abruptly changing tenses in a passage is a common scribal practice.

174–92 The invective of the oiselet against the villein recalls particularly the *Fablel dou Dieu d'Amors* (ed. Jubinal, lines 57–64) and a romance (Bartsch, Bk. 1, no. 27, pp. 22–23) where the presence of a villein in the garden is an insult to the bird (a nightingale) who is singing. The conjunction *car* before the imperative registers impatience (also in lines 175 and 177). Cf. Foulet, *Syntaxe*, 293 and Nyrop 1: 147. In the *Rose* (ed. Lecoy), *Amors* speaks against the *vilenie* of the *vilains* (2074a–j), and *Dangiers*, of course, is the villein (*Rose*, 2809–12, 2904; 2927–34; 3652–742). The sin of gluttony is implied by the accusation of the bird that the villein wants only to eat (cf. *Rose*, 11303–308). The dialogue here between the bird and the villein recalls the dialogue between *Amors* and *Faux Semblant* (*Rose*, ed. Lecoy, 11193–987).

178 *Ci* = ici, "here." *D* has *Ceus*, which anticipates the subject nouns that follow in the next line. In 189 *Ci* is emended to *Cil* in *B* since the reference is clearly back to the previously mentioned *dames* and *chevaliers* of 179 and contrasts with *cist* in line 192.

178–83 Mss *AC* have a couplet 182*ab*, *Si en fesoient les larguesces Les cortoisies les proëces*, absent in *BDE*, that influences the syntax of this passage. The problem is with line 183, *Maintenoient chevalerie*, where the subject of the verb has to be understood as following from 179 and the relative pronoun *Qui* of 180. *E* does not have 183 and ends the sentence at 182. *D* has a different line 183: *Et tenoient chevalerie*, so that the presence of *Et* at the beginning of the line maintains the flow from *Qui* (subject of *tenoient*) in 180. With the couplet 182*ab* in the passage, the line 182*b* can be seen as furnishing a subject for 183. Without the couplet 183*ab* in *B*, line 183 seems abrupt. In order to understand the verb standing alone at the beginning of 183, several elements have to be considered as unexpressed but understood: 183 can be considered as having a subject *ils* understood, referring back to the *Gentis dames et chevaliers* of 179. The line can also be seen as a relative clause with the *qui* of 180 understood, so that it becomes the third in a list of actions beginning with 181; or an *Et* at the beginning of 183 can also be understood. Lacking the smoothness of the reading either with 183*ab* or without 183 and 183*ab* altogether, the reading in *B* is an instance of *lectio difficilior*. Cf. Foulet, *Syntaxe*, 313–15.

185–86 I have emended 185 *Que* to *Qui* since I believe that the relative clause was intended to characterize the villein, not just his action (*Que* = "car," for). In 186 the subject should be expressed, so *Qui* is emended to *Qu'il*.

187–92 This passage in *ABC*, absent in *E* and expanded in *D* (by 20 lines after 192 and 2 lines after 190), illustrates clearly an instance of amplification in the poem. The bird's invective in *E* ended with the *pointe* of 185–86. It was increased by 6 lines in *AB* and ends with the *pointe* of line 192. *C* has a slightly different version, without 187-88 and with line 192 inverted so that the line ending the song is "Por miex boire et por gloutoier." *D* continues the vein of *gloutoier* with its longest addition of the poem of 20 lines after 192.

188 *sougis* p p *sogire* See T.-L., 9: col. 744, 50-col. 746, 30.

189 *Cil* < *Ci* By not using *Cil* in line 189, the scribe does not have the nice distinction between *Cil* 189 and *Cist* 192. The scribe of *B* may have been distracted from his context by making a large initial here, or he might have recalled the similar line of 178 where *Ci* was used. The change to *Cil* is also supported by *ACD*.

191 *aaisier* For this form, cf. Foulet's *Glossary* to *Continuations*, 3. 2: 1 and 5. On p. 5, Foulet gives the expression *por lor cors . . . aesier* with the meaning "pour se soigner (dans une période de repos)." Cf. T.-L., 1: cols. 27–29. T.-L. have entries for *aaisier* with both *cuers* and *cors*. With *cuers* the meaning is "gladden," "please," and with *cors* "delight," "please," "restore to health."

195 *pöuet* This imperf 3 of *pooir* is probably a deviant spelling of *pöoit* in which the ending -*oit* > -*uet*. The form *pooit* occurs in 197. See Fouché, 241.

196 *[A]ssez* The initial letter of this line is obscured by the decorative flourish from the large capital at the beginning of line 189.

197 *ce* = *se* = "si," "if."

198 *En jaiole le meteroit* < *En la jaiole le metroit* The scribe of *B* first wrote *la* with *jaiole* and then "fixed up" the line by using *metroit*, an alternate form of *meteroit*. *E* has a defective line (−1), using both *En jaiole* and the short form of the verb *metroit*. *C* uses a different verb altogether: *En jaiole l'enfermeroit*. *A* has a correct line, *En jaiole le meteroit*, and *D* changes the line to: *En sa gëolle le metroit*. On the poetic license of *meteroit* for *metroit*, see Nyrop, 2:160 (§ 209 rem.). *B* also uses the short forms *metrai*, 296, and *donra*, 227.

199 *Si l'i chanteroit tart et tempre* < *Si l'i tendroit main et tempre* On this occasion *B* lost track of the context. His line continues with the idea of setting up the trap, and, combined with the expression *et main et tempre*, it is nonsense. The line should begin a new idea with *chanteroit*. Line 199 is thus emended to *chanteroit*, which is in *ACDE* as well. Cf. God., 4: 628*a*, and T.-L., 4: col. 1545, 8–11, who cite lines 198–99 from the *Oiselet* (s.v. *jaiole*).

200 *atempre* God., 1: 468*b* cites this line from the *Oiselet* (s.v. *atemprer*), with the meaning "régler," "adjust, set." Cf. 205 *atempree*.

204 *laz* The word is plural in this line, singular in 209, and plural in 210. T.-L., 5: cols. 249–54, give over five columns of examples, in which *laz* or *las* (mod. Fr. *lacs*) is singular or plural almost at random. The meaning here is "snare" or "trap."

205–06 *atempree : vespree* < *atrempee : matinee* The reading of ms *B* originally had a line 206 with *matinee* that was emended to bring the line into conformity with the sense (see notes to lines 73, 124, and 199 for slips similar to 206). The resulting rhyme *atrempee : vespree* with the metathesis of *r* in *atrempee* would have been acceptable. However, the word is used in line 200 with the rhyme *tempre : atempre*, so that 205 *atrempee* is emended to *atempree*, the form it would have had if the scribe had not anticipated writing *matinee* in 206. T.-L., 1: col. 627, 42–44, cite lines 200 and 205 from the *Oiselet* (from Méon, 1808).

209 *erroment* Other spellings of this word are in T.-L., 3: col. 779, lines 8–52: *erranment, erraumant. Erec* (ed. Foerster) 1587 *erraumant* (ed. Roques 1567 *araumant*); *Yvain* (ed. Foerster) 3170 *erraumant* (ed. Roques 3165 *araumant*); *arroment* (Montaiglon and Raynaud, *Fabliaux: De Guillaume au Faucon*, 2: 112, 113); Ruelle in his ed. (1960) of *Huon de Bordeaux*, 459 (s.v. *erraument*) lists six examples of the spelling *erroment*.

210–11 Mss *A* and *B* have the series of substantives *li chaitis, li dolenz* and *li las* in line 210, and *CDE* have *li vilains* (*D le maus vilains*) instead of *li dolenz*. It is clear in *CDE* that the subject for the verb in 211 is *li vilains*, but in *A* and *B*, the string of three substantives could apply either to the bird or to the villein. I have solved the problem in *B* by retaining *chaitis* and *dolenz* for the bird and using *Li las* for the villein as subject of *Monte amont*. I did not remove *dolenz* and add *vilains* since that would be a more drastic change of *B*. The three words *chaitis, dolenz,* and *las* are often used together and as such have the meanings "miserable," "wretched," "grieving." Cf. T.-L., 5: cols. 205–10. *Caitis*, however, can also have a pejorative sense: one can be *caitis* (miserable) or accuse someone of being a *caitis* (a wretch). In the context of the *Oiselet chaitis* could apply either to the bird or to the villein. The word *dolanz*, however, seems only to mean sad and grieving, and as such, can be applied only to the bird. The word *las* also has two meanings, "wretch" and "wretched," and in God., 4: 731*a, las* is applied to Judas in one citation. With this pejorative interpretation of *las*, punctuation alone can provide a subject for 211: *Li las Monte amont,* and the substantives *chaitis* and *dolenz* refer back to the bird in line 209. Referring to the bird, *caitis* can also have its meaning of "wretched captive" as well. Other uses of *chaitis* in the text show how it has two meanings: in 364 the villein applies it to himself as he wrings his hands, and in 371 the bird applies it to the villein as he upbraids him.

212 Proverb: Le Roux de Lincy, 2: 105; Morawski nos. 1986 (166, 725, 1805, 1987); Ulrich 289. Cf. God., 5: 18*c*-19*a* (s.v. *loier*).

213–14 These two lines are inverted in *B. ACE* have *avis : pris* (*D pourpris : pris*). Since line 213 is at the bottom of a column (78*b*) and 214 at the top of the next column and page, the scribe causes the inversion by anticipation.

214 Ms *D* (line 214*c* = D283) has an interesting idiomatic expression, *Malesgré vostre nes devant* (in spite of yourself, whether you want to or not). T.-L., 6: col. 609, 51-col. 610, 27, give numerous examples (s.v. *nés*). The form *malesgré* is unusual. Almost all the examples in T.-L., 6, are *maugré*, but they cite a similar form (4: col. 595, 48–50, s.v. *gré*) from the *Vie de saint Martin* 2818–21 by Péan Gatineau: "Puis li manda qu'eneslepas Venist a lui, ou si ce non, Il l'amenreit par le grenon, Malegré son, sanz atendue." See also *Perceval* (ed. Roach), l. 812: "maleoit gre mien" = "malgré moi."

218–19 The repetition of a form of *servir* in *ABC* 218–19 may reflect the repetition of the same verb in the *Donnei*, 962–63, and the *Trois Savoirs*, 48–49.

220–23 The text of this passage illustrates a pattern of divergence, mistakes, and bad lines among the manuscripts. Line 220 is unique in *B. EC* have a line using *cheance* (*E* is −1) and *AD* have a line using *chançon(s)*. After 220, *E* has four lines of the same rhyme: *avis : pris, devis : porpris; C* has *avis : devis;* and *B* has *pris : devis. A* changes the rhyme further with *emprise* : *devise*, and *D* uses *prise* : *devise* (preceded by two very bad lines).

222 *seul* This form of the ps ind 1 of *soloir* (*souloir*) is not attested (cf. Fouché). T.-L., 9: cols. 807–10, give three columns of quotations for the verb *soloir*, but the only instances of the ps ind 1, spelled *soil*, are from the *Vie de St. Thomas* (3022) by Guernes de Pont-Sainte-Maxence (ed. Walberg, 1922), and from the *Roman de Rou* (ed. Holden), part 3, vol. 1, lines 635, 636. Cf. *Roman de la Rose* (ed. Lecoy), 7778, 7975, 11565, ps ind 1 spelled *seull*; and the *Romanzen und Pastourellen* (ed. Bartsch), 3, 35, 39 (p. 284), ps ind 1 spelled *sueil*. Forms like imperfect *soloie* 226 are quite common. This verb frequently occurs in the ps ind 3 when the meaning is past, even though the impf ind 3 existed (*soloit*). See Foulet, *Glossary* to the *First Continuation* (ed. Roach), 283 (s.v. *soloir*).

227 *donra* Cf. Nyrop, 2: 156–57. For another example of alternate forms, see note to 198.

231 *Ja em prison ne chanterai* Cf. *Rose* (ed. Lecoy) 13911–28 and note to these lines where Lecoy cites Boethius, *Philosophiae consolationis*, Bk. 3, pt. 2, lines 17–26, as the source of this motif.

232 *Par foi et je vous mengerai!* Cf. Hesiod, *Works and Days*, "The Hawk and the Nightingale," in Hesiod (Loeb, *Classical Lib.*, 18–19) for what is considered the earliest instance of this fable.

233 *tor* The meaning here is "tour" (m), "trick" or "ruse." God., 10: 788*b* (s.v. *tourn*). T.-L., 10: col. 395, 11, cite this line from Méon, 1808, and give the definition "Ausweg" for *tor*. Cf. *Donnei* (971–94) and *Trois Savoirs* (55–74) for a *feintise* proposed by the bird.

238 *m'aler* < *m'ester* The sense of this line and *ACDE* all support this change, although *lessiez m'ester* with the meaning "give me up" would be acceptable. Cf. lines 229, 250.

241–42 Proverb: Le Roux de Lincy, 2: 106–107; Morawski no. 2290 (cf. no. 1418).

245 *Douce* < *Toute* Proverb: Le Roux de Lincy, 2: 486, cites four lines (245–48) of the *lai de l'Oiselet*; Ulrich no. 206. God., 1: 195*c* (s.v. *airier*) cites the *Oiselet* 245–46 (from Méon, 1808). T.-L., 1: col. 255, 28–29, cite this line from the *Oiselet*. (See note to 248.)

246 *ACD* have *Mainte foiz l'avez oï dire*, which is a slightly more satisfactory line than in *B* (*E* follows *B*), but no change is made.

247–48 *chose* : *chose* Only *B* and *E* have this identical rhyme. *ACD* have *glose* : *chose* and line 247 *Mes uns diz nous enseigne et glose* is more expressive than the lines in *EB*. No emendation is made in *B*, however, since there is no real error. On rhyme *du même au même*, see Elwert, 90; Tobler, *Vers fr.*, 167–73; Roach, *Continuations*, 5: note to 36733–34.

248 Proverb: Le Roux de Lincy, 2: 486 (cites *Oiselet* lines 245–48); Hassell no. *B* 49; Ulrich no. 152.

252 [*hons*] Hole in manuscript. The form *hons* is also used in lines 277 and 316. In line 96, the abbrevation *hō* is solved as *hom* with the expression *nus hom*.

261 *hericiez* This passage (lines 259–65) is cited by T.-L. 4: col. 1082, 9–14 (s.v. *hericier*), and the word means "disheveled, with the hair in disorder." The line in ms *D* (345) is: *Touilliez fu, et touz hericiez.* The word *touilliez* in God., 7: 745–46 (s.v. *tooillier*) and T.-L., 10: cols. 350–53 (s.v. *toëillier*), has the general meaning of "to soil." In the infinitive and p p, most of the examples are trisyllabic, but some are dissyllabic. Cf. the *Roman de la Rose* (ed. Lecoy), 6355, *tooullier*, defined as "plonger dans l'eau sale."

263 *contre lainne* This expression is recorded in T.-L., 5: col. 71, 40–45, whose only example is from the *Lai de l'Oiselet* (ed. Méon, 1808). They define the expression "gegen den Strich der Haare," "against the grain," "the wrong way"; or, referring to feathers, "ruffled" or "mussed." Gaston Paris gives the meaning "à contre-poil" (line 265).

265 *rasiet* God., 6: 612*b* and T.-L., 8: col. 318, 7–8 (s.v. *rasseoir*), cite lines 264–65 from the *Oiselet* (ed. Méon, 1808).

266 *estuet* Ms D may have miscopied *estuet* and used *voulet* as an impf ind, but this form of *voloir* is not attested in Fouché.

267 *semont* < *comment* B probably misread *semont* in his copy since both words have the same general outline. On this type of error cf. Roach, *Continuations*, 5: notes to 35265, 36767, 27971, 40465.

270 *i puez* It is tempting to change B here since all the other mss agree on *porras*. The future is appropriate for an "if clause," and the removal of *molt* from B would not be a great alteration. However, the line is grammatical and conveys the sense, and so it is not changed.

270–312 In this passage *EC* and *ABD* group themselves according to the order of the first two sens: *EC* have *croire* as the first sens and *ABD* have *pleurer*. The following table, using the line numbers of *B*, provides a concordance for this passage. The most striking feature of this passage is that the greatest differences between the two versions are not the wording of the lines but their arrangement. *E* represents the short version and *C* the longer version of *croire pleurer*, and *ABD* have essentially the same version of *pleurer croire*, with a few exceptions that will be noted. The lines in parentheses for *E* indicate lines not in *E*. *D* adds a couplet 270*ab* not recorded in the table. The boxed lines indicate the texts of the sens *croire* and *pleurer* and graphically show their relative positions to each other.

E		C		ABD	
270		270		270	
301–304	*croire*	301–304	*croire*	271–78	*pleurer*
(305–10)		305–10		279–82	
283–84				283–84	
(285–86)				285–86	
287–94				287–94	
295–96				295–96	
296*a–b*					
296*c–d*		296*c–d*			
297					
297*a*–98		297*a*–98		297–98	
(299–300)		299–300		299–300	
271–78	*pleurer*	271–78	*pleurer*	301–10	*croire*
(279–82)		279–82			
		283–84			
		285–86			
		287–94			
311–12		297–311	(2 lines)	311–12	
		312–12*a*			
		296–95			
(313–14)		313–14		313–14	
315–16		315–16		315–16	

The long version of *croire pleurer* in *C* adds 305–10 to the text of *croire* and has 283–84 and 287–94 apply to *pleurer*. *C* also has additional lines 285–86 and 279–82 applied to the text of *pleurer*. The transitional lines in *E*, 296a–b, 296c–d, and 297a–98 are 296c–d, 297a–98, and 299–300 in *C*. The transition to the third *sens* in *E* consists of lines 311–12 and 315–16. *C* has an expanded version: 297–311 (2 lines), 312–12a, 296–95, and 313–14. In *E* 311–12 rhymes *couvent : sens*. In *C* this couplet is expanded to two couplets 297–311 *gabant : couvant* and 311–12a *sen : assen*.

In the version in *ABD* the whole text of *pleurer* in *C*, 271–94, now comes first, i.e., after line 270. Lines 296c–d and 297a are eliminated, leaving 297–300 as transition to *croire*. The text of *croire*, 301–10, now follows. Lines 311–12 begin the transition to the third *sens*, as in *E* (*D* changes the rhyme and so this couplet is 310a–b in *D*).

The couplet 295–96 is one key to understanding the rearrangements of text in this passage. In *E* the couplet 295–96 is part of the transition of the texts from *croire* to *pleurer*. In *C* the couplet (inverted) is in the transition between *pleurer* and the third *sens*. In *ABD* 295–96 is in the passage from *pleurer* to *croire*. It has, in a sense, remained stationary while the *croire* and *pleurer* texts "changed places." From *E* to *C croire* expanded from four lines, 301–304, to ten lines, 301–10, and the extended text of *pleurer* in *C* (271–94) now fits in between 297a–98 with the addition of 299–300 and 297 *gabant*–311 *couvant*. In *ABD* the whole text of *pleurer* in *C* is placed first after 270 and the whole text of *croire* is placed after 300. It is possible that other slightly different arrangements of text existed in the copies from which *ABD* descend that would show even more graphically how the transition passages surrounded the reversed portions of the texts and how the transition lines were rearranged. Some similar problems of accounting for lines moved from one place to another in different manuscripts were also encountered in the passage 335–60 (see Textual Note to this passage).

The following table of pronouns in this passage indicates that there was a certain amount of confusion concerning how many *sens* had already been mentioned by the bird at a given moment. The use of singular for plural or plural for singular is a clue to the fact that lines had been rearranged in this part of the text.

PRONOUNS IN THE TEXT OF THE FIRST TWO SENS

E	C	B	A	D
(croire)	(croire)	(pleurer)	(pleurer)	(pleurer)
303 le	303 le	278 ce	278 ce	278 en
304 *les*	304 le	283 jel	283 jel te	283 le
283 je le (+1)	305 l'	284 l'	284 l'	284 l'
284 l'	309 ce	286 l'	286 l'	286 l'
287 ne le (+1)		287 nu	287 *nes*	287 nel
288 le		288 le	288 *les*	288 le
298 Cestui	298 cestui	298 cestui	298 cestui	298 *Ces deus*
(pleurer)	(pleurer)	(croire)	(croire)	(croire)
278 se (= ce)	278 ce	303 le	303 le	303 le
	283 les	304 le	304 le	304 les
	284 les	305 l'	305 l'	305 ne l' (nes?)
	286 l'	309 ce	309 ce	309 ce
	287 nes			
	288 les			

Pronouns in italics indicate the use of a plural where a singular would be expected in the context. Neither *C* nor *B* makes any such errors, and *B* uses no plurals at all, thus avoiding entirely the problem of how many sens have already been mentioned at any given moment in this portion of the text. The errors in *E* 304, *A* 287, 288 and *D* 298 are significant clues that there were different arrangements of lines for these two sens since the same lines have correct pronouns in the other manuscripts. The errors suggest that lines were lifted "bodily" and rearranged without correction for the new order. Unfortunately, the discovery of these errors does not solve the problems of "which came first" in an "original," since the error in *E* suggests a text with *croire* second, and the errors in *A* and *D* suggest a text with *pleurer* second!

271 Proverb: Morawski no. 1346; Ulrich no. 439 (cf. no. 87).

272 *Li vilains fu molt irascus* Ms *B* stands alone here. *ACDE* all have *Li vilains ne fu mie mus* for line 272. As a result, only *B* has the same reaction (anger) of the villein after both the sens *pleurer* and *croire* (302 *Li vilains fonce le nez d'ire*) are given. In the *Trois Savoirs* (174) and *Donnei des Amants* (1108) the villein is also referred to as *irascu*.

278 *ce est* Not elided (also 193 *ce ot*).

284 *B* has a grammatically correct line whereas *A Grant paor ai que ne l'oublie* (rhymes with 283 *redie*) is incorrect since the *-s* ending for ps sg 2 is omitted for the rhyme. The correct form is *obliz* (cf. Fouché, 101).

292 On the omission of *si*, the first term of a comparison, see Roach, *Continuations*, 5: note to 42198–99. See also my note to 33.

296 Unique line in *B*. See note to 270–312.

301 Proverb: Le Roux de Lincy, 2: 387, 483; Morawski nos. 982, 2389, 2394 (cf. nos. 1389, 1433); Hassell no. *C* 348.

311 Ms *B* has *covens*, but *C* has *couvant* which G. Paris gives as *convant* (314). See my note to line 157.

313–14 Notice the use of *orrai* 313 and *Entent* 314 that later is made explicit in 392 where "he who listens" (*ot*) does not hear or understand (*entent*).

316 Ms *E* has two similar passages, one after 316 and one after 360, that suggest *E* added couplets where they did not belong either because of the similarity of context or inattention to context when he was copying. The passages in *E* are as follows:

315	Li tiers est tex qui le feroit		359	Que li hom qui la porteroit
316	Que james pouvres ne ceroit		360	Jamais povrete n'avroit (–1)
add	Ne savrez demander ceste (–1)		362	Ne ne savoit demander ceste
add	Que maintenant ne li fust prestre		361	Qui maintenant ne li fust prestre
317	Et quant li vilains l'oi (–1)		*add*	Quan li vilains a ce oi
318	Molt durement c'en esjoi		*add*	Sachiez qu'il n'est pas esjoi
			add	Ainz est a pou enragiez d'ire
			add	Ses drapiaus deront et decire

None of the other manuscripts has these repeated lines. The corresponding passages are given from the manuscript readings in *B*:

315	Li tierz est tiez qui le saroit		359	Qui en son demainne l'aroit
316	James povres hons ne seroit		360	Ja chose ne demanderoit
317	Et quant li vilains l'entendi		361	Que maintenant ne li fu preste
318	Molt durement s'en esjoi		362	Qant li vilains entendi ceste

Since *E* seems to "borrow" couplets back and forth in these two passages, it is possible that *E* could have copied from a manuscript where the passages beginning at 315 and 359 were on the same page in columns across from each other. This kind of situation exists in *A* and *B*, and it would be tempting to conclude that *E* actually copied from *A* or *B*. The most that one can conjecture, however, is that a similar arrangement of lines could have existed in the text or texts from which *E* copied and thus caused the scribe of *E* to insert the lines he did.

Another possible explanation for the added lines in *E* is that *E* amplified similar passages in a similar way, with the "nucleus" of these two passages being 317 and 361*a*. (These two lines recall the *Donnei* 1021 and 1087 and the *Trois Savoirs* 95 and 155.) If this were the case, similar contexts led to similar development, although the couplet *E* 316*ab* clearly is out of place in the context. All these added lines are unique to *E*, although *C* 318-17 maintains the rhyme *esjoi* : *oi* of *E* 317-18 and 361*ab*.

323 *erroment* See note to 209.

325 *chastoi* God., 2: 86c–87c (s.v. *chastier*) gives the following definition of *chastiement*: "Ce mot a désigné en particulier une espèce de fiction ayant pour but de moraliser à l'aide d'apologues, d'histoires et de contes, et dont . . . le premier modèle: *le Chastoiement d'un père à son fils.*"

326-27 Proverb: Le Roux de Lincy, 2: 491; Morawski no. 1343; Ulrich no. 438.

331 *paroles AB* have *paroles*, *C adavinal*, *D enseignement* and *E sanz* (-2 and inverts). The most expressive word is in *C*, "childish riddles."

332 Ms *C* has an interesting use of *saches* imperative 2 of *savoir* (*Et si saches a esciant*) instead of the normal *sache*, which would leave the line a syllable short. Cf. *Perceval* (ed. Roach), note to 2310; and *Chanson de Roland* (ed. Bédier), 3902, where final *s* also saves the line from being –1.

335-60 This passage demonstrates a strong similarity of pattern of lines between *E* and *C* and illustrates the amplification of text in *ABD*.

E	C	ABD
334	334	334
(335–38)	335–38	335–38
339	339	339
340	340	340
(341–46)	(341–46)	341–46
		347
		348
(349–52)	349–52	349–52
353	353	353
354	354	354
348	*348*	
347	*347*	
355	355	355
356	356	356
(357–58)	357–58	357–58
359	359	359
360	360	360

The lines in parentheses are not in *E* and/or *C* and are in *ABD*. The most striking aspects of this passage are the placement of the couplet 347-48 in *EC* and the amplification of the passage: from 10 lines in *E*, to 20 in *C*, and 26 in *ABD* (not counting unique lines added in *D*). What is also striking in this passage is that the essential outline of the dialogue exists in the 10 lines of *E*. The lines in *C* not in *E*: 335–38,

349–52, and 357–58, elaborate but do not alter what is in *E*: 349–52 adds "If you had killed me" and 357–58 adds the detail about the stone weighing three ounces. The lines in *ABD* not in *C*: 341–46 also add details, but again, they do not change the overall effect of the lines. The different pattern of lines 347–48 in *EC* and *ABD* also involves the altering of the wording of lines 347 and 353 and the shift of lines 347-48 from after 354 to before 349. The added line 346 in *ABD* ends with the word *comment*, and the beginning of line 347 has *Comment*, suggesting that 348–47 was moved up to follow 346, while the rest of line *EC* 353, *que sez tu dont fere*, was left in *ABD* in the same place as in *EC*. Line 348 is also moved up and now follows 347. Its placement in *ABD* has the admonition: *Tu ne sez que t'est avenu* now precede both the passage "if you had killed me" (349–52) and the passage "there is a three-ounce precious stone in me."

Because *E*, *C*, and *ABD* all have plausible dialogues conveying the same essential scene (cf. *Chastoiement A*, for example), most of the added lines in *ABD* seem like padding, and it is possible to see *E* and *C* as abridging a longer text in this passage. In such a scenario *C* would have skipped from 340 to 349 and then used *comment* for 353, kept 354 in place, added *Tu ne sez qu'il t'est avenu* that was 348 in *ABD* and kept a remodeled 347. Eyeskip would be involved in this passage, from *seüsses : eüsses* 339–40 to *eüsses* 349. An abridgment from *C* to *E* is easier to envisage, since it merely involves the omission of blocks of text: 335–38, 341–46, 349–52, and 357–58, without any changes of order.

Although I believe that the poem of the *Oiselet* grew by means of the amplification of a short poem, it is not inconceivable that the shorter versions of manuscripts *E* and *C* in this passage could have omitted or abridged lines in their copy, in much the way that *A* probably omitted 39–50 and 391–98.

Since it is most likely there were manuscripts intervening between the versions in *EC* and *ABD* that we have and those of the original poem, we cannot know for certain at which stage a passage may have been added, or whether that passage could also have been later omitted. Although the poem was clearly amplified, this does not necessarily mean that the shorter version of a given passage may not also be the result of abridgment.

340 *Lessié* < *Lessier AD* correctly have *Ja laissié*, but *C* has the same error *laissier* as in *B* and also has the *Ja* of *A*. In this line the first word in *E* is illegible.

346 *Comment?* There is a similar use of dialogue with *comment?* in the *Roman de la Rose* (ed. Lecoy), 11383, 11959. Cf. also *Chastoiement A*, 3469-71 (Hilka-Söderjhelm; 3375-77 Montgomery).

Ms *D* (346*b* = *D* 440) has an interesting expression *ne ce ne quoi*. T.-L., 2: col. 83, 29-30, refer to the study by Lommatzsch, *Deiktische Elemente im Altfranzösischen*, 2, 219ff., in the *Jahrbuch für Philologie*, ed. V. Klemperer and E. Lerch (Munich, 1925). Cf. also God., 2: 164*a*: *ne ço ne quoi*, with the definition "rien du tout." The first example cited by God. is from line 20643 of the Second Continuation, where eight of nine mss have "Ne li respont ne ce ne coi." The ninth ms (*Q*) has "Ne ne li respont ce ne coi." Other examples occur in *Bueve de Hantone* (ed. Stimming), Fassung 3, vol. 1, 14877 (cf. note to this line in Fassung 3, vol. 2).

347 *malostru* The word in *A* is *durfeü* and is cited by T.-L., 2: col. 2110, 11 (from Méon, 1808), meaning "worthless scamp." (*D* omits, *C* has *mescheü*, and *E* has *mesavenu*). In the *Donnei des Amants* the villein calls himself *mal[e]ürez* (1092).

350 *empensé* T.-L., 3: col. 99, 40-col. 100, 19, give entries which support this as one word. Cf. *Cleomadés* (ed. Henry), 10733, 12303, and *enproposé*, *Cleomadés* 6463. Cf. God., 3: 58*a*. The meaning is "to plan or intend to do."

353 *Ha* < *Hai̯* The scribe showed by his expunctuation that he erred in anticipation of the next line.

357 *de trois onces* < *demie once* *B* forgot his context or anticipated the dénouement, line 375. *E* does not have this information (357–58), but the message is still conveyed when the bird says he has a precious stone inside him (355–56). Cf. note to 335–60.

362 *ceste* A neuter pronoun equivalent to something like *ceste chose*. Cf. *Erec* 3559 (ed. Roques; 3569 ed. Foerster). See also T.-L., 2: col. 147, 10-26, where this line from the *Lai de l'Oiselet* was cited from Méon, 1808. More examples in Tobler, *Vermischte Beiträge*, 5: 303–304. In English, "this thing."

367 *de sor* This expression means "from on top of." As one word, *desor* means "on top of" or "upon." See Roach, *Continuations*, 5: n. to 37967; also 4: n. to 32322.

373–74 The scribe of *E* wrote *moine que moisson* in line 373. God., 5: 362*b*, cites these lines (373-75) under the heading "*moine*, s. m. moineau" (only entry in God. for "moine")! The *moine* in *E* is probably just a slip, and the scribe probably meant to write a form *menre* (cf. *E* 80 *maindres d'un moisson*). Under *moisson* (5: 366*a*) God. gives lines 77–81 from the *Oiselet* (from Méon, 1808). (Cf. Bloch-Von Wartburg, *Dict. Etym.*, *moine*.)

In 374 *E* has *Qu'aloue ne que pinçons* (−1), and the other mss use *mesenge* and *pinçon*. *E* not only makes a faulty line (−1), but *aloue* (lark), a much bigger bird (up to 7½ inches), is also much less satisfactory for the comparison. (See note to lines 80–92.)

375 *demie* Mss *AB* use *demie* and *CDE demi*. *B* also uses *demie* in 357 although the text must be emended to *trois onces*. On the variability of *demi*, see Nyrop, 5: 100–101.

376 *gronce* T.-L., 4: col. 682, 16-19, cite the *Lai de l'Oiselet* for this instance of *groncier* (alternative form of *grocier*) = to "growl, grumble, scold," with the rhyme-word *once*. God., 4, lists *groucier* and has three instances of *groncier* where he says a form of *groucier* is printed as *groncier*. The *Donnei*, 29 and 65, uses *grucer* with the villein.

377 Both *E* and *D* have –2 for this line, suggesting that *D* was influenced by the version in *E*. Since what is missing is a banal *Li dist*, it is not surprising that such a formula was dropped. However, there are many such formulae in this text, and it seems highly unlikely that two manuscripts would drop the same expression in the same line by chance. For other instances of a suggestion of a relationship between *D* and *E*, see notes to 10 and 220–23.

382–98 This passage contains the end of the admonition by the bird to the villein and is a passage showing much divergence:

E	C	B	A	D
382	382	382	382	382
a–b				
c–d				
e–f				
	383–84	383–84	383–84	383–84
	385–86	385–86	385–86	385–86
387–88	387–88	387–88	387–88	387–88
a–b				
c–d	a–b			
	389–90	389–90	389–90	389–90
	391–92	391–92		391–92
	393–94	393–94		393–94
	395–96	395–96		395–96
	397–98	397–98		397–98
399	399	399	399	399

The passage begins with line 382 where the bird says he will prove (*BCD*) or has proved (*A* 382, *E* 382*b*) the three truths. *E* then has a couplet 382*c–d* alluding to the sens *croire*. Lines 382*e–f* and 387–88 in *E* allude to the sens *pleurer*, and then lines 388*a–d* allude to the third sens, not in the previous words of the poem (326–27) but in words similar to the *Trois Savoirs*:

Li autre sen tantost orrez:
Ceo qe aver ne poez nïent
Ne coveitez trop durement.   (126–28)
Ceo vi jeo par ton marrement
Dit vos a voi apertement
Qe ja ne covetisset por voir
Chose qe vos ne poez avoir   (197–200)

Other texts also have wording similar to *E* 388*a–d*: the *Castoiement A* (ed. Hilka):

Ne ja mar trop grant duel feras
Quant la toue chose perdras,
Quer bien seiz que par doloser
Ne porreies rien recovrer   (3399–402)

the *Donnei*:

Sun travail perd sanz recovrer   (1149)

and the *Disciplina* (ed. Hilka):

quoniam dolore nichil erit recuperabile   (Heidelberg, p. 33)

The additional couplet in *C*, 388*ab*, makes the only allusion of the five *Oiselet* manuscripts to the third sens in the words of the poem (326–27), but does not have an allusion to *croire* in this passage, as does *E* 382*cd*.

In *ABD* only the sens *pleurer* is alluded to directly (385–88), and, as mentioned in the note to 270–312, this passage may reflect an emphasis on the sens *pleurer* that led to the placing of *pleurer* first among the three sens in that passage.

The idea of *folie* in *E* 388*b* is expanded in the passage 391-98 in *BCD* (absent in *A*). The idea of *folie* is in the ending of the *Chastoiement A* (ed. Hilka):

"Pere," dist li fiz, "fous esteit
Li vilains quant il duel feiseit
De ce que il aveit perdu
Ce qu'il onques n'aveit veü."   (3555–58)

and the *Donnei*:

Trop creire en haste est folie   (1160)

387 *ce* On this use of *ce* for *il*, see Ménard, 32–33, who calls it "une variante expressive de l'article" (32).

389 *abosmez* God., 1: 29*c*-30*a* (s.v. *abosmer*) cites 389-90 of the *Oiselet* (ed. Méon, 1808) and gives a special meaning to *être abosmé des trois sens* as "avoir les trois sens égarés, perdus."

392 Proverb: Psalms 115:6, 135:17; Isaiah 6:9–10, 42:20; Ezekiel 12:2; Matthew 11:15, 13:9, 13:43; Mark 4:9; Luke 14:35; Corinthians I, 2:9 (etc.).

393-98 Proverb: Le Roux de Lincy, 2: 104-107, 490, cf. 1: 235; Morawski nos. 2346, 2347.

399-410 The final passage of the poem shows the following pattern of verses:

E	C	B	A	D
399	399	399	399	399
		400		
	401	401	401	401
		402		
	403	403	403	403
				a
	404	404	404	404
				a
	402		402	402
405	405	405	405	405
		406		
404				
407	407	407	407	407
	408	408	408	408
409	409	409	409	409
410	410	410	410	410
	a–b			
	c–d			

The text in E has the unlikely coupling of *pint* and *deduit* (404 and 407) that leads one to assume that E has abridged and perhaps rearranged his copy (or that he had a copy as bad as his own!). The lines in the text of E, however, do convey the essential conclusion: The bird went away (399), the fountain dried up (405), the leaves fell from the pine (404), the villein lost his pleasure (i.e., pleasure of his garden) (407), and he who covets all loses all (409–10).

The texts of CAD have an expanded version that conveys the same message (not counting the added lines in C 410*a–d* and in D 403*a* and 404*a*). In CAD, after the bird flies away (399), the events are in the following order: The leaves fall (404), the garden withers (402), and the fountain dries up (405). The text of B stands alone in this passage in the order of events: the garden withers (402), the leaves fall (404), and the fountain dries up (405). If we assume B rearranged lines, then we see that the withering of the garden (402) was moved up to precede the falling of the leaves (404) so that two new lines (400 and 406) were needed to complete the rhyme scheme. These two lines unique to B merely repeat the message of 403 and as such have the banality of filler lines, which they indeed are. The order of the lines in B, however, now expresses events in the following order: the bird flies away (399), the garden withers (402), the leaves fall (404), and the fountain dries up (405). This order reflects lines 121 and 122 of the poem where the withering of the garden and the drying up of the fountain were given in that order, so that the reordered lines in B can be seen as the result of a desire to harmonize the conclusion with the preceding text of the poem. Another possible source of the reordered text in B could be the use of the word *eür* in 401 where ACD have *heure*. With its meaning of "fortune" or "result," the word *eür* in B reinforces the notion of cause and effect: The bird left, and as a result (401 *de tel eür*) the garden withered (402), etc. In ACD a line intervenes between 401 *a tele eure* and the effect on the trees (404), thus diluting the cause and effect in two ways, with the less expressive "a tele heure" and in the arrangement of lines. Although B has a unique passage here, the uniqueness is in the arrangement of the lines, not in their overall content. The insertion of two banal lines (400 and 406) seems to be offset by the perceived intention of the scribe to reflect a previous passage in the poem (121–22), and to reinforce the message with a more direct coupling of cause and effect. Conversely, *D* also has two added lines (403*a* and 404*a*) that add no special meaning whatsoever to the text. They are the result of the scribe's effort to separate the rhyme (*re*)*vint* : *pin* into two more acceptable rhymes — *revint* : *devint* and *pin* : *matin* — so that *pin* now also has an eye rhyme. (Cf. note to 127–28.) It is to be noted that with the exception of *A*, lines 193 and 399 have the same wording in each of the manuscripts, using either *ala* or *vola* for both. Only *A* has *ala* for 193 and *vola* for 399.

The unique four-line conclusion in *C* (410*a–d*) seems to owe its existence to an inspired desire by the scribe to twit the villein one more time. On the other hand, he may merely have wanted to fill up the page a little more (there are only eight lines plus the *Explicit* on this page of ms *C*). Another inspiration for the unique conclusion of *C* could be in the texts of the *Trois Savoirs* and the *Donnei des Amants* where the texts do not end with a proverb, but continue on for some 20 or so lines after the proverb is stated (*Trois Savoirs* 215–16, *Donnei* 1149–50):

> Son travaille piert saunz recoverir
> Qe aprent asne a harper   (*Trois Savoirs* 215-16)

Another line, "N'avez jagunce ne oisel" (*Trois Savoirs* 1154; *Donnei* 230), could have inspired *C* 410*cd*. As for 410*ab*, the tone may owe something to that of the *Trois Savoirs* 213–20 (not in the *Donnei*) which, like *C*, is far from courtly. . . . See the Introduction, pp. 22–23, for further discussion of the effect of the four-line conclusion in ms *C*.

405 *restancha* God., 7: 122*a* (s.v. *restanchier*) cites lines 400-402 (= *B* 404, 402, 405) from the *Oiselet* (ed. Méon, 1808); in 10: 555*a* (s.v. *resecher*), God. cites lines 399, 405, 404 from the *Oiselet* (from ms 1593); in 3: 598*c* (s.v. *estanchier*), God. cites lines 118–122 from the *Oiselet* (ms 1593). Cf. T.-L., 8: col. 1080 (s.v. *restanchier*), who cite lines 121-23 and 402, 405 and 407, from the *Oiselet* (ed. Méon, 1808).

407 In the *Rose* (ed. Lecoy) the garden is "deduit": *ou biau vergier qui est Deduit* (2994).

409 *proverbes ABD* have *proverbe(s)*, *C* has *prodons*, and *E* *profetes*. *Proverbe(s)* is used in *Donnei* 150, 217, 1147, and *Trois Savoirs* 213; *prodom* in *Donnei* 783 and *Chastoiement B* 2513 (ed. Hilka); *Philosophe* in *Disciplina* (ed. Hilka, Heidelberg, 1911, 34, line 8), and French prose *Disciplina* (ed. Hilka, 26, line 27).

The use of *prodons* in *C* and *profete* in *E* are final links suggesting the origins of the *Oiselet* in the *Disciplina*, the *Chastoiement* and ultimately in the *Barlaam*. The story of the *Oiselet* was originally a parable or exemplum taught by a wise man (*profete, prodom, philosophe*). When the frame story is removed and the context generalized, the sayings are merely "proverbs." As we have seen in previous discussions of *E* and *C* (in the Introduction), *C*, with *prodons*, and *E*, even more so with *profete*, betray their sources, whereas *ABD*, with *proverbe(s)*, remove a final link to their sources in the *Disciplina* and the *Barlaam*.

410 Proverb: Le Roux de Lincy, 2: 488; Tobler, *Proverbe*, 222; Morawski no. 2165; cf. Ulrich nos. 52, 251, 303, 374; Hassell no. C 288. Ms *C* adds four lines; see note to 399–410 for discussion.

GLOSSARY

aaisier *tr* 191 to ease, refresh; *v* note to 191

abosmez 389 *p p m sg nom of* **abosmer** to bewilder

aert 211 *ps ind 3 of* **aerdre** to seize

afaitiez 88 *p p m sg nom of* **afaitier** to prepare, instruct

afiert 7 *ps ind 3 of* **aferir** to be suitable

ains *adv* 252, 277, 388 never

ainz *adv* 21, 216 rather

aïre 245 *ps ind 3 of* **aïrier** to anger, irritate

alainne *f* breath : *loc adv* **a grant alainne** 130 at the top of [one's] voice

aloe *f* 85 sky or meadow lark

ame *f* 34 whosoever, anyone

amis *m pl* 152 lovers

amont *adv* 211 up high

amor *mf* : *adv loc* **par amors** 182 willingly, readily

assenez 306, 398 *p p of* **assener** to instruct

atant *adv* 258 then, thereupon

atempre 200 *ps ind 3 of* **atemprer** to adjust, set; *p p* **atempree** 205

avant *adv* 145 first of all

avenanz *adj* 142 pleasing

avenir *impers* 150; *p p* **avenu** 348; *pret 3* **avint** 1 happen

aver *m pl nom* 161 miserly

avis *m* : *loc* **estre avis** 84, 213 to seem

avoir *tr* 143, 222, 254 to have; *p p* **eü** 280, 386; *ps ind 1* **ai** 221, 246, 286, 295, 379, 2 **as** 274, 281, 3 **a** 2, 205, 212, 355, 368, 369, 394, 5 **avez** 214, 218, 335, 336, 342; *impf ind 3* **avoit** 19, 31, 41, 50, 53, 61, 93, 95 6 **avoient** 180; *pret 2* **eüs** 271, 350, 388, 3 **ot** 10, 22, 28, 113, 193, 280, 386, 399; *fut 1* **avré** 216, 225, 2 **avras** 388, 5 **avrez** 234; *cond 3* **aroit** 359; *ps sbj 3* **ait** 290 *impf sbj 2* **eüsses** 340, 349, 3 **eüst** 100, 105; *inf used substantively* 320 wealth

bandon *m* : *adv loc* **a bandon** 56 freely

beaus *v.* **biaus**

bel *adv* 82 well

biaus *adj m* 27, 51, 71, 77, 110, 133, 229, 304, 390, **beaus** 300, **bel** 58, **biau** 270; *f* **bele** 155, **beles** 142 beautiful

biere *f* 34 sickbed

bousist 56 *impf sbj 3 of* **bolir** to boil

c' = **qu'** *conj* 38, 271 that; 392, 400 for

car *conj and adv* 95, 117, 149, 235, 241, 244, 262, 320, 349; **qu'** 215 for; *with imper* 174, 175, 177 therefore

ce *pro* 167, 169, 193, 278, 309, 399 this, that; *impers* 63, 206, 213, 387 it

cel *dem adj m sg obl* 45; *f sg obl* **cele** 126; *m sg nom* **cil** 184, 207 this, that

cenele *f* haw, hawthorn berry : *loc* **ne pas valoir une cenele** 92 to be worthless

chaitis *adj and subs* 210 unhappy captive; 364 unfortunate; 371 wretched

chant *m* 85, 93, 107, 117, 169 **chans** 95, 187 song, singing

chastoi 325 *ps ind 1 of* **chastoier** to warn, teach a lesson

cheïrent 404 *pret 6 of* **cheoir** to fall; *p p* **cheüe** 120; *imper 2* **chiez** 175

chiere *adj f sg* 356 expensive; *loc* **tenir chier** 66 to like; **avoir chier** 180 cherish; **vendre chier** 196 sell for a high price

choisir *tr* 64 to see, perceive

ci *adv* 178, 331 here

cil *dem pr m sg nom* 20, 48, 258, 376, 392, 410 that one, he; *m pl nom* **cil** 189 those, they

cist *dem pro m sg nom* 192, 344 this one; *m sg obl* **cestui** 298, 319 this (thing); *f sg nom* **ceste** 362 this (thing)

claimme 364 *ps ind 3 of* **clamer** to call, declare

coitier *tr* 321 to goad

com *conj* 56, 57, 241, 276, 293, 350, **come** 103, **comme** 87, 228, 256, **con** 334 like, as

compas *sg m* : *loc* **a compas** 52 perfectly

contrement *adv* up : *loc* **d'un grant contremont** 43 very high on top

corouciez 328 *p p m sg nom of* **coroucier** to anger, irritate

corre *intr inf used as subst* 174 running

cors *m* 191, 355 body; *loc* **por lor cors miex aaisier** 191 better to restore, refresh themselves

covens *m* 311 promise

covoiteus *adj m sg pl used as subst* 162 covetous

covoitier *tr used as subst* 188 covetousness; *ps ind 3* **covoite** 157, 410 covets

creant *ps ind 1* 144, 257 *of* **creanter** to promise

cui *dat of qui* 124, 266 to whom

cuidai 381 *pret 1 of* **cuidier** to believe; *ps ind 1* **cuit** 14, 287, *3* **cuide** 397

dahez *m sg* : *formula of malediction* 290 cursed (be)

dechieent 26 *ps ind 6 of* **decheoir** to fall down; *v* **cheïrent** (**cheoir**)

deduire *intr* 190 rejoice

deduit *m* 225, 407 pleasure, diversion

delitable *adj* 11 pleasing, lovely

deliteus *adj m sg nom* 71, 132 delightful, wonderful

demainne 154 *ps ind 3 of* **demener** to show, display; *m* 359 power

denier *f* 185 coin, penny, farthing

deporter *intr and refl* 190 to rejoice

deputaire *adj* 354 vile, low

desouz *prep* 171 underneath

despiece 365 *ps ind 3 of* **despecier** to scratch, tear; *p p* **despeciez** 369 torn to pieces

destruiemenz *m* 78 detriment, delay (to my story)

detenir *tr* 309 to retain

deüs 275 *pret 2 of* **devoir** to be supposed to, have to

devant *adv* 337 before

devis *m* : *loc* **a mon devis** 222 at my disposal

devise *f* : *loc* **a devise** 27 marvelously, as one could wish

dire *tr* 89 to recite

dolans *adj* 96 sorrowful, grieving; *subst* **dolens** 210 grieving one

donoier *vb used as subst* 186 paying court

donques *adv* 304 then

donra 227 *fut 3 of* **doner** to give; *v* note to this verse

doz *adj* 116 sweet, **douce** 245 gentle

duites 60 *p p f pl of* **duire** to arrange

durement *adv* 318, 352 very, very much

einsi *adv* 24, **ainsi** 244 thus

el = en + le *art* 37, 44, 63, 207, 400 in

em *prep* 34, 231 in

em *pro* 254 of it

emparlez 240 *ps ind 5 of* **emparler** to plead, to be a great talker

empensé 350 *p p of* **empenser** to plan or intend to do

emporterez 168 *fut 5 of* **emporter** to obtain

en *pro* 227, 228, 291 one

enclooit 17 *impf 3 of* **enclore** to enclose

enferme *adj* 35 ill

engin *m* 200 snare

engingnié 335 *p p of* **engingnier** to fool

enmi *adv* 53 in the middle

enquiert *ps ind 3 of* **enquerre** 201 to seek

enserrez 224 *p p m sg nom of* **enserrer** to enclose, lock up

entendez a 285 *ps ind 5 of* **entendre a** to be preoccupied with

entor *adv* 16 around; *prep* 62 towards

entremetez 139 *ps ind 5 refl of* **entremetre** to care about, occupy oneself with

enuieus *adj* 172 disagreeable

envie *f* 184 envy

envïeus *adj* 161 envious

erroment *adv* 209, 323 immediately, right away

escïant *m* : *loc adv* **a escïant** 74, 332 with certainty

esforce 69 *ps ind 3 refl of* **esforcier** to make an effort

esgarde 201 *ps ind 3 of* **esgarder** to look at, examine; *imperf 3* **esgardoit** 367

esjoïst 98 *impf sg 3 refl of* **esjoïr** to rejoice *pret 3* **esjoï** 318

essample *m f* 134 moral lesson

esté *m* 62 summer; 263 *p p of* **estre** to be

estornel *m* 84 starling

estre *intr* 66, 102, 110, 397 to be; *p p* **esté** 263 *ps ind 1* **sui** 4, 224, 235, 292, 306, *2* **es** 294, *3* **est** 84, 86, 103, 208, 213, 243, 279, 291, 300, 313, 315, 322, 329, 333, 348, 356, 357, 358, 370, 385, 387, 398, *5* **estes** 142, 389, *6* 123, 152, 161, 163, 164, 331; *impf ind 1* **estoie** 337, **iere** 373; *3* **ert** 5, 131, **estoit** 47, 52, 54, 57, 65, 67, 80, 132, 172, 330, *6* **estoient** 43, 60; *pret 3* **fu** 18, 20, 21, 27, 39, 48, 49, 51, 71,

77, 88, 124, 133, 187, 188, 209, 260, 262, 268, 272, 279, 328, 343, 385; *cond 1* seroie 241, *3* seroit 78, 316; *impf sbj 3* fust 35, 38, 96, 101, 104, 106, 109, 111, 119, 120, 351, 352, 361; *imper 5* soiez 230

estres *m* 124 garden

estuet 266, 319 *ps ind 3 of* estovoir to be necessary

eür *m* 401 reason

euz *m pl* eyes: *loc* par mes euz 351 by my eyes

eve *f* 19 water

fable 12 *f and adj* fable, fabulous

fel *adj* 172, 354 perverse, perfidious, violent

felon *m pl* 164 felons

felonnie *f*: *loc* par felonnie, 273 de felonnie 376 with violence

fere *tr* 248, 353, 396 to do, make, cause; *p p* fet 49, 214; *ps ind 2* fez 308, *3* fet 204, 228, 248, 366, 391, *verbum vicarius* 137, 213, 243, 255, 257, 289, 299, 307, 322, 342, 380 says; *impf ind 3* fesoit 58; *pret 2* feïs 276, *3* fist 20, 48; *fut 1* ferai 255, *5* ferez 220, 238; *cond 1* feroie 242, 251, *5* feroiz 239; *ps sbj 3* face 14, 186

ferme *adj* 36 healthy, strong

finez 106 *p p of* finer *intr* to die

fis *adj* 230 certain; *loc* de fi 380 assuredly

flors *f pl* 31, 118, 176 flowers

fontainne *f* 53, 122, 127, 129, 405 fontaine 180 fountain, spring

fos *adj m nom* 20 fox 279, 385 foolish, crazy

fronce *ps ind 3 of* froncier to snort, scowl : *loc* froncier le nes d'ire 302 to snort in anger

fueille *f* 61, 68, 70, 404 leaf, foliage

gabant 297 *pr p of* gaber to mock

ge, g' *pro 1 sg nom* 141, 380, 373 I

gent *adj* 11, genz 77 pretty, well-born

gentis *adj sg* 21, *pl* 179 gentle, high-born

giete 327 *imper 2 of* geter to throw (down); disdain

gigue *f* 91 fiddle

gisent 34 *pr p of* gesir to lie down; *impf sbj 3* geüst 37

graindre *adj* 81 bigger

grant *subst* 43 great size; *v* note to this verse

gre *m* : *loc* savoir gre 290 to be grateful

gronce 376 *ps ind 3 of* groncier to grumble; *v* note to this verse

ha *interj of surprise* 353 ah!, what?

haï *interj* to attract attention, to warn 354 I say!

hericiez 261 *p p m sg nom of* hericier to ruffle

het 153 *ps ind 3 of* heer to hate

honis *adj* 40 even

honor *f* 165 honor

humors *m f*: *fig* 117 substance, essence; *v* to this verse

irascus *adj* 272 angry

issoit 117 *impf ind 3 of* issir to come out, emanate

itant *adv* : *loc* a itant 338 then

itel *adj* 10 its equal

ja *adv* 45, 96, 231, 233, 236, 287, 360, 388, never, 310 still; jamés 316, 351 never

jaiole *f* 198, jeole 224 cage

jel = je + le *pro* 283, 314 I + it

jus *adv* 327 down

kalandre *m* 85 calandra lark

lai *subst* 138 layman

laienz *adv* 50 inside

lainne *f* fleece, nap : *loc* contre lainne 263 against the grain, the wrong way

laiz *adj m sg nom* 261 ugly, made ugly

largesce *f* 157 largess

las *m sg* 209, *m pl* laz 204 snare, trap

las *adj and subst* 210, 364 miserable wretch, miserable; *v* note to 210

lasches *adj* 235 of no account

latin *m* 136 birdsong

leesce *f* 366 joy, rejoicing

lesse 258 *ps ind 3 of* lessier to let go, leave off; *p p* lessié 340; *impf ind 5* lessié 250; *imper 2* lai 174, *5* lessiez 177, 229, 238

leus *m* 370 places

li *f pro after prep* 358 it

loier *m* 212 recompense, return

lons *adj m sg nom* 51 long

lors *adv* 328 then

mains *adv* 242 less

maintenant *adv* 98, 101, 121, 361, meintenant 387; de maintenant 108 immediately, right away

maintient 166 *ps ind 3 of* maintenir to preserve, uphold; *impf 6* maintenoient 183

mainz *adj* 370 many a

reançon *f* 215 ransom

recort 151 *ps ind 1 of* **racorder** to announce

remainne 264 *ps ind 3 of* **remender** to repair, restore

reons *adj* 52 round

restanchast 122 *impf sbj 3 of* **restanchier** to dry up; *pret 3* **restancha** 405

retien 304 *imper 2 of* **retenir** to retain; *fut 5* **retendrez** 287 keep, retain

riche *adj* 15, **riches** 3, 5 rich, mighty

rien *indef pro f* 237 nothing, insignificant thing

roëtel *m* 81 wren

ront 363 *ps ind 3 of* **rompre** to tear

rotrüenges *f* 90 rotrouenge, song with refrains

rueves 309 *ps ind 2 of* **rover** to ask

sagement *adv* 60 with art

sauvages *adj* 292 ignorant, uncouth

savoir *tr* 266, 319, 378 to know; *pr p* **sachans** 48; *ps ind 1* **sai** 29, 288, 298, 332, 380, *2* **sez** 348, 353, *3* **set** 334, *5* **savez** 25; *impf ind 1* **savoie** 303; *cond 3* **saroit** 315, **savroit** 396; *impf sbj 2* **seüsses** 339; *imper 5* **sachiez** 74, 87, 242, *6* **sachent** 408

se, s' *conj* 8, 30, 100, 105, 107, 119, 167, 195, 197, 237, 239, 250, 254, 269, 294, 311, 339, 349 if; **com s'** 56 as if; **se tant non que** 115 unless

semont 267 *ps ind 3 of* **semondre** to press, urge, exhort

senez *adj* 397 wise

sens *m* 251, 267, 270, 275, 307, 312, 339, 389, 393 truth, truths, precept

seoit 203 *impf 3 of* **seoir** *refl* to sit; *pr p* **seant** 170

seul 222 *ps ind 1 of* **soloir** to be used to; *impf ind 1* **souloie** 226, *6* **soloient** 178, 189 (*v* note to verse 222)

seul *adv* 165 only

sez 348, 353 *ps ind 2 of* **savoir** to know

si *adv* 36, 47, 55, 57, 67, 74, 82, 101, 110, 148, 173, 193, 199, 200, 204, 238, 253, 269, 297, 325, 330, 363, 364, 390, 399 thus, so, and

siecle *m* 106, 143, 333 the present world as opposed to heaven, this earth

soautume *f* 126 sweetness, sweet music

soloir *v* **seul**

sons *m* 89, 116, **son** 132 music, song

sor *prep* 131, 208, 259 on, 295 over; **de sor** 367 from on top of

sordoit 55 *impf ind 3 of* **sordre** to gush, well up

soufroitos *adj* 333 poor, indigent

sougis 188 *p p of* **sougire** to be subject to

suens *poss pro* 87 his

tans *m* 1, 47, **tens** 68, 322 time

tant *adv* 69, 285, 356 so much; *conj* **por tant que** 37 provided that; **tant que, c'** 38 until (+ *sbj*), 202, 368 until (+ *indic*); **se tant non que** 115 unless

tart *adv* : *loc adv* **tart et tempre** 199 late and early

teche 158 *f* blemish, spot

tempre *adv* 199 early; *v* **tart**

tenant *subst* 162 avaricious

teüz 329 *p p of* **taire** to be quiet

tenser *tr* 249 to defend, protect

tent 320 *ps ind 3 of* **tenter a** to possess, seek

tex *m sg of* **tel** *indef pro* 393, 395, 397, **tiex** 315, 333 such a one, such

tor *m* 233 trick

tor *f* 15 tower

tort 363 *ps ind 3 of* **tordre** to twist, wring

tot *adj and pro m sg obl* 10, 17, 68, 410 **tout** 47, 410; *m sg nom* **toz** 278; *f sg obl* **toute** 157; *m pl nom* **tuit** 42, 408; *f pl nom* **toutes** 408; *m pl obl* **toz** 369; *adv* **tot** 49, **toute** 36, **touz** 261 all, completely

valoir *intr* 253 to be worth; *ps ind 3* **vaut** 344; *cond 3* **vaudroit** 135; *impf sbj 3* **vausist** 92

veil *v* **voil**

verité *f* : *loc* **par verité** 151 in truth; *v* **voir** *adv*

vertu *f* 95, 358 power, virtue, property; *loc* **en vertu** 118, 123 alive, flourishing

vïele *f* 91 viol, hurdy-gurdy

vis *m* 129, 365 face; *loc* **m'est vis** 387 seems to me

vo 252 *poss pro* your

voil 8 *ps ind 1 of* **voloir** *tr* to want; *ps ind 1* **veil** 30, *5* **volez** 143, 283; *cond 1* **voudroie** 310

voir *adv* : *loc* **dire voir** 342, 377 tell, speak the truth; **or voir** 144 in truth

voir *m* 30 truth

voisdie *f* 268 skill, finesse, subtlety, wiliness